Rethinking Investment Law

Rethinking Investment Law

Perspectives and Prospects

Edited by

DAVID SCHNEIDERMAN & GUS VAN HARTEN

OXFORD
UNIVERSITY PRESS

OXFORD
UNIVERSITY PRESS

Great Clarendon Street, Oxford, OX2 6DP,
United Kingdom

Oxford University Press is a department of the University of Oxford.
It furthers the University's objective of excellence in research, scholarship,
and education by publishing worldwide. Oxford is a registered trade mark of
Oxford University Press in the UK and in certain other countries

First Edition published in 2023

Published in the United States of America by Oxford University Press
198 Madison Avenue, New York, NY 10016, United States of America

British Library Cataloguing in Publication Data

Data available

Library of Congress Control Number: 2023945863

ISBN 978–0–19–287108–4

DOI: 10.1093/oso/9780192871084.001.0001

Printed and bound in the UK by
Clays Ltd, Elcograf S.p.A.

Acknowledgements

The editors would like to thank the contributors to this volume, each of whom endured our editorial entreaties. We also thank Fay Gibbons and Kathryn Plunkett of Oxford University Press, and the anonymous peer reviewers, for their work in support of the project. David Schneiderman wishes to thank colleagues at Stockholm University Department of Law, where he was an Affiliated Professor, and at Gothenburg University Department of Law, where he held the Torgny Segerstedt Visiting Professorship, at the time he was soliciting and editing contributions, in addition to writing his own contribution for this volume. Gus Van Harten thanks colleagues who were supportive in the relevant period, early in the pandemic, when he served as Associate Dean (Academic) at Osgoode Hall Law School. Both are deeply grateful to their families.

Contents

Table of Cases

List of Contributors

Fola Adeleke, Senior Research Fellow, Wits University

Juan Carlos Boué, Counsel, Curtis, Mallet-Prevost, Colt & Mosle LLP

Jimena Sierra Camargo, Fellow, York University

Ibironke T. Odumosu-Ayanu, Professor, University of Saskatchewan

Josef Ostřanský, Policy Advisor, International Institute for Sustainable Development

Nicolás M. Perrone, Professor, Universidad de Valparaíso

Mavluda Sattorova, Professor, University of Liverpool

David Schneiderman, Professor, University of Toronto

M. Sornarajah, CJ Koh Professor, University of Singapore

Federico Suárez, Professor, Universidad Externado de Colombia

Gus Van Harten, Professor, York University

Anil Yilmaz Vastardis, Senior Lecturer, University of Essex

1
Introduction

David Schneiderman and Gus Van Harten

International investment law and arbitration establish the most robust of international treaty regimes. Together, they entitle foreign investors to enforce a panoply of rights—the regime's 'standards of treatment'—directly against states. Investor claims have led to enormous sums of monetary compensation at the expense of states when they regulate foreign-owned assets. The regime reaches deep into the policy space of even the most powerful states to a degree not seen since the early twentieth century.[1] In turn, investor–state dispute settlement (ISDS) tribunals have been given the power to second guess all variety of state measures, no matter how essential to social or economic well-being. In their first thirty years, ISDS tribunals also have shown a lack of restraint in the review and disciplining of domestic institutions. As one of us has put it, the arbitrators' enforcement of the treaties amounts not to a 'gentle civilizer' of nations but rather to their 'strict controller'.[2]

Despite the regime's muscularity, much investment law scholarship treats it as instituting tolerable and justified limits to state policy.[3] The treaties, and the arbitrators' readings of them, are approached as one would any other set of legal sources and judicial interpretation. This apologetic stance is widespread even in the long absence of compelling evidence that the treaties' disciplines attract new investment or improve governance or the rule of law. The orthodoxy treats investment law as a desirable restraint on undesirable politics. The fact that the regime was consolidated by lawyers and arbitrators so rapidly in the 1990s and early 2000s, and since then allowed by governments to endure and expand, has helped to give cover for such convictions.

[1] We have in mind the *Lochner* era in the United States associated with the famous 1905 Supreme Court case concerning the hours of work of bakery workers in New York State.

[2] Gus Van Harten, *Sovereign Choices and Sovereign Constraints: Judicial Restraint in Investment Treaty Arbitration* (OUP 2013) 164, referring to Martti Koskenniemi.

[3] For example, August Reinisch (ed), *Standards of Investment Protection* (OUP 2008); Marc Bungenberg and others (eds), *International Investment Law* (CH Beck/Hart Publishing/Nomos 2015); Rudolf Dolzer and Christoph Schreuer, *Principles of International Investment Law* (2nd edn, OUP 2013); and Campbell McLachlan, Lawrence Shore, and Matthew Weinigar, *International Investment Arbitration: Substantive Principles* (2nd edn, OUP 2017).

David Schneiderman and Gus Van Harten, *Introduction* In: *Rethinking Investment Law*. Edited by: David Schneiderman and Gus Van Harten, Oxford University Press. © David Schneiderman and Gus Van Harten 2023.
DOI: 10.1093/oso/9780192871084.003.0001

This volume offers a more complete view than the orthodox one. Focusing on the core treaty standards, the contributors lay out how investment law operates to constrain states and compensate investors while signalling approaches that challenge the hyper-investor friendly direction of ISDS since its explosion a few decades ago. Thus, they return to a more balanced vision of how international law can protect individuals in general, not just foreign owners of assets, while also accepting the role of states as representatives of their people and mediators of relations with other states and peoples. Core treaty standards are considered alongside the state's decision-making role, often framed as the 'right to regulate', and the treaties' radical remedy of uncapped damages awards against the state. In each area, the contributors aim to present the conventional law and its limitations in order to help shape a more respectful approach to the state in the international law for protection of foreign nationals. They give new takes on leading cases and the underlying texts. Collectively, the analysis shows how doctrines taken for granted in the descriptive accounts that permeate the literature could have been taken, and could still be taken, in a better direction. Put differently, it reveals how the regime has been allowed to take far too many wrong turns.

This project is not one that dominant voices in the field would leap to embrace.[4] Such voices have often used their influence to marginalize other perspectives. Access to scholarly 'spaces of reason' is typically closed to those seeking to question the basic legitimacy of the current regime. The 'normative power of the factual' is offered as a defence against trying to think differently.[5] One is asked, 'what is the alternative?', without constructive acknowledgement and diagnosis of the root disease. Yet, change begins with a clearer understanding of the origins and trajectory of the regime, an understanding that, for many of the contributors, leads away from the existing regime. For our part as editors, we do not think the goal of protecting foreign nationals calls for such exceptionally robust safeguards of the most powerful economic actors in opposition to the institutions charged with protecting everyone else. Such a task of rethinking protections should be undertaken in concert with a wider range of constituencies than have been heard in the present regime, including those who are most impacted; namely, the governments and other representatives of targeted capital-importing states.

[4] David Schneiderman, 'The Paranoid Style of Investment Lawyers and Arbitrators: Investment Law Norm Entrepreneurs and their Critics' in Chin Leng Lim (ed), *Alternative Visions of International on Foreign Investment: Essays in Honour of M. Sornarajah* (CUP 2016) 131–55.

[5] Rainer Forst, 'Noumenal Power' in Rainer Forst, *Normativity and Power: Analyzing Social Orders of Justification* (OUP 2017) 42, 45.

To understand investment law, one must undertake close analysis of investment treaties and ISDS awards. That task is impossible for many observers of the regime because of how deeply its wrong turns are buried in impenetrable legalese and volumes of paper. Besides outlining the regime, the contributors to this volume offer ways to see the problems that are otherwise obfuscated by orthodoxy, teaching us not only about the regime's design but also its quiet failures. Thus, the volume explains the leading standards of investment law and the main remedy under the bilateral investment treaties (BITs) and regional economic agreements that authorize ISDS; that is, asymmetrical investor–state arbitration which is compulsory for states but optional for investors.

We see four key themes emerging from the volume. The first is that states succumbed to a 'gotcha' tactic during the late-1980s to the mid-1990s when they accepted a furious pace of investment treaty-making without studying actual ISDS claims and without understanding the risks and liabilities for states. The second is that the newly minted treaties opened the way for radical interpretations of vague standards, divorced from the customary norms, which then exploded the scope and intensity of disciplines for states and entitlements for investors. The third is that states have been lumbering in their responses to the resulting crisis of international law, leaving innumerable minefields for decision-making in the public interest. Even when states have tried to clarify the treaties, ISDS arbitrators have been able to manipulate their revised terms in favour of foreign investors and the ISDS industry at extreme risk to public budgets. The fourth theme is that the dangers posed by the regime, in its skewed approach to international law and its lopsided process, will not be alleviated without changing the incentivization of those who wield adjudicative power in ISDS. Investment law needs to be recreated. To understand why and how, one must start with understanding what went so wrong, as this volume helps us to do.

Besides considering the origins of the standard or remedy and referring to contemporary debates about interpretation, the chapters that follow cumulatively identify a range of pivotal moments where the regime took a wrong turn, whether in the rulings of tribunals or the treaties of governments. The overall goal is to comprehend investment law as a contingent project that could have turned out differently. The regime's outcomes were not inevitable or preordained. They were a consequence of choices by those who were given, or who assumed, the power to make them.

As implications of the wrong turns, for example, we note a few of the key findings of the volume.

Following this introductory chapter, Chapter 2 discusses national treatment, a non-discriminatory standard that is customarily central to the protection of foreign nationals once they have been admitted to the host state. Yet, in today's investment law, David Schneiderman argues, it has been selectively expanded so that it now serves to protect immense wealth at the expense of everyone else, thus contradicting the underlying norm of equality.

Chapter 3 concerns most favoured nation (MFN) treatment. This standard has a complex history that calls for vigorous assessment, in every instance, of the relevant treaty texts and precise language used to extend protections of investors in one treaty to those covered by another. Unfortunately, tribunals have short-circuited the analysis of MFN clauses, observes Anil Yilmaz Vastardis. The clauses have been converted, instead, into baskets of protection and privilege from which investors can effectively pick and choose.

For the major capital-exporting states, protection against expropriation and nationalization was perhaps the clearest motivation for the spread of investment treaties in the decolonization era. In Chapter 4, Nicolás Perrone explains how this standard puts fundamental questions of economy and society in the hands of ISDS arbitrators. They have answered these questions by expanding the standard to over-compensate investors, thus deterring state-led democratic transformation.

The minimum standard of treatment, the topic of Chapter 5, has a rich history aimed at ensuring a fair balance between the interests of foreign nationals and a state's citizenry in customary international law. In investment treaties, states abandoned this equilibrium by expanding the grounds for review of state action and paving the way for a vast growth in foreign investor protections. Folo Adeleke and Gus Van Harten argue that the implications for African states, emerging from colonialism and searching for stability and prosperity, are unsettling.

Chapter 6 discusses the issue of denial of justice. Applied broadly, a protection against expropriation or against unfair and inequitable treatment allows arbitrators to judge a state's own court system. Mavluda Sattorova reveals how some tribunals have shown deference in this context, such as by requiring investors to exhaust local remedies before challenging a judicial act of the state. Others have found ways to avoid these limitations by allowing investors creatively to 'dress up' claims of judicial misconduct as violations of other treaty standards. The resulting divergence lays bare a profound disagreement about the threshold for triggering state responsibility under investment treaties for judicial misconduct.

The concept of fair and equitable treatment, supplemented by the related term 'full protection and security', has become the arbitrators' explosive substitute for more balanced norms of treatment of foreign investors and, in turn, the weapon of choice for investors in ISDS. Using this device, Josef Ostřanský warns in Chapter 7 that arbitrators have invented a range of far-reaching novel grounds to review state acts, thus disregarding or radically diminishing their regulatory capacity.

Ibironke Odumosu-Ayanu explains umbrella clauses in Chapter 8. These treaty clauses were originally intended to protect colonial-era concession contracts from changes by newly independent countries. Built into many treaties, arbitrators have used them to turn contractual disputes into international treaty claims. In turn, they have made the 'political' space of decolonized countries subservient to a restyled politics of ISDS that privileges foreign investors while stripping away the agency of the state and its citizenry in contractual decision-making.

As a central concept in relation to state, the right to regulate is advanced as a potential antidote to pro-investor standards and interpretations. Jimena Sierra-Camargo and Federico Suárez-Ricaurte argue in Chapter 9 that the results in ISDS are disappointing. Tribunals, guided by norms of investor protection rather than public law, use the right, paradoxically, to reinforce an overarching dynamic of restriction of regulation where it creates costs for investors. The right to regulate appears more likely to relegitimize than to rebalance an inequitable system.

Of all the wrong turns in the field, none has been more acutely devastating for states than the quantum of damages awards, discussed in Chapter 10 by Juan Carlos Boué. Quantum is a tool by which all the other wrong turns have been unmoored from economic fundamentals and even common sense. The ISDS trend towards escalating colossal awards against states is premised on flimsy rationales from both a legal and a business perspective.

Since the 1990s, investment treaties and ISDS awards have turned international law into an instrument for control of the resources and economies of most countries. In the concluding chapter, Chapter 11, M. Sornarajah (who has long been an inspiration for independently minded scholars of investment law) argues that the 'obvious injustices' in the field should be confronted directly, without the usual 'pompous niceties' or 'pretentious decorum'. While there has been tinkering with aspects of the system, the legal establishment prefers to ignore the harsh outcomes under which poorer countries continue to suffer.

Our hope is that this volume proves to be a corrective for much of what passes as conventional wisdom in the field. Rather than lending legitimacy to the project of protecting foreign investors, our aim is to enlighten readers about alternative ways of envisaging legal relations between foreign investors, states, and citizens. By opening that conversation, alternative pathways forward may be mapped out, beyond the cramped field of vision that inhibits our imagination.

2
National Treatment

David Schneiderman

1 Introduction

Governing calls upon governments to make distinctions. The investment treaty standard of national treatment typically requires that there should be no distinction in the treatment accorded to foreign investors and investments that are in like circumstances to national investors and investments. The standard is premised on notions of equality and wrongful discrimination. It assumes that foreign nationals may be the subject of economic discrimination favouring locals and that such a distinction should be irrelevant in economic spheres. National treatment is meant to serve as a prophylactic against such unjust discrimination.[1]

A significant challenge to these assumptions is that, while states may engage in condemnable behaviour, large empirical data sets reveal that non-national investors typically are not vulnerable to discrimination even after having a well-established presence in host states. Indeed, the evidence suggests that such firms exercise outsized influence over host state behaviour.[2] From this angle, the assumption that states are likely to target foreign nationals looks like a form of 'stereotyping' of host states.[3] Discrimination law censures stereotyping

[1] National treatment has been eclipsed by other standards, like fair and equitable treatment. According to the data generated by the United Nations Conference on Trade and Development (UNCTAD), tribunals found violations of fair and equitable treatment (including minimum standard of treatment and denial of justice) in 133 cases and national treatment in nine cases. See https://investmentpolicy.unctad.org/investment-dispute-settlement/ (accessed 17 March 2020); and findings in Gus Van Harten, *Sovereign Choices and Sovereign Constraints: Judicial Restraint in Investment Treaty Arbitration* (OUP 2013) 101.

[2] Relying on World Bank data drawing on the experience of companies operating in eighty countries during the period from 1999 to 2000, Aisbett finds that foreign firms are 'no more or less influential' than domestic firms and that 'both foreign and domestic multinationals are significantly more influential' than other firms. See Emma Aisbett, 'Powerful Multinational or Persecuted Foreigners: "Foreignness" and Influence over Government' Centre for Economic Policy Research Discussion Paper No 638, Australian National University (April 2010) 19.

[3] Stereotyping arises in circumstances where negative characteristics are attributed to an individual merely by virtue of group membership. See *Law v Canada* [1999] 1 SCR 497 [64].

David Schneiderman, *National Treatment* In: *Rethinking Investment Law*. Edited by: David Schneiderman and Gus Van Harten, Oxford University Press. © David Schneiderman 2023. DOI: 10.1093/oso/9780192871084.003.0002

unless it is 'premised upon informed statistical generalizations'.[4] In this case, statistics simply do not support the premise.

There is a further problem with the idea of equality that is promoted by investment law. Not only are foreign investors required to be treated no worse than locals; investment law also ensures that foreign investors receive treatment *better* than that received by locals. As discussed below, in some circumstances national treatment results in preferential treatment compared to that received by local economic actors. The problem is compounded by the panoply of other protections available to foreign investors under investment treaty law. These protections, in the aggregate, impose not merely equal but vastly unequal treatment.[5] Levelling as between nationals and foreigners is, therefore, inadequate to the mindset of investment treaty lawyers and arbitrators. How this preferential treatment for foreign investors is to be squared with the principle of non-discrimination has not been the subject of arbitral decision-making or of much scholarly discussion.[6]

As national treatment is only a relative, and not an absolute, standard of treatment it is typically considered a modest restriction on state policy space.[7] It will be seen, however, that this standard authorizes intrusive international control of state action. Investment law, as will be discussed, is not so much concerned with unjust discrimination as it is with maintaining open markets for powerful economic actors.

This chapter scrutinizes features of national treatment doctrine that are revealed in treaty text and arbitral interpretation. Various problems with the doctrine will be highlighted, two in particular. First, as both direct (de jure) and indirect (de facto) discrimination are encompassed by the standard, the widest possible range of government action is subject to arbitral review. Second, this breadth of review is compounded by the restricted availability of the defence of justification. Instead, the standard of scrutiny applied by tribunals, and endorsed by many scholars, insists that even non-discriminatory objectives cannot be justified by states unless the discriminatory impact is

[4] ibid 106. On stereotyping as marker of discrimination and over-inclusive generalizations see Sophia Moreau, 'Equality Rights and Stereotypes' in David Dyzenhaus and Malcolm Thorburn (eds), *Philosophical Foundations of Constitutional Law* (OUP 2016) 283–303, para 291.

[5] This can be likened to Georg Simmel's 'most favoured position' in 'Superordination and Subordination' in Kurt H Wolff (ed), *The Sociology of Georg Simmel* (The Free Press 1950) 101–85, para 275.

[6] It could be argued, for instance, that differential treatment is necessary so as to promote equality, as was argued by South Africa in the Foresti dispute (discussed below), but this argument has not been favoured by investment law scholars and arbitrators.

[7] See Don Wallace Jr and David B Bailey, 'The Inevitability of National Treatment of Foreign Direct Investment with Increasingly Few and Narrow Exceptions' (1998) 31 Cornell International Law Journal 615, 619.

insignificant, no matter how valuable the public policy objective that is being pursued. So long as discrimination plays some role in the measure—in the OECD's words, as long as the measure is 'motivated, at least in part' by discrimination against foreigners[8]—it will not survive scrutiny under national treatment. Both of these moments, when the arbitral jurisprudence has taken a wrong turn, result in foreign investors being granted a degree of solicitude typically available only to the most vulnerable groups in society—those 'discrete and insular minorities'[9] who have suffered historic disadvantage at the hands of majorities. Such problems point to the merits of the Calvo doctrine, which insists not only on equality between nationals and foreigners but also on ensuring that claims of discriminatory treatment be settled in local courts according to local law.[10]

Various tribunals have focused on three questions in their national treatment analysis: is the claimant or his investment in like circumstances with locals; has there been less favourable treatment; and is there a justification for that treatment?[11] With few exceptions,[12] the first and second questions have been compressed into a single inquiry. This is probably because it is unusual for a charge of discrimination not to involve some degree of differential treatment. Even the third question of justifiable discrimination often gets squeezed into the first ('like circumstances') stage of the analysis. While the following discussion does not follow this typology precisely, it does examine these and other questions posed by tribunals. The emphasis is on recurring interpretive problems that have plagued national treatment analysis, particularly those arising from incorporating indirect, and not just direct, discrimination, identifying proper comparators, and determining acceptable justifications. In addition, some largely neglected issues are addressed, including standards of scrutiny and the claim that the standard confers no greater rights than those available to locals. I turn first to a brief discussion of the origins of the treaty text.

[8] OECD, *National Treatment for Foreign-Controlled Enterprises* (Paris 1993) 22.

[9] This is the language in *United States v Carolene Products Co* 304 US 144 (1938) [153], fn 4.

[10] See Donald R Shea, *Calvo Clause: A Problem of Inter-American and International Law and Diplomacy* (University of Minnesota Press 1955); Carlos M Calvo, *Le droit international théorique et pratique* (Guillaumin 1880). For a translation of a part of Calvo's treatise see Edward M Gallaudet, *A Manual of International Law* (H Holt 1879).

[11] *Grand River Enterprises Six Nations Ltd and Others v United States of America*, UNCITRAL, Award (12 January 2011) 163.

[12] See eg *ADF Group Inc v United States*, ICSID Case No ARB AF/00/1 (9 January 2003).

2 Origins

The origins of investment law's national treatment standard can be found in both national constitutional law and international law. National constitutions, at least since the French Declaration on the Rights of Man, have emphasized equal treatment as a foundational principle of legitimate law. At its origins, equality was mostly a formal requirement.[13] Many things could be done by the state, so long as there was no distinction between persons, for instance, in their ability to contract or own property.[14] As the principle came to be understood in the US Reconstruction era, equal treatment in the fifth and fourteenth amendments mandated no distinction between 'classes'. For instance, economic legislation disturbing the distribution of wealth and power between employers and employees was constitutionally forbidden.[15] Investment law's standards of treatment exhibit, in some material respects, a similar prejudice against class legislation.

With the advent of Roosevelt's New Deal, strict scrutiny of economic legislation came to be viewed as illegitimate, as it is now in many jurisdictions. Modern equal protection doctrine has reversed these earlier priorities, concerning itself mostly with the protection of vulnerable groups. In the language of famous footnote four in the US Supreme Court's ruling in *Carolene Products*, which justified the new paradigm, a more 'searching judicial inquiry' is warranted for laws that exhibit 'prejudice against discrete and insular minorities' as these tend 'seriously to curtail the operation of those political processes ordinarily to be relied upon to protect minorities'.[16] Yet, there are limits even to the circumstances giving rise to this more searching judicial inquiry—or 'strict scrutiny'—in US constitutional law. Only intentional, or direct, discrimination is cognizable to courts applying US equal protection doctrine. Unintentional, or indirect discrimination, apart from one narrow exception,[17] is not of much

[13] 'Men are born and remain free and equal *in respect of their rights*' in National Assembly, 'Declaration of the Rights of Man and Citizen' (1789) art 1 (emphasis added).

[14] What are called civil rights in TH Marshall, 'Citizenship and Social Class' in TH Marshall, *Class, Citizenship and Social Development: Essays by T.H. Marshall* (Anchor Books 1965) 71.

[15] *Lochner v New York* 198 US 45 (1905). On this critical period see Howard Gillman, *The Constitution Besieged: The Rise and Decline of Lochner Era Police Powers Jurisprudence* (Duke University Press 2003).

[16] *United States v Carolene Products Co* 304 US 144 (1938).

[17] The exception concerns indirect burdens on interstate commerce which are cognizable under 'dormant' commerce clause doctrine. Implied in the grant of Congressional power to 'regulate commerce … among the several States' (US Constitution, art 1, s 8, cl 3.) is a negative prohibition against states disrupting interstate trade (this is the commerce clause in its dormant state). While the standard of review under the dormant commerce clause lacks clarity and consistency, Congress can always fix, via its positive grant of power to regulate commerce, what may be flawed judicial reasoning. By contrast, the corrective of unilateral legislative supervision is not available in the case of investment arbitration.

constitutional interest. This is because of a worry, as the US Supreme Court has expressed it, that expansive constitutional review would be too 'far-reaching' and disrupt dominant social and economic expectations.[18] The Court came around to endorsing a heightened standard of scrutiny—an intermediate tier—only for sex-based discrimination. In a sequence of cases argued by then Professor Ruth Bader Ginsburg in the 1970s, this heightened scrutiny had the effect of rooting out formal legal distinctions between the sexes.[19]

The US version of equal protection falls well short of other newer constitutional regimes, such as the 1996 South African Constitution, which captures both intentional and unintentional discrimination as a means of rooting out vestiges of racism in South African society.[20] The same is true for many of the world's operative democracies, rendering US equal protection doctrine more of an outlier in today's world. To the extent that constitutional orders are interested in unintentional as well as intentional discrimination, they will have wide-ranging socio-economic impacts as a broader spectrum of government behaviour is subject to constitutional scrutiny. Much turns, then, on the standard of scrutiny that is adopted.

The international law origins of national treatment are traceable, it is said, to the twelfth and thirteenth centuries.[21] Though there may be numerous historic parallels, Vandevelde's study of the origins bilateral investment treaties (BITs) looks to more recent friendship, commerce, and navigation treaties (FCNs) for guidance. Vandevelde reveals that the US intention in signing FCNs was to internationalize US constitutional law.[22] Standards analogous to those in the Bill of Rights were considered suitable for other countries to adopt. Vandevelde reports that the State Department would not 'recommend a treaty provision which would go beyond' US constitutional principles in order to avoid granting to foreign investors 'more favorable treatment' than that available to US citizens.[23] We can surmise that only intentionally

[18] It 'would raise serious questions about, and perhaps invalidate, a whole range of tax, welfare, public service, regulatory, and licensing statutes that may be more burdensome to the poor and to the average black than to the more affluent whites' in *Washington v Davis* 426 US 229 (1976).

[19] For a discussion see Wendy W Williams, 'Ruth Bader Ginsburg's Equal Protection Clause: 1970–80' (2013) 25 Columbia Journal of Gender and Law 1.

[20] The state nor any person 'may not unfairly discriminate directly or indirectly against anyone' in Constitution of the Republic of South Africa (1996) art 9, ss 3, 4.

[21] United Nations Conference on Trade and Development (UNCTAD), National Treatment (United Nations 1999) 9.

[22] Kenneth J Vandevelde, *The First Bilateral Investment Treaties: U.S. Postwar Friendship, Commerce, and Navigation Treaties* (OUP 2017) 23, 26, 379.

[23] ibid 287. Vandevelde admits that the treaties did in some ways go beyond these constitutional protections by, for instance, 'incorporating certain rights under customary international law and providing limited protection against exchange controls' which were less robust than US law. But, he insists, 'any substantive protections essentially replicated the treatment that foreign investors already received under existing US law and policy' 385.

discriminatory violations of national treatment were intended to be caught. In other words, it was not a program to go beyond what equal protection doctrine provided under the fifth and fourteenth amendments of the US Constitution.

Scholars have occasionally looked to trade law in order to inform their analyses of national treatment in investment law. Some arbitrators, however, have been reluctant to draw on that experience, distinguishing sharply between the two regimes.[24] It is claimed that they serve different purposes even as they invoke nearly identical language.[25] To this end, DiMascio and Pauwelyn distinguish between the trading regime, promoting economic efficiency and competition between traders, and the investment law regime which, they say, is 'remarkably different', focusing almost exclusively on the rights of investors. From this angle, they argue, investment law is 'about protection, not liberalization'.[26] Their argument, however, elides the principal aim of those promoting investment law strictures. Once internalized, those norms are expected to discipline states so that they exhibit the behaviour of 'well-ordered' states.[27] States are expected to withdraw from the 'job of shaping events' and retire, instead, 'to the role of observers'.[28] For this reason, Kurtz more accurately captures the common aim of thwarting 'distortion in the domestic political process', namely lobbying by well-organized domestic interests.[29] According to this public choice account, there will be a decisive tilt in both trade and investment law that favours market liberalization and economic freedom. Newcombe and Paradell similarly pinpoint 'equality of competitive opportunities' as the animating purpose of national treatment.[30] It is in the service of these objectives, ones associated with the promotion of economic liberalism, that the standard of national treatment can potentially

[24] See eg *Pope & Talbot v Canada*, UNCITRAL–NAFTA, Interim Award (26 June 2000).

[25] 'WTO law cannot simply be transposed onto investment law' in José Alvarez, 'Beware: Boundary Crossings' in Tsvi Kahana and Anat Scolnicov (eds), *Boundaries of State, Boundaries of Rights: Human Rights, Private Actors, and Positive Obligations* (CUP 2016) 43, 63.

[26] Nicolas DiMascio and Joost Pauwelyn, 'Nondiscrimination in Trade and Investment Treaties: Worlds Apart or Two Sides of the Same Coin?' (2008) 102 American Journal of International Law 48, paras 56, 58.

[27] Thomas W Wälde, 'The Umbrella Clause in Investment Arbitration' (2005) 6 Journal of World Investment and Trade 183, para 188.

[28] Franz Böhm, Walter Eucken, and Hans Grossman-Doerth, 'The Ordo Manifesto of 1936' in Thomas Biebricher and Frieder Vogelmann, *The Birth of Austerity: German Ordoliberalism and Contemporary Neoliberalism* (Rowman & Littlefield 2017) 27, para 31.

[29] Jürgen Kurtz, *The WTO and International Investment Law: Converging Systems* (CUP 2016) 87–90.

[30] Andrew Newcombe and Lluis Paradell, *Law and Practice of Investment Treaties: Standards of Treatment* (Kluwer Law 2009) 152, 162. See also Wallace and Bailey (n 7) 616 (the goal being the 'ultimate elimination of all barriers to market access for all foreign economic actors in all sectors').

stand in the way of policy priorities opposed to the logic of the movement of capital.

These comparative exercises, having reference to other international law as well as national constitutional law, continue to attract controversy. It turns out, however, that the roots of national treatment doctrine have not played much of a role in its interpretation and application. The next section turns to the distinction between direct (de jure) and indirect (de facto) discrimination, followed by discussion of the issues of identifying comparators, allowing justifications for differential treatment, specifying standards of scrutiny and, finally, addressing the paradox of conferring greater rights on foreign investors.

3 Discrimination

Investment treaties are opaque on the issue of whether both intentional (de jure) and unintentional (de facto) discrimination are intended to be captured by national treatment. Typically, there will be no specificity about whether intentional or unintentional discrimination is covered or whether different considerations apply in each case. An example is the (relatively new) language in the EU–Canada Comprehensive Economic and Trade Agreement (CETA):[31]

> Article 8.6: National treatment
>
> 1. Each Party shall accord to an investor of the other Party and to a covered investment, treatment no less favourable than the treatment it accords, in like situations to its own investors and to their investments with respect to the establishment, acquisition, expansion, conduct, operation, management, maintenance, use, enjoyment and sale or disposal of their investments in its territory.

By now, lack of clarity on this issue must be considered deliberate. Many states appear content with the capacious scope of national treatment obligations in the treaties. As an example of a different approach, the draft Indian Model BIT text incorporated a number of innovations, including an intentionality

[31] In 'Section C' entitled 'Non-Discriminatory Treatment'.

requirement that confined coverage to de jure discrimination.[32] This innovation was abandoned in the final version of the text.[33]

Despite the ambiguity, investment arbitrators have not hesitated to proscribe both types of discriminatory conduct, albeit without much explanation.[34] The *SD Myers* tribunal, one of the first tribunals to offer a fulsome interpretation of national treatment, represents a watershed moment in this regard. Six years after the coming into force of the North American Free Trade Agreement (NAFTA), the tribunal concluded, in a series of short bullet points, that among the factors to be considered were: (a) 'whether the practical effect of the measure is to create a disproportionate benefit for nationals over non-nationals' and (b) 'whether the measure, on its face, appears to favour its nationals over non-nationals who are protected by the relevant treaty'.[35]

It is interesting that the tribunal addressed, first, the possibility of unintended discrimination (disproportionate impact) and, second, intentional discrimination, as if these were the only two possible categories. They are not. While facial distinctions on prohibited grounds, like nationality, are typically prima facie prohibited, *purposeful* discrimination 'may often be inferred from the totality of the relevant facts, including the fact, if it is true, that the law bears more heavily' on a targeted group than another, observed the US Supreme Court.[36] For the US Supreme Court, the task is to root out invidious discrimination. This may appear on the face of the law or it may be 'inferred' from the facts. It is pretty clear that the *SD Myers* tribunal considered the first category of disproportionate impact to be the all-encompassing one. The tribunal noted that: 'Intent is important, but protectionist intent is not necessarily decisive on its own.'[37]

[32] The text directed (1) that the parties do not accord 'less favourable treatment in the application of laws and (2) that a breach of national treatment occurs only in the case of 'intentional and unlawful discrimination on the basis of nationality'. See 'Model Text for the Indian Bilateral Investment Treaty', art 4 (April 2015) at https://www.mygov.in/sites/default/files/master_image/Model%20Text%20for%20the%20Indian%20Bilateral%20Investment%20Treaty.pdf (last accessed 17 December 2019).

[33] See 'Model Text for the Indian Bilateral Investment Treaty' (December 2015) in Martins Paparinskis, *Basic Documents in International Investment Protection* (2nd edn, Hart Publishing 2019) 735.

[34] This explanation was offered in *Standard Chartered Bank (Hong Kong) v Tanzania*, ICSID Case No ARB/15/41, Final Award (11 October 2019) [408]: it would 'reduce the scope of protection without explicit mention'.

[35] *SD Myers Inc v Canada*, Ad hoc–UNCITRAL Arbitration Rules, First Partial Award and Separate Opinion (13 November 2000) [252]; The tribunal reversed the order of inquiry proposed by the Government of Canada in *SD Myers Inc v Canada*, Government of Canada Counter Memorial (5 October 1999) 274. SD Myers argued only that the 'effect' of the order was to violate national treatment in *SD Myers Inc v Canada*, Investor's Supplemental Memorial (15 December 1999) [99].

[36] *Washington v Davis* 426 US 229 (1976) (Justice White).

[37] *SD Myers Inc v Canada* (n 35) [254].

This interpretive approach, originating in *SD Myers*, has been faithfully replicated in many subsequent arbitral awards.[38] With few exceptions, it is mostly taken for granted that investment law's national treatment standard encompasses the widest possible scope of state action. Authorizing scrutiny of measures that, both de jure and de facto, impact on investors and their investments is probably the most significant development in the jurisprudence, as it grants to arbitrators a supervisory role over the widest possible range of policy measures. Foreign investors are entitled to the same solicitude available only to discrete and insular minorities in some host states, all of whom will have experienced historic patterns of prejudice. In contrast, foreign investors are generally among the most privileged actors in the contemporary world.[39]

4 Likeness

As investment treaty arbitration took off in the late 1990s and early 2000s, it became necessary to answer the question of whom to compare to whom in disputes founded in national treatment. This analysis would determine whether differential treatment, giving rise to discrimination, had occurred. What soon became apparent was the problem of identifying the appropriate comparator for the purposes of conducting a defensible analysis. A similar problem has arisen in national constitutional contexts.[40] Recognizing that this choice can be determinative of many outcomes, the issue became a considerable preoccupation for the Supreme Court of Canada—a jurisprudential 'battleground', according to one justice of the Court.[41] In a challenge to the citizenship requirement to practice law in the province of British Columbia, a 'formal equality' approach,

[38] There is 'weak support from other tribunals for the proposition that intention to disfavour or discriminate is an essential element to establish less favourable treatment or discrimination' in *Standard Chartered Bank (Hong Kong) v Tanzania*, ICSID Case No ARB/15/41, Award (11 October 2019) [407], a contract-based arbitration.

[39] I have addressed the faulty claim that investors are analogous to vulnerable minorities in David Schneiderman, 'Investing in Democracy: Political Process and International Investment Law' (2010) 60 University of Toronto Law Journal 909.

[40] This will be the case even if only a 'class of one' alleges discrimination, eg *Village of Willowbrook v Olech* 528 US 562 (2000) (asking whether a claimant 'has been intentionally treated differently from others similarly situated'). That investment law claims are inherently comparative is underscored by the fact that it is structured to secure not special privileges from states but withdrawal of states from interfering in markets. That is, the purported aim is to ensure state 'neutrality' as between locals and foreigners rather than expanding any state's distributive functions; On the disguised role of equality analysis in 'levelling up' distribution. See Denise Reaume, 'Dignity, Equality, and Comparison' in Deborah Hellman and Sophia Moreau (eds), *Philosophical Foundations of Discrimination Law* (OUP 2013) 7–27.

[41] *Hodge v Canada (Minister of Human Resources Development)* [2004] 3 SCR 357 [18] (Justice Binnie).

associated with Aristotle (that likes should be treated alike), was rejected by the Court in *Andrews*.[42] The Court observed that formal equality would vindicate abhorrent discrimination like Nazi Germany's Nuremburg laws; so long as all members of the sub-class of German Jews had been treated similarly, there was no discrimination. Rather than adopting a fixed formula, the Court's majority adopted a contextual approach—what has come to be characterized as 'substantive equality'. In conducting equality analysis, the Court now takes into account not only 'the context of the law which is subject to challenge' but also 'the context of the place of the group in the entire social, political and legal fabric of our society'.[43] It is not far removed from the US Supreme Court's inquiry into 'prejudice against discrete and insular minorities' as laid down in *Carolene Products*.

This contextual approach turned out to be a cramped inquiry. The Court sought out for comparison those who were identical to the claimant in all respects but for the impugned characteristic (eg nationality, sex, etc.). This 'mirror comparator' inquiry resulted in outcomes that, despite the Court's references to context, were highly formalistic, focusing heavily on treating like cases alike. Responding to academic criticism, the Court subsequently rejected the search for mirror comparators in favour of a more nuanced and contextual inquiry.[44] The Court even concluded that the identification of a comparator may not be necessary in some cases.[45]

In the international context, the OECD noted the significance of this exercise for investment law when it offered an interpretation of the circumstances in which a foreign investor is 'in a like situation' to a national economic actor. Such a comparison, the OECD advised, 'is only valid if it is made between firms operating in the same sector'.[46] It was appropriate, the OECD continued, to examine '[m]ore general considerations, such as the policy objectives' of the host state in order to help 'define the circumstances in which comparison between foreign-controlled and domestic enterprises is permissible'.[47] The advice issuing out of the OECD was that economic competitors were the best-suited comparators for national treatment analysis in investment law.

[42] That 'things that are alike should be treated alike, while things that are unalike should be treated unalike in proportion to their unalikeness' in *Andrews v Law Society of British Columbia* [1989] 1 SCR 143, quoting Aristotle, *Ethica Nichomacea* (W Ross tr,) Book V3, at p 1131a-6 (OUP 1925).

[43] *Andrews* (n 42).

[44] *Withler v Canada (Attorney General)* [2011] 1 SCR 396 [58]; *Fraser v Canada (Attorney General)* 2020 SCC 28 [94].

[45] *Withler* (n 44) [65].

[46] Quoted in *SD Myers Inc Inc v Canada* (n 35) [248].

[47] ibid [248].

This method of analysis was, in turn, embraced by the tribunal in *SD Myers*. In this NAFTA dispute, the Government of Canada had closed the US-Canada border to hazardous waste, with a view to protecting the business of the only facility that had capacity to dispose of PCB waste in Canadian territory. The tribunal concluded that US and Canadian hazardous waste operators were 'in like circumstances'—NAFTA's language, which the tribunal treated as equivalent to 'in like situations'—and that the US-based operator had been expecting to 'attract customers' away from its Canadian competitor. This is the reason why, the tribunal surmised, the Canadian company lobbied the government to close the border to exports in order to check its competition.[48] Notably, the tribunal also invoked the Supreme Court of Canada's reasoning in *Andrews* to support a contextual approach to its comparison, eschewing a 'purely mechanical . . . similarly situated' test in favour of a more contextual and flexible one that was intended to protect marginalized vulnerable groups.[49]

The identification by tribunals of a proper comparator has led to both underinclusive and overinclusive inquiries. To illustrate, in *Methanex*, the tribunal sought a mirror comparator to a Canadian investor that produced methanol for use as a gasoline additive in order to reduce fuel emissions. The additive had been prohibited for sale in California on the basis that it posed a 'significant risk to the environment'.[50] Methanex claimed that the ban intentionally favoured a US competitor who produced ethanol for use as a substitute fuel additive, amounting to a violation of NAFTA's national treatment standard. The Canadian investor, however, failed to establish that California had intentionally discriminated against the company—the ban, after all, was supported by a variety of independent scientific studies. Vitally, the tribunal declined to seek out a comparator in competition with Methanex to produce an additive that would reduce gasoline emissions, namely, the US-based producer of ethanol. Instead, the tribunal chose a domestic comparator that was 'most like' the foreign investor, that is, other producers of methanol. As all the producers of Methanol had been treated similarly, there was no discrimination. According to the tribunal, it would be 'perverse to ignore identical comparators if they were available and to use comparators that were less "like"' the investor'.[51] By limiting itself to a mirror comparator, the tribunal effectively

48 ibid [251].
49 ibid [122].
50 *Methanex Corporation v United States*, Ad hoc—UNCITRAL Arbitration Rules, Final Award on Jurisdiction and Merits (3 August 2005), Part IV, Chapter B art 1102.
51 ibid [17].

dodged the discrimination claim, marking a very different approach from that in *SD Myers*.[52]

Beyond investment arbitration, one could accuse the European Court of Justice of a similar dodge. It was asked to consider whether the CETA, between Canada and the European Union, treated nationals of EU member states differently from Canadian nationals, in part because European nationals would be unable to launch investment disputes against European states under CETA. This differential treatment, it was argued, contravened the declaration in Article 20 of the European Convention of Human Rights that 'everyone is equal before the law'. The Court declined to resolve whether CETA conferred rights greater than those available to European citizens. Doing so might have required more work than the Court was willing to undertake, namely, a comparison of the rights and protections in CETA to those in European legal instruments and an assessment of the respective quality of their enforcement. It was no doubt easier to reject the comparison laid out in the referral to the Court. To this end, the Court redefined the comparator for the purposes of its discrimination analysis. European nationals were not 'comparable to that of enterprises and natural persons of Member States that invest within the Union', the Court declared in a short discussion of the point.[53] They were instead more 'similar to Canadian persons within Canada' as they simply 'are not foreign investors'.[54] By redefining the comparator group in this way, employing a formalistic analysis that strictly treated like cases alike, the European Court of Justice was able to define away the equality problem.

If this European Court ruling and the *Methanex* award were instances in which the decision-maker chose a comparator that was underinclusive, the *Occidental* tribunal moved in the opposite direction, adopting an overinclusive group for comparison.[55] Ecuador had instituted a Value Added Tax (VAT) rebate for manufacturers involved in the export of goods. The program was expanded to include a wide swath of industrial and agricultural goods and services, including oil exports. The Ecuadorian taxing agency revisited this

[52] It is not mere coincidence that the United States managed to dodge liability, as it has in every other investment dispute where it appears as respondent, through a constrained reading of an investment treaty standard of protection. This can be explained, in part, as the product of strategic arbitral decision-making. See discussion in David Schneiderman, 'International Investment Law's Unending Legitimation Project' (2017) 49 Loyola University Chicago Law Journal 229, 254–55.

[53] Court of Justice of the European Union, Opinion 1/17 (30 April 2019) ECLI:EU:C:2019:341, para 180.

[54] ibid para 181.

[55] *Occidental Exploration and Production Company v Ecuador*, LCIA Case No UN 3467, Award (1 July 2004).

tax holiday for oil exporters, ultimately reversing its policy, and requiring that US-based Occidental repay, with interest, deductions that had already been granted. In these circumstances, the tribunal accepted Occidental's claim that there was a violation of national treatment by distinguishing between exporters. Instead of seeking a domestic comparator in the same sector, however, the tribunal compared Occidental's treatment to all exporters in a wide variety of sectors. Any comparative need for 'like situations', the tribunal concluded, 'cannot be interpreted in the narrow sense advanced by Ecuador as the purpose of national treatment is to protect investors as compared to local producers, and this cannot be done by addressing exclusively the sector in which that particular activity is undertaken'.[56] Had the tribunal chosen to seek out actual competitors that were, like Occidental, producing oil for export, it would have found only the Ecuadorian national oil company, Petroecuador, as a candidate. The state-owned oil company was also unable to take advantage of the VAT rebate. Moreover, Ecuador argued, in place of a VAT rebate for foreign investors, the government had incorporated a comparable discount to calculate royalties owed by Occidental to the state.[57] The most dismaying aspect of the tribunal's analysis was that it failed to identify any discrimination at all between foreign and domestic investors. Without analysis, the tribunal simply stated that the investor had received less favourable treatment 'than that accorded to national companies'. As the tribunal admitted, this less favourable treatment, broadly compared, was not purposeful discrimination. On the contrary, the taxing authority had acted in a 'very professional' manner in accordance with 'what it thought was its obligation ... under the law'.[58] By implication, the tribunal mandated that the taxing authority should have set aside its domestic legal obligations in order to protect the revenues of a multinational oil company.

From this survey of comparators, we can observe that there is inconsistency in the approaches taken. That recommended by the OECD appears to be favoured by most arbitrators.[59] *Methanex* and *Occidental*, for this reason, can be considered outliers. Comparing actors in the same sector makes sense if one focuses on state behaviour that limits equality of economic competition. The promotion of economic equality, after all, is the predominant

[56] ibid [173].

[57] It is curious that DiMascio and Pauwelyn claim that there was, in this dispute, an 'absence of any legitimate reason to distinguish to distinguish between the foreign and domestic investments' in DiMascio and Pauwelyn (n26) at 85.

[58] *Occidental* (n 55) [177].

[59] As declared in Campbell McLachlan, Laurence Shore and Matthew Weiniger, *International Investment Arbitration: Substantive Principles* (2nd edn, OUP 2017) 343.

purpose of national treatment protections. Such a market ideal—of firms freely in competition—underscores how international investment law relies on economic modalities to condemn behaviour it sees as irrational. From this point of view, national treatment is a quintessentially market-friendly human right.[60]

Yet, the market-focused perspective may elide other, non-economic rationales for differential treatment. For this reason, it is worth heeding the advice of the *Grand River Enterprises* tribunal that all of the 'legal regime(s) applicable to a claimant and its purported comparators' serve as 'a compelling factor' in national treatment analysis.[61] In other words, the larger national legal context in which the investor and investment operate is relevant to a tribunal's analysis.[62] Decision-makers are warranted in examining the whole of the circumstances that give rise to complaints of discrimination and not exclusively treatment vis-à-vis any set of comparators. One can then examine whether distinctions are defensible from a public policy point of view. It also raises the possibility that exceptions from equal treatment may, in some instances, be warranted or desirable, an issue to which we next turn.

5 Justification

In *SD Myers*, the tribunal acknowledged that an assessment of like circumstances 'must also take into account circumstances that would justify governmental regulations that treat them differently in order to protect the public interest'.[63] Put differently, there will be circumstances where distinctions, whether intentional or not, will be justified based on the public interest. Nothing more was said by the *SD Myers* tribunal on this key point, other than to acknowledge that the Canadian government's goal to maintain an ability to process PCBs in Canada 'was a legitimate goal' consistent with Canada's duties under the Basel Convention, an international convention committing states to

[60] Upendra Baxi, *The Future of Human Rights* (2nd edn, OUP 2016).

[61] *Grand River Enterprises Six Nations Ltd et al v United States of America* (n 11) [167].

[62] See 'Model Text for the Indian Bilateral Investment Treaty' (December 2015) art 5, fn 2 in Paparinskis (n 33) 69 (The 'totality of the circumstances' should be considered in order to determine whether 'legitimate regulatory objectives' are being pursued). USMCA, cl 14, art 14.4(4) ('For greater certainty, whether treatment is accorded in "like circumstances" under this Article depends on the totality of the circumstances, including whether the relevant treatment distinguishes between investors or investments on the basis of legitimate public welfare objectives') https://ustr.gov/sites/default/files/files/agreements/FTA/USMCA/Text/14-Investment.pdf (accessed 22 December 2019).

[63] *SD Myers* (n 35) [250]. The same considerations will apply when the 'like situations' language is used.

dispose of their own hazardous waste within their own borders.[64] Even so, according to the tribunal, this goal was not a direct 'legitimate environmental reason for [Canada] introducing the ban' on PCB exports but, rather, an 'indirect environmental objective'.[65] Moreover, the means employed by Canada were themselves said to be illegitimate. A number of 'equally effective' alternative measures had been available to Canada to achieve its 'indirect goal' which, for the tribunal, would not have run afoul of national treatment.[66] Here, the tribunal appears to have applied a strict proportionality analysis (discussed further below), blending its analysis of the validity of a claimed justification by the state with the question of whether there were less restrictive alternatives available to the state.[67]

Few tribunals have followed *SD Myers* in acknowledging this justificatory step in the analysis.[68] When doing so, they have typically considered justifiable departures from equal treatment in the course of answering the question of whether foreign investors were in like circumstances to national comparators.[69] Ortino describes this approach as a 'second function' served by the analysis of like circumstances.[70] Yet, the exercise of identifying comparators seems ill-suited to an evaluation of justifications.[71] In so far as justifiable distinctions do not amount to a violation of national treatment, it would be preferable to treat justifications as exceptions.[72] That is, public policy justifications in national treatment doctrine

[64] ibid [255].

[65] ibid [195].

[66] ibid [195], referring to NAFTA, art 104 (1) and at *SD Myers Inc v Canada* (n 35) para [255].

[67] As standards of scrutiny are addressed in the next section, this discussion is confined to rationales that justify departures from national treatment.

[68] Titi advises that a 'right to regulate' (which the justification exception to national treatment implicitly recognizes) is confined mostly to expropriation and FET and is overly reliant on 'arbitral discretion' in Aikaterini Titi, *The Right to Regulate in International Investment Law* (Nomos 2014) 301.

[69] This is aside from what Titi (n 68) at 134 describes as 'idiosyncratic exceptions' to non-discrimination. She includes South Africa's equality-promoting exception, introduced in 2000, as an example of this. See discussion of this practice in David Schneiderman, *Constitutionalizing Economic Globalization: Investment Rules and Democracy's Promise* (CUP 2008) 155.

[70] The first is identification of an appropriate comparator. See Federico Ortino, 'Non-Discriminatory Treatment in Investment Disputes' in Pierre-Marie Dupuy, Ernst-Ulrich Petersmann, and Francesco Francioni (eds), *Human Rights in International Investment Law and Arbitration* (OUP 2009) 360. The first function serves as a directive to compare foreign to local nationals.

[71] For an argument in favour of a 'separate justificatory step after prima facie inconsistency [with national treatment] see Andrew D Mitchell, David Heaton, and Caroline Henckels, *Non-Discrimination and the Role of Regulatory Purpose in International Trade and Investment Law* (Edward Elgar Publishing 2016) 160.

[72] The OECD contemplated public policy 'exceptions' to national treatment in OECD, *National Treatment for Foreign-Controlled Enterprises* (n 8) 21–22 ('key to determining whether a discriminatory measure applied to a foreign investor constitutes an exception to National Treatment'). However, the pamphlet also suggested that these were 'taken into account to define the circumstances in which comparison … is permissible' (ibid). The WTO jurisprudence treats justification as operating 'outside' of national treatment, on which see Federico Ortino, 'From "Non-Discrimination" to "Reasonableness": A Paradigm Shift in International Economic Law?' (2005) Jean Monnet Working Paper 10/05 25.

should be examined independently as are exercises of police powers to excuse alleged expropriations.[73]

Having been relatively neglected, the justification step has not been fully developed or applied consistently by tribunals. The treaties also tend to be silent on the issue,[74] with little added clarity from the arbitral jurisprudence. In UNCTAD's parlance, these matters remain 'open to further refinement',[75] while Dolzer and Schreuer describe the justification exercise as imprecise and 'unclear'.[76] The *Pope & Talbot* tribunal adopted a similar approach to *SD Myers* by acknowledging that the full legal context requires an examination of whether the measure has 'a reasonable nexus to rational government policies that (1) do not distinguish, on their face (or de facto), between foreign-owned and domestic companies, and (2) do not otherwise unduly undermine the investment liberalizing objectives of NAFTA'.[77] That is, once a distinction is found, it can 'be justified by showing that it bears a reasonable relationship to rational policies not motivated by preference of domestic over foreign owned investments'.[78] States can, therefore, escape liability for differential treatment, including intentional discrimination,[79] if the impugned measure is reasonably connected to 'rational' government policy. So long as the state can point to a neutral objective, independent of discriminatory intent or effect, the state will be excused for any unequal treatment of foreign investors.[80]

Among the tribunal decisions that considered the issue of justification, the *GAMI* tribunal excused the Government of Mexico for its expropriation of sugar mills, both locally and foreign owned, on the basis that the 'measure was plausibly connected with a legitimate goal of policy (ensuring that the sugar

[73] It remains difficult, nonetheless, to identify a workable categorical rule in this instance just as it is in characterizing measures as falling within police powers jurisdiction.

[74] The Indian model BIT has incorporated express language in a footnote, directing interpreters to consider 'legitimate regulatory objectives' based on the 'totality of the circumstances'. These circumstances include 'impact ... on third persons, the local community or the environment' in 'Model Text for the Indian Bilateral Investment Treaty' (December 2015) art 5, fn 2 in Paparinskis (n 33) 69.

[75] United Nations Conference on Trade and Development, *Investor–State Dispute Settlement and Impact on Investment Rulemaking* (United Nations 2007) 51.

[76] Rudolf Dolzer and Christoph Schreuer, *Principles of International Investment Law* (2nd edn, OUP 2012) 202–203.

[77] *Pope & Talbot* (n 24) para 78.

[78] ibid para 79.

[79] Even if *Pope & Talbot* (n 24) acknowledges this possibility, tribunals seem unlikely to do so in the case of facial distinctions; Caroline Henckels, *Proportionality and Deference in Investor-State Arbitration* (CUP 2015) 135.

[80] Similarly see Sylvie Tabet, 'Beyond the Smoking Gun: Is a Discriminatory Objective Necessary to Find a Breach of National Treatment?' in TJ Grierson Weiler (ed) *Investment Treaty Arbitration and International Law*, vol 1 (JurisNet 2008) 299–313; If, as some commentators suggest, plausible non-protectionist discrimination is drawn from the WTO experience, then the same considerations will apply outside of the NAFTA context, eg Kurtz (n 29) 132.

industry was in the hands of solvent enterprises) and was applied neither in a discriminatory manner nor as a disguised barrier to equal opportunity'.[81] In *Archer Daniels Midland*, the tribunal considered whether the foreign investor had 'unreasonably been treated less favourably than domestic investors in like circumstances'.[82] Imposing a tax on fructose sugar sweeteners (foreign-owned), but not on cane sugar sweeteners (locally owned), could not be justified with reference to any public policy other than a protectionist one that was designed to 'favor the domestic sugar market'.[83] An objective independent of discrimination was available to Canada in *Pope & Talbot*. 'Market conditions' and 'underlying economics' dictated the 'unlike circumstances' between softwood lumber producers in one Canadian province as compared to another. Both by conferring privileged access to new entrants, and by allotting decreasing shares in production and export to the United States for existing participants, the policy 'had a reasonable nexus with the rational policy ... and it had no elements of discrimination against foreign-owned producers'.[84] In summary, tribunals have the option to excuse discrimination, de jure or de facto, 'on the basis' that it pursues 'legitimate public welfare objectives'.[85]

Baetens identifies the few instances where justifiable distinctions are discussed by tribunals, including *SD Myers*, and argues that the more 'legitimate aims' are those that advance 'internationally accepted standards, in particular treaties with quasi-universal adherence'.[86] While international treaties generate good grounds for justifiable differentiation, this criterion looks too cramped. A polity may choose to pursue policy goals that are not yet, and may have little prospect of being, incorporated into a ratified treaty.[87] There is no good reason to limit 'rational government policies' only to those expressed in widely adopted international treaties. All variety of policy initiatives, including those following from national constitutions, even those initiatives characterized as bold and innovative,

[81] *Gami Investments Inc v Government of the United Mexican States*, UNCITRAL (15 November 2004) [114].

[82] *Archer Daniels Midland Company and Tate & Lyle Ingredients Americas Inc v The United Mexican States*, ICSID Case No ARB AF/04/5 (21 November 2007) [205].

[83] ibid [211]–[212].

[84] *Pope & Talbot* (n 24) [93].

[85] It was proposed (by US negotiators, it is said) that this language be expressly incorporated into a footnote to the national treatment clause in the Transpacific Partnership Agreement. See 'Drafters' Note on Interpretation of "In Like Circumstances" under Article 9.4 (National Treatment) and Article 9.5 (Most-Favored-Nation Treatment)' in Paparinskis (n 33) 792–93. With the election of President Donald Trump, the US withdrew from the agreement and the text was omitted.

[86] Fraya Baetens, 'Discrimination on the Basis of Nationality: Determining Likeness in Human Rights and Investment Law' in Stephan Schill (ed), *International Investment Law and Comparative Public Law* (OUP 2010) 279–315, 313. For examples of wider permissible objectives including implementation of international treaties see Mitchell, Heaton, and Henckels (n 71) 166, fn 299.

[87] For example, consider the case of black economic empowerment in South Africa, discussed below.

should be candidates for justification in the face of discrimination under national treatment.

Might the proliferation of 'right to regulate' clauses (RTR) in the treaties change this evaluation?[88] If one accepts the characterization of the Canada-EU CETA as representative of a 'state of the art' agreement, the relevant RTR clause does not add much to the present discussion.[89] It merely reaffirms the right of the parties to 'achieve' a non-exhaustive list of 'legitimate policy objectives' including measures to secure environmental, public morals or social protections.[90] A joint interpretive instrument, meant to respond to those who were holding up CETA approval in the European Parliament, declared further that the parties 'recognize the importance of the right to regulate in the public interest and have reflected it in the Agreement' and that they 'continue to have the ability to achieve the legitimate policy objectives that their democratic institutions set', including a longer list of objectives than the ones noted in CETA's text.[91] That same list of objectives is also included in a separate RTR clause in the joint interpretive instrument, reiterating again that the parties are entitled to 'adopt and apply ... laws ... that regulate economic activity in the public interest, to achieve legitimate public policy objectives'.[92] The RTR is, furthermore, repeated in a supplemental instrument, under the heading of 'Investment Protection', which declares that the CETA 'includes modern rules on investment that preserve the right of governments to regulate in the public interest'. Yet, there is little here to change the evaluation of what are justifiable distinctions that otherwise violates national treatment standard.[93]

[88] Titi answers this question by stating this 'exception is not necessary' as justifications are available in the 'like circumstances' inquiry. See Aikaterini Titi, *The Right to Regulate in International Investment Law* (Nomos 2014) 184 and the discussion of Sierra-Camargo and Suárez-Ricaurte in this volume.

[89] While this discussion is specific to national treatment, the chapter by Sierra-Camargo and Suárez-Ricaurte, in this volume, provides a more fulsome examination.

[90] CETA, art 8.9.1.

[91] Preamble (c) and (d) to the Joint Interpretative Instrument on the CETA Between Canada and the European Union and its Member States.

[92] Section 2 of the Joint Interpretative Instrument on the CETA Between Canada and the European Union and its Member States.

[93] Annex 8-A, s 3 of CETA concerning expropriation indicates that a proportionality inquiry is called for in cases of indirect expropriation, where a measure is 'so severe in light of its purpose that it appears manifestly excessive'. There is no such guidance in CETA despite the Joint Interpretative Instrument's declaration that CETA 'provides clear guidance to dispute resolution Tribunals on how these [clearly defined] standards should be applied' (s. 6 [c]).

5.1 Standard of Scrutiny

What standard of scrutiny is suggested by use of the qualifiers such as 'reasonable', 'rational' or 'plausible' in defence of justifiable discrimination? This question preoccupies equality law in national constitutional orders. With few exceptions,[94] it has not been of much concern to the interpretation of national treatment in investment law. Instead, arbitrators have taken for granted that the degree of scrutiny will mostly be strict. To illustrate, the *SD Myers* tribunal, near the conclusion of its award, acknowledged that maintaining an ability to dispose of PCB waste in Canada was a 'legitimate' objective as it was in accord 'with the policy objectives of the Basel Convention'. However, there 'were a number of legitimate ways by which Canada could have achieved' this objective, the tribunal opined. Closing the border to the export of hazardous waste was not one of them because 'the method contravened Canada's international commitments under the NAFTA'. The tribunal declared that the 'right to source all government requirements and to grant subsidies to the Canadian industry are but two examples of legitimate alternative measures', without further discussion.[95]

What the *SD Myers* tribunal appears to have applied was a version of the second step of a proportionality inquiry: the inquiry into 'necessity' or 'less restrictive' or 'alternative' means available to the state. It may be that the tribunal was merely following the textual directive in NAFTA Art. 104, which speaks of departures from NAFTA that aim to adhere to a handful of international environmental and conservation 'obligations' (including the Basel Convention) adopted by the parties. On such occasions, when a NAFTA party seeks to depart from obligations it must select, among the 'equally effective and reasonably available' means available, 'the alternative that is the least inconsistent with the other provisions of this Agreement'. Others advocate a similar least restrictive means inquiry, even when there is no such textual directive.[96]

[94] Henckels (n 79); Generally, see Gus Van Harten (n 1); Joshua Paine 'Standard of Review: Investment Arbitration' in *Max Planck Encyclopedias of International Law* (OUP 2018).
[95] *SD Myers Inc v Canada* (n 35) [255].
[96] See Mitchell, Heaton, and Henckels (n 71) 146, who insist that a measure be the 'least restrictive means reasonably available to achieve a legitimate objective'. See also Ortino, who, despite arguing against application of the final branch of the proportionality inquiry (*stricto sensu*), insists that the second branch of the proportionality inquiry, a strict 'necessity' test, be applied to determine whether the action taken is the 'most effective or efficient measure' amounting to 'meaningful substantive review' in Federico Ortino, 'Investment Treaties, Sustainable Development and Reasonableness Review: A Case Against Strict Proportionality Balancing' (2016) 30 Leiden Journal of International Law 71, para 90.

Yet, even here, NAFTA's directive grants some room to manoeuvre.[97] The process of choosing among reasonably available means that are equally effective and least restrictive is open to a variety of outcomes. One can, after all, almost always imagine less restrictive means. Moreover, how is a tribunal to determine whether means are equally effective?[98] The exercise calls for an assessment of policy alternatives and some measure of deference by tribunals.

In *SD Myers*, the tribunal evinced little understanding of this analytical step. If, by the 'right to source government requirements', the tribunal was envisaging disposal of government waste at particular sites, this approach would not have achieved the objective as effectively since it would have omitted any possibility for domestic private sector waste disposal. As for the tribunal's idea of granting governmental subsidies, even if such subsidies were expressly excepted from national treatment,[99] it was unclear (with no elaboration from the tribunal) why such measures would not run afoul of other standards in NAFTA's investment chapter.[100]

An inquiry into alternative means goes well beyond the justification inquiry suggested by the *Pope & Talbot* tribunal, that is, an inquiry into whether the distinction is for a purpose independent of discriminatory impacts. In *SD Myers*, the tribunal admitted that such a purpose was available to Canada—compliance with the Basel Convention—but this goal was downplayed as 'indirect'. Why is maintaining a country's capacity to dispose of PCBs and other dangerous substances safely, in its own territory, not a matter of direct national interest?[101] How could any country achieve that objective without ensuring that PCB waste could be disposed at an

[97] Inquiries even into 'necessity' can entail a variety of approaches, from 'strict scrutiny to a high degree of deference' in Andrew D Mitchell and Caroline Henckels, 'Variations on a Theme: Comparing the Concept of "Necessity" in International Investment Law and WTO Law' (2013) 14 Chicago Journal of International Law 93.

[98] It may be that policy decisions based upon scientific or technical expertise call for more deference. This has not been the experience to date. Instead, Paine (n 94) para 13 notes tribunals have focused upon the 'process' by which states adopt regulatory measures.

[99] NAFTA, art 1108(7)(b), which exempts 'subsidies or grants provided by a Party or a state enterprise, including government supported loans, guarantees and insurance' from art 1102 (national treatment). Kulick describes the tribunal as having 'internalized to a quite remarkable degree' elements of a proportionality test in Andreas Kulick, *Global Public Interest in International Investment Law* (CUP 2012) 244.

[100] See the discussion in Anne van Aaken and Jürgen Kurtz, 'Prudence or Discrimination? Emergency Measures, the Global Financial Crisis and International Economic Law' (2009) 12 Journal of International Economic Law 859. See generally OECD (n 8) 30, identifying subsidies that can comprise exceptions to national treatment as being confined to circumstances where the state is a shareholder, offsetting costs imposed by the state, or state aid in the form of grants, low interest loans, interest subsidies, and state guarantees. The case of subsidies that favour only locals, in other words, is not likely justifiable under a strict standard of scrutiny.

[101] This was the stated Canadian policy before SD Myers began to court Canadian customers in SD Myers (n 35) [108], [109]; The direct/indirect distinction is reminiscent of discredited Lochner era jurisprudence in the US; see eg *ALA. Schechter Poultry Corp v United States* 295 US 495 (1935).

existing facility located in the state? This was precisely the goal specified in the Minister's interim order justifying the ban on hazardous waste exports.[102] In response, the tribunal appears to have felt compelled to find a violation of national treatment because of the Minister of the Environment's statement in the House of Commons that the handling of PCBs should be 'done in Canada *by Canadians*'.[103] Why can't this statement be treated simply as a rhetorical flourish by an outspoken politician?[104] The government's written policy had been laid down six years earlier by a national council of environment ministers, following ratification of the Basel Convention. It was not an after-the-fact justification, as many commentators have insinuated. Indeed, the policy of the US Environmental Protection Agency (EPA) was also in accord with this objective, having imposed an 'absolute ban' on PCB imports until the government was successfully lobbied by SD Myers to open the US–Canada border. The border was closed not long after by court order. This is because the EPA had issued its directive opening the border in violation of federal law controlling admission, on a temporary basis, of toxic substances.[105] Yet, in *SD Myers*, the tribunal insisted, dismissively, that the shared policy rationale for closing the border was not a 'legitimate environmental reason' and only an 'indirect' objective.[106]

The apparent consensus among investment law specialists is that *SD Myers* was correctly decided.[107] This consensus has emerged despite the tribunal's highly restrictive standard of scrutiny and its eliding of arguments that closure of the border to hazardous waste served important purposes. The dominant view rejects that the state's purposes in this case were reasonable, rational, and plausible and aimed at objectives for which other measures would not have been as effective. In turn, there has emerged a corresponding view that

[102] 'On becoming aware of information indicating that the U.S. Environmental Protection Agency is allowing PCB imports into the U.S. from CANADA for destruction, the Minister of the Environment made this Interim Order to Amend the PCB Waste Export Regulations on November 20, 1995. 'The purpose of the Interim Order is to ensure that Canadian PCB Wastes are managed in an environmentally sound manner in CANADA and to prevent any possible significant danger to the environment or to human life or health', quoted in *SD Myers* (n 35) [123].

[103] ibid [116] (emphasis added). The minister is quoted in Hansard as stating that: 'It is still the position of the government that the handling of PCBs should be done in Canada by Canadians.'

[104] Should the principle of ministerial 'responsibility' (Kurtz (n 29) at 128) have greater weight than sound environmental policy? One is left wondering if the outcome would have been different had Minister Copps received proper legal advice about the matter and had exercised more discretion in expressing government policy.

[105] In *Sierra Club v United States Environmental Protection Agency* 118 F3d 1324 (9th Cir 1997), mentioned in *SD Myers* (n 35) [128].

[106] *SD Myers* (n 35) [195].

[107] See eg Kurtz (n 29); Andrea K Bjorklund, 'National Treatment' in August Reinisch (ed), *Standards of Investment Protection* (OUP 2008) 29–58, 39–40; August Reinisch, 'National Treatment' in Marc Bungenberg and others (eds), *International Investment Law* (CH Beck/Hart Publishing/Nomos 2015) 846–69, paras 18–23.

distinctions made by states should be closely scrutinized under the rubric of national treatment. The OECD, for instance, declares that measures will violate national treatment whenever 'discrimination is motivated, *at least in part*, by the fact that the enterprises concerned are under foreign control'.[108] There may be any number of motivations for state measures. Condemning all those that are partly motivated by discrimination appears highly intrusive, particularly when there may be other legitimate policy reasons for the measure. The penchant for strict standards of scrutiny is also manifest in Mitchell, Heaton, and Henckels' argument that permitting merely '*one* non-discriminatory, legitimate regulatory purpose' to escape the charge of discrimination would 'defeat' the object of the standard of protection. Only if the discriminatory measure is '*de minimis* or totally insignificant compared with other purposes', they argue, could a measure escape a charge of national treatment violation.[109] Nor is the analysis made easier by characterizing a measure's dominant purpose, as Kurtz and others recommend.[110] This, again, is often difficult to accomplish given the multitude purposes that can be served by an impugned measure. Some laws serve multiple constituencies; some even achieve contradictory purposes.[111]

This desire to impose strict standards of proof reveals an anti-regulatory disposition. It demands that a state act for no other purpose than a non-discriminatory one. So long as discrimination against foreign investors plays some role in policy design that is not totally 'insignificant', then the measure violates national treatment.[112] Insubstantial discriminatory side-effects are permissible if they are not a primary purpose of a measure. If the resulting adverse impact is anything more than de minimis, even if in pursuit of an important non-discriminatory objective, it will not be tolerated.[113] Anything less, it is said, would defeat the object of national treatment.

[108] OECD (n 8) 22 (emphasis added).

[109] Mitchell, Heaton, and Henckels (n 71) 166–67. Apart from *Clayton*, they argue, arbitrators have not second-guessed regulatory objectives provided they are 'plausible and non-discriminatory' (at 166).

[110] Jürgen Kurtz, 'Balancing Investor Protection and Regulatory Freedom in International Investment Law: The Necessary, Complex, and Vital Search for State Purpose' in *Yearbook on International Investment Law and Policy 2013–14* (OUP 2015) 251–304 at para 301; Mitchell, Heaton, and Henckels (n 71) 88, 90–91; also Kurtz (n 29) 127 where, applying a public choice account of investment law, he calls upon tribunals to evaluate the dominant political forces at work promoting the measure.

[111] Robert C Farrell, 'Legislative Purpose and Equal Protection's Rationality Review' (1992) 37 Villanova Law Review 1, 166, para 18 ('It is even possible that a law will have two purposes that pull in opposite directions'); Henckels admits that a measure of deference may be owed in such circumstances in Henckels (n 79) 136.

[112] On the distinction between *animus* playing 'some role' in decision-making (resulting in a lesser burden on plaintiffs) and showing 'but for' causation (resulting in a stricter burden) see *Comcast Corp v National Association of African American-Owned Media* 589 US (2020).

[113] This is not an argument meant to advocate for discriminatory conduct. Rather, it is an argument that tolerates discriminatory treatment, de jure or de facto, so long as a valid non-discriminatory objective is being pursued.

What is specifically intolerable for this school of thought is a standard of scrutiny that confines itself to rationality review or, as in the first stage of a proportionality analysis, rational connection. For such a standard of review, the burden of justifying limitations on investor rights is more easily satisfied than under the stricter standard promoted by most investment law scholars and lawyers. For instance, the US Supreme Court has ruled that such a burden of proof can be discharged, in a case involving a violation of religious freedom, 'so long as it [the policy] can reasonably be understood to result from a justification independent of unconstitutional grounds'.[114] Out of mutual respect, the Court presumes that other constitutional branches are proceeding primarily on firm constitutional ground. By imposing a low threshold on the state, rationality review allows for constitutionally valid objectives otherwise to be pursued. Such respect for host state governments is rarely on display in investment law discussions.[115]

Thus, it is not entirely convincing when Mitchell, Heaton, and Henckels describe their approach to national treatment as advocating only for a 'rational or reasonable connection' to satisfy the national standard.[116] This is because elsewhere, as mentioned, they insist on more: that there be no evidence of protectionist purpose beyond the *de minimis*.[117] To similar effect, Di Mascio and Pauwelyn argue that a rational relationship test is appropriate only if the non-protectionist purpose is relatively unimportant. In other cases, the burden of proof rises to what they call a 'substantially related to' test, analogous to a test of 'necessity'.[118] For these authors, the ruling in *SD Myers*, applying a strict standard of scrutiny, was undoubtedly correct.

Unexpectedly, Dean Ronald A. Cass, in a separate statement in the *UPS* award, declined to apply strict scrutiny in an inquiry into justifiable discrimination.[119] At issue was the Canadian federal government's support for Canada Post's courier delivery service, Purolator. In addition to preferential treatment at Canadian border points of entry, Canada Post also received indirect support via a publication assistance programme (PAP), which provided subsidies to Canadian publishers who used Canada Post to distribute their periodicals. This

[114] *Trump v Hawaii* 138 S Ct 2392, 2420 (2018) (applying rational basis review to President Trump's executive order closing the US border to select Muslim countries).

[115] Van Harten (n 1) 73.

[116] Mitchell, Heaton, and Henckels (n 71) 160.

[117] ibid 166.

[118] Di Mascio and Pauwelyn (n 26) 87.

[119] *United Parcel Service of America Inc v Canada*, Ad hoc–UNCITRAL Arbitration Rules, Award and Separate Opinion (24 May 2007). Unexpectedly, because Dean Cass has been appointed exclusively by claimants according to IA Reporter's 'Arbitratror Profile and Appointments' (last accessed 31 August 2023).

indirect support was unavailable to Purolator's US competitor, United Parcel Service (UPS). A majority of the tribunal concluded that UPS and Canada Post were not in like circumstances given Canada Post's statutory obligation to deliver to every corner of the country. Rather, UPS was in like circumstances to other courier delivery services, Canadian and foreign owned, that were not responsible for comprehensive delivery. Furthermore, Canada was entitled to take advantage of the cultural industry exemption in NAFTA.[120] Dean Cass dissented on these points and would have issued an award of damages in favour of the investor. In the course of so doing, he articulated a standard of review for determining 'reasonableness' in the context of a national treatment claim. This review should be undertaken, Cass declared, with something less than strict scrutiny. He characterized the UPS argument as inviting the tribunal to adopt a 'less restrictive means' test.[121] The test was rejected by Cass as it would 'severely constrain NAFTA Parties in pursuit of their own objectives and would greatly expand the power of NAFTA tribunals to evaluate the legitimacy of government objectives and efficacy of governmentally chosen means'; likewise, it would 'intrude ... forcefully on government prerogatives'.[122] While 'bald discrimination on the basis of nationality cannot be salvaged' by an assertion of reasonableness, a different standard should apply 'where the claim of national treatment violation rests on the effects of decisions not expressly predicated on nationality'. This call for respect for the other branches of the state resembles a direction taken in the initial draft of the Model Indian BIT. Although subsequently abandoned, that draft would have instructed tribunals to grant 'substantial deference' when considering factors justifying departures from equal treatment.[123]

In *UPS*, arbitrator Cass preferred not to specify 'a precise formula for the degree of justification required'. Instead, he adopted an alternative argument attacking the 'legitimacy' of Canada's justification for confining the publication assistance program benefits only to customers of Canada Post. That rationale was never clearly articulated when Canada 'framed the current structure for delivery'. The government had never questioned *why* it was important to pursue these 'broader public policy goals' and, instead, crafted a plan 'that on its face

[120] ibid paras 177, 172. The cultural industries exception can be found in NAFTA, art 2106 and Annex 2106.

[121] *United Parcel Service* (n 119) Separate Statement, para 113.

[122] ibid paras 117–18.

[123] This direction was abandoned in the final version of the model text. See 'Model Text for the Indian Bilateral Investment Treaty' (April 2015) art 4, fn 2 https://www.mygov.in/sites/default/files/master_image/Model%20Text%20for%20the%20Indian%20Bilateral%20Investment%20Treaty.pdf (accessed 17 December 2019) and the India–Colombia BIT (2016) art 4 for the final version.

seemed to ask only *how* to give PAP benefits to Canada Post'.[124] Cass declined to defer to Canada's assertion that this was a justifiable policy choice. Otherwise, Cass claimed, the NAFTA parties could 'craft rationales during the course of a dispute that would be tailored to the legal issues arising in the proceeding'.[125] Canada's simple assertion, without more, meant that it had not rebutted the prima facie case that UPS and Canada Post were in like circumstances.

Just the opposite lesson to that recommended by Cass is drawn by Baetens from her inquiry into what investment lawyers can learn from international human rights law. To determine whether it is appropriate to find 'likeness' (non-justifiable discrimination), she argues that arbitrators should inquire into whether 'alternative (entirely different) measures are available'. Even if no other measures achieve the same objective, that is, 'even if this particular measure is the only option available, the state needs to ensure that it is not enacted in a more restrictive manner than is required to achieve this legitimate aim (the proportionality principle)'.[126] Here, she declares that any claimed exceptions to national treatment must be scrutinized closely, recalling the strictest test available in national constitutional orders.[127] Notably, Baetens does not appear to derive this onerous standard directly from international human rights practice, even as she purports to draw lessons from these international obligations. Missing from her list of factors, for instance, is the margin of appreciation that is typically granted to states in meeting their human rights obligations.[128] Indeed, Baetens affords little deference at all to the state, instead, favouring the most intrusive standard of scrutiny.

In this stream of anti-regulatory scholarship and arbitral awards, it is as if state measures were directed at the most vulnerable groups in society, those who are 'anonymous', 'diffuse', and 'systematically disadvantaged in pluralist democracy'.[129] Of course, these descriptors are hardly credible. Foreign investors, particularly those able to finance investment claims, have a variety of means to influence states in both operative and non-operative democracies.[130]

124 *United Parcel Service* (n 119) Separate Statement, para 130 (italics in original).

125 ibid para 132.

126 Baetens (n 86) 305.

127 Baetens may have been inspired by the International Law Commission's draft articles for determining whether a state is entitled to invoke a defence of necessity. States can preclude wrongfulness of an international act if the action is 'the only means ... to safeguard against a grave and imminent peril'. See art 25(1)(a) reproduced in Paparinskis (n 33) 134, cited in CMS Gas Transmission Company c. República Argentina, Award, ICSID Case No ARB/01/08 (12 May 2005) para 316.

128 This is discussed in Baetens (n 86) 294–96.

129 Bruce A Ackerman, 'Beyond Carolene Products' (1985) 98 Harvard Law Review 713, 724.

130 Further on this see David Schneiderman, 'Investing in Democracy? Political Process and International Investment Law' (2010) 60 University of Toronto Law Journal 909.

The standard of scrutiny to assess reasonableness in national treatment analysis calls for a rethink. Far more deference to regulators and legislators is warranted.

6 No Greater Rights

The CETA joint interpretative instrument declares that 'CETA will not result in foreign investors being treated more favourably than domestic investors'.[131] The object of this declaration was to reassure Europeans (and, perhaps, Canadians) that the CETA did not entitle Canadian investors to greater rights than those available to the citizens of EU states. This 'no greater rights' claim has been relied on by European and US political leadership to defend various trade and investment agreements. The claim has not been an entirely successful one.[132] As mentioned above, the ambit of national treatment standards exceeds constitutional protections under the US equal protection clause. In Canada, there are national and sub-national legal protections against discrimination (on grounds of national origin, for instance) in addition to constitutional protections against discrimination. Absent intentional discrimination of the most objectionable sort (on the grounds of race, for instance), these protections typically do not attract strict scrutiny but rather a more deferential standard of review. The same could be said of the rights of European citizens; equality violations typically do not attract strict scrutiny as doctrines of subsidiarity and margin of appreciation, for instance, serve to soften the standard of review. The case that foreign investors gain greater rights is made even more convincing once other standards of protection, such as expropriation and fair and equitable treatment, are brought into the discussion. Clearly, the CETA's declaration of 'no greater rights' is, at the very least, disingenuous.

The case of *Clayton v Canada* demonstrates how national treatment can deliver better treatment for foreign investors. The Bilcon Company of Delaware sought damages against Canada for its reliance on an allegedly flawed independent environmental review consisting of public hearings, scientific evidence, and the production of a lengthy, detailed report. The review panel had recommended that the investor be refused permission to construct a rock

[131] See s 6(a) of the CETA's Joint Interpretative Instrument.

[132] As I have argued elsewhere. See eg David Schneiderman, '"Writing the Rules of the Global Economy": How America Defines the Contours of International Investment Law' (2018) 6 London Review of International Law 255.

quarry, along with a processing and ship-loading facility, on sensitive coastline in Nova Scotia. Comprised of three scientists, the panel advised against approval because of the proposed project's adverse environmental effects to land, marine, and human environments. The principal investors, the Clayton family, claimed that the panel failed to apply Canadian environmental law by having taken into account 'community core values', a consideration not mentioned in the authorizing statute. A majority of the tribunal agreed. Having relied on the panel's flawed decision, the government's conduct was found to be 'arbitrary', falling foul of NAFTA's minimum standard of treatment.[133]

The majority also decided that Canada offended NAFTA's standard of national treatment for having subjected the investor's proposal to public scrutiny under the auspices of an independent environmental review. The Clayton investment, it was argued, had been treated differently from similar projects that were granted approval through more expeditious processes, such as environmental screening or simple comprehensive study. Those investments had not been subject to the spotlight of public hearings. There was no ground for this differential treatment, the investor claimed, other than vocal community opposition to its proposal.[134] Minimal scrutiny, despite the proposal's significant impacts on the environment, would have been more appropriate, according to the claimant's expert in Canadian environmental law. What the investor alleged, and the tribunal accepted, was the pernicious argument that, because the government employed a process that dug deeper into adverse environmental effects and afforded an opportunity for transparency and community input in the approval process, Canada had discriminated against the investor on nationality grounds.[135]

There are many troubling elements to the *Clayton* decision.[136] Having regard only to the claim that investors have no greater rights than locals, the tribunal granted an award of damages that would not have been available to claimants in Canadian courts. As the dissenting arbitrator McRae put it, the tribunal imported a 'damages remedy not available under Canadian law'.[137] If successful in a Canadian court, the remedy for the Claytons would have been a judicial order

[133] *Clayton v Canada*, PCA Case No 2009-04, Award on Jurisdiction and Liability (17 March 2015) para 591.

[134] *Clayton v Canada*, Expert Report of David Estrin, PCA Case No 2009-04 (8 July 2011) para 101 www.italaw.com/sites/default/files/case-documents/italaw6286.pdf.

[135] *Clayton v Canada* (n 133) para 724.

[136] For instance, it is not beyond question that the joint review panel misapplied Canadian law. The Federal Court of Canada might only have 'potentially' been interested in the claim, observed dissenting arbitrator McRae.

[137] *Clayton*, Award on Jurisdiction and Liability, Dissenting Opinion of Professor Donald McRae (n 33) para 48.

to reconsider their application under the relevant statute. This opportunity for more favourable treatment helps to explain the investor's launching of a direct NAFTA dispute without prior resort to the local courts. It reveals the hollowness of CETA's declaration that foreign investors are not 'treated more favourably than domestic investors'.[138]

The *Foresti* dispute also reveals how investment treaties confer privileged rights on foreign investors. The South African government had initiated a plan to support black economic empowerment[139] in furtherance of its constitutional commitment to equality and to advancing the interests of 'categories of persons, disadvantaged by unfair discrimination'.[140] There were various elements to the plan, but the one that triggered the dispute was a requirement that existing mineral rights be replaced with new licences, resulting in the sale of 26 per cent of the ownership in mining companies to historically disadvantaged South Africans. This forced divestiture, it was claimed, amounted to an expropriation (direct or indirect[141]) and a denial of national treatment. The dispute was not ultimately resolved. After it was revealed that one of South Africa's lawyers had solicited a substantial bribe, conditional on him convincing the government to settle the case, the investor's claim was discontinued. The tribunal ended up awarding costs in favour of the state.[142]

The choice of comparator group would have been critical to the claimant's success in *Foresti*. Where foreign investors are required to give up part of their investment to locals, such a measure could be characterized as discriminatory. The scheme, after all, was structured precisely in ways that favoured South African nationals, exhibiting the kind of 'capture' that worries public choice accounts of investment law. Were foreign investors entitled to the best treatment available to any domestic investor in the mining sector, including those owned by historically disadvantaged South Africans? Or was the appropriate comparator those most similarly situated to the Foresti group, that is, South Africans who owned investments in the mining sector but were not historically

[138] This was a question the Court of Justice of the European Union (n 53) also preferred not to ask.

[139] For an evaluation of BEE and its non-conformity with investment treaty obligations, see David Schneiderman, *Constitutionalizing Economic Globalization: Investment Rules and Democracy's Promise* (CUP 2008) at 147–156.

[140] See art 9 of the Constitution of the Republic of South Africa.

[141] Compensation under the investment treaty would be immediate, fully transferable, and at fair market value which was well beyond the constitutional standard of what was equivalent to 'appropriate' compensation. For more on this see Schneiderman (n 139) at 137–47.

[142] See *Foresti and Others v South Africa*, ICSID Case No ARB AF/07/, Award (3 August 2010) [31], [133].

disadvantaged?[143] The latter approach would have been endorsed by South Africa's Constitutional Court, having adopted interpretations that would have supported the scheme in any constitutional challenge. Given the remedial nature of the country's constitutional guarantee of equality, the measure would be considered consonant with the Constitution's transformative agenda. Those who are more advantaged, Justice Albie Sachs has written, are expected to 'bear a larger portion of the burden of transformation than others'.[144] Equality is not merely about treating everyone the same. It also is about tolerating unequal treatment so as to protect vulnerable groups and advance their social position for the purpose of remedying historic disadvantage.

On these grounds, South Africa's measure bore a 'reasonable relationship to rational policies' not motivated by a discriminatory preference. Put differently, the rule had a justification that was independent of its discriminatory impact. Yet, among its non-*de minimis* purposes, it also differentiated between foreign investors who, by definition, could not benefit from the scheme and a sub-set of locals who could.[145]

The *Foresti* dispute isolates a number of unsettled difficulties in national treatment analysis. First, it reveals that policies, not primarily motivated by *animus* toward foreign investors, cannot be saved if they unintentionally have the effect of discriminating against foreigners. Secondly, the dispute points to the difficulty of identifying an appropriate comparator and, thirdly, to the difficulty of articulating and applying a justification test. Fourthly, it points to the fact that the claimants sought an exemption from the constitution's promise of substantive equality. All other local firms had to comply. Under the logic of national treatment, however, foreign investors would be excused from the shared burden of reversing widespread economic inequality.

These criticisms point to the merits of the Calvo doctrine. Its key premise, articulated by Argentinian jurist Carlos Calvo, is that foreign actors have no absolute right to diplomatic protection under international law. They are entitled only to equal treatment with locals and any complaint about differential treatment is to be settled by local courts: '[n]o alien has a right to demand

143 This was the comparator proposed by in Luke Eric Peterson, 'South Africa's Bilateral Investment Treaties: Implications for Development and Human Rights' (November 2006) *Dialogue on Globalization* Occasional Papers No 26, 31 http://library.fes.de/pdf-files/iez/global/04137-20080708.pdf (accessed 20 October 2019).

144 *Minister of Finance and Another v Van Heerden* (2004) 6 SA 21(CC) [154].

145 Were South Africa to claim that BEE was not motivated by an *animus* directed at foreign investors, this would not salvage the measure in so far as it had de facto discriminated.

more'.[146] Even if Calvo's views were complicated by arguments about civilized justice in Latin America,[147] his doctrine is predicated on the principle of equality and non-intervention among states—that, 'as a matter of international law, no state may intervene, diplomatically or otherwise, to enforce its citizens' private claims in a foreign state'.[148] It also presupposes that nationals in host states will be treated similarly to foreigners. This equality principle, however, is jettisoned once treaties bind states to provide treatment beyond that which is binding on locals and not for the purpose of protecting members of a vulnerable group that has experienced historic disadvantage. Unless, that is, investment law requires that we treat foreign investors as similarly situated to black South Africans seeking to overcome the vestiges of apartheid?

7 Conclusion

This examination of national treatment doctrine has revealed an evolving and inconsistent set of understandings about how equality principles operate in investment law. An optimistic assessment suggests that arbitrators may be on a learning curve, slowly acquiring more nuanced understanding of how discrimination analysis operates in theory and practice. Arbitrators could, with this knowledge, retreat from capacious review of state policy in favour of a more carefully calibrated review. They could undertake their review function with an understanding that foreign nationals do not experience discrimination solely because a measure negatively impacts them on the grounds of nationality. More of this type of learning is needed before national treatment can be tailored to its function of policing unjust discrimination.

At present, problems persist. Tribunals are too quick to rush to judgment in cases of indirect discrimination. The search for appropriate comparators has proven especially challenging. The readiness of scholars and arbitrators to condemn state measures that intermingle discriminatory and non-discriminatory purposes is disquieting. It is particularly so when non-discriminatory objectives pursue important policy goals. Connected to these problems is the indeterminate standard of review that is applied to scrutinize the justifications for state measures. Whether the path forward shifts away from strict scrutiny will

[146] See Shea (n 10) 109.

[147] Liliana Obregón, 'Between Civilization and Barbarism: Creole Interventions in International Law' (2006) 27 Third World Quarterly 815.

[148] Gloria Sandrino, 'The NAFTA Investment Chapter and Foreign Direct Investment in Mexico: A Third World Perspective' (1994) 27 Vanderbilt Journal of Transnational Law 259, 268.

determine whether, in future, national treatment is an obstacle to measures aimed at ameliorating economic inequality. With strict scrutiny, states are disarmed from pursuing what could be characterized as just discrimination.

There is an irony in the invocation of national treatment by foreign investors to escape responsibilities imposed upon local economic actors. The special treatment bestowed upon foreign investors is compounded by the many other treaty protections to which they can avail themselves. Cumulatively, they have the effect of shifting investment law from the promotion of equality of opportunity to the generation of more privileges for international elites. One can reasonably conclude that investment law norm entrepreneurs are little more than strategically egalitarian.[149] It comes as no surprise that, in locales around the world, people are dismayed by public power's inability to resist the demands and priorities of the economically powerful few.

[149] Norberto Bobbio, *Left and Right: The Significance of a Political Distinction* (Polity Press 1996) 70.

3

Most Favoured Nation Treatment

Anil Yilmaz Vastardis

1 Introduction

The interpretation of investment treaty standards by arbitral tribunals is infamous for its lack of consistency and legal certainty.[1] Most favoured nation (MFN) treatment clauses in investment treaties reflect this trend. MFN treatment is one of the most inconsistently applied standards in investment treaty arbitration.

In essence, MFN treatment is a component of the non-discrimination principle under international law.[2] MFN clauses in a variety of treaty types typically contain a promise by the contracting states that the beneficiaries of that treaty (the 'basic treaty') will receive the most favourable treatment that is extended by the contracting states to any third state or its nationals under the relevant state's domestic law or treaties.[3] Historically, MFN clauses were most typically included in economic treaties (governing trade, navigation, or investment) and consular treaties.[4] Today, MFN clauses are common in international economic

[1] See United Nations Commission on International Trade Law Working Group III (Investor–State Dispute Settlement Reform) Thirty-sixth session Vienna (29 October–2 November 2018) 'Possible reform of investor–state dispute settlement (ISDS): Consistency and related matters Note by the Secretariat' (A/CN.9/WG.III/WP.150).

[2] Suzy H Nikièma, 'The Most-Favoured-Nation Clause in Investment Treaties' IISD Best Practices Series (February 2017) 2 (explaining that the MFN standard reflects the external component of the non-discrimination principle, while the national treatment standard reflects its internal component).

[3] The 1978 ILC Draft Articles on MFN Clauses of the International Law Commission (ILC) provide the following definition in Article 4.a: 'treatment accorded by the granting State to the beneficiary State, or to persons or things in a determined relationship with that State, not less favourable than treatment extended by the granting State to a third State or to persons or things in the same relationship with that third State'. See Draft Articles on MFN clauses with commentaries, adopted by the ILC at its third session in 1978, A/CN.4/SER.A/1978/Add.1 (Pt 2) 18.

[4] See Stanley K Hornbeck, 'Most-Favored-Nation Clause' (1909) 3 American Journal of International Law 395, 398. See also Umut Ozsu, 'The Ottoman Empire, the Origins of Extraterritoriality, and International Legal Theory' in Anne Orford and Florian Hoffmann, *The Oxford Handbook of the Theory of International Law* (OUP 2016) 130–32 (discussing the uses of MFN clauses extending to civil and criminal matters concerning the citizens of contracting parties in the other state. For instance, the capitulations used by major powers in the nineteenth century allowed foreign states to exercise consular jurisdiction over civil and criminal matters concerning their citizens either by explicit treaty provisions or via expansion of jurisdiction under the MFN standard in countries that were considered

Anil Yilmaz Vastardis, *Most Favoured Nation Treatment* In: *Rethinking Investment Law.* Edited by: David Schneiderman and Gus Van Harten, Oxford University Press. © Anil Yilmaz Vastardis 2023. DOI: 10.1093/oso/9780192871084.003.0003

law.[5] In that field, their primary aim is to ensure that states afford consistently favourable treatment to economic actors of different nationalities.

Despite this basic framing of MFN treatment, it is widely acknowledged that there is no uniform usage of an 'MFN standard' in international law. Indeed, the content and scope of MFN treatment can vary widely depending on the wording of a treaty clause.[6] Under international investment law, the interpretation of MFN treatment has been influenced, for example, by debates over how much the idea of a general MFN standard in international law should have bearing on an MFN clause in the treaty.[7] The interpretation of MFN treatment in investment law has also been driven by creative efforts of claimants to 'import' substantive standards and procedural rights from third-country investment treaties of the respondent state. This ambitious reliance on MFN clauses to import external treaty standards has now become accepted by many arbitral tribunals and scholars as conventional wisdom,[8] practically allowing investors to pick and mix investment treaty standards. This position has attracted criticism from a minority of scholars and arbitral tribunals, and states as being inconsistent with treaty law and the general principles of international law applicable to the MFN standard.[9]

'semi-civilized'); Georg Schwarzenberger, 'The Most-Favoured-Nation Standard in British State Practice' (1945) 22 British Yearbook of International Law 97.

[5] ILC, 'Final Report of the Study Group on the Most-Favored-Nation Clause' (2015) 2 Yearbook of the International Law Commission(Pt Two) UN Doc A/70/10 [20].

[6] Tanjina Sharmin, 'The MFN Clause in Investment Law and Arbitration: A Developing Countries Perspective' in Julien Chaisse and others (eds), *Handbook of International Investment Law and Policy* (Springer 2019) 4; ILC Draft Articles on MFN, Article 4 Commentary, para 13; M Paparinskis, 'MFN Clauses and Substantive Treatment: A Law of Treaties Perspective of the "Conventional Wisdom"' (2018) 112 American Journal of International Law Unbound 49–54, 50.

[7] Alejandro Faya Rodriguez, 'The Most-Favoured-Nation Clause in International Investment Agreements: A Tool for Treaty Shopping?' (2008) 25(1) Journal of International Arbitration 89, 92; Paparinski (n 6). In the area of trade, the ILC (n 5) has observed that the balance between the words used and the general concept of MFN treatment tipped more in favour of the latter ('[n]otwithstanding the fact that MFN provisions in the WTO are worded differently, the approach of the Appellate Body has been to treat them as having the same meaning. The textual interpretation of the words has less importance than the underlying concept of MFN treatment') para 45.

[8] *Bayindir Insaat Turizm Ticaret Ve Sanayi AS v Pakistan*, ICSID Case No ARB/03/29, Award (27 August 2009) [153] ff; *Rumeli Telekom AS v Kazakhstan*, ICSID Case No ARB/05/16, Award (29 July 2008) [575]–[681]; *Emilio Agustín Maffezini v Kingdom of Spain*, ICSID Case No ARB/97/7, Award (13 November 2000); Paparinskis (n 6); Simon Batifort and J Benton Heath, 'The New Debate on the Interpretation of MFN Clauses in Investment Treaties: Putting the Brakes on Multilateralization' (2018) 111 American Journal of International Law 873. See for a critique of this position Tomoko Ishikawa, 'Interpreting the Most-Favoured-Nation Clause in Investment Treaty Arbitration: Interpretation as a Process of Creating an Obligation' in Charles Sampford, Spencer Zifcak, and Derya Aydin Okur (eds), *Rethinking International Law and Justice* (Routledge 2016).

[9] *İçkale İnsaat Limited, Şirketi v Turkmenistan*, ICSID Case No ARB/10/24, Award (8 March 2016); *Methanex Corporation v USA*, Response of Respondent United States of America to Methanex's submission Concerning the NAFTA Free Trade Commission's 31 July 2001 Interpretation (26 October 2001) 9 https://2009-2017.state.gov/documents/organization/8252.pdf; Facundo Perez-Aznar, 'The Use of Most-Favoured-Nation Clauses to Import Substantive Treaty Provisions in International

In this chapter, I unpack these creative approaches and debates about MFN treatment, exploring key aspects of MFN clauses' application in investment law and highlighting the need to pull MFN back to its non-discrimination origins. I discuss pivotal moments when the meaning of MFN treatment was redirected towards worse outcomes in international investment law, blurring the ideal of non-discrimination. The discussion begins with a brief overview of the origins of MFN clauses. It then turns to the 'non-discrimination' principle in international economic law. These introductory sections serve as guideposts for how MFN treatment, by its interpretation, has been extensively side-tracked in international investment law. They set the stage for an examination of basic features of MFN clauses as interpreted in investment treaty awards. Patterns are identified in the face of the many variations in the wording of MFN clauses in the treaties. After this analysis, I return in more detail to debates about the interpretation of MFN clauses by arbitral tribunals. Here, I shed light on the misconceptions surrounding the application of MFN treatment in investment law. Finally, an optimistic note is sounded in the concluding section by reviewing some recent investment treaties and models which have sought to learn from the unfortunate experience with MFN clauses at the hands of arbitrators, and adapt accordingly.

2 Origins of MFN Treatment

The first ancestors of modern MFN clause have been traced to trading relationships among cities in the eleventh century.[10] From the fifteenth century on, MFN clauses were standard in commerce treaties between states, especially so-called friendship, commerce, and navigation (FCN) treaties.[11] Despite this medieval pedigree, MFN clauses never became uniform in treaty practice. FCN treaties between states of comparable bargaining power tended to have reciprocal and conditional clauses, focused on ensuring tariff reductions for all trading partners on a going-forward basis.[12] Among states

Investment Agreements' (2017) 20(4) Journal of International Economic Law 777; Ishikawa (n 8); Rodriguez (n 7); Christopher Greenwood, 'Reflections on 'Most Favoured Nation' Clauses in Bilateral Investment Treaties' in David D Caron and others (eds), *Practising Virtue: Inside International Arbitration* (OUP 2015).

[10] First Report of the Special Rapporteur, Mr Endre Ustor (21st session of the ILC 1969) A/CN.4/213 (in (1969) 2 Yearbook [10]; Michael Trebilcock, Robert Howse, and Antonia Eliason, *The Regulation of International Trade* (4th edn, Routledge 2013) 54.

[11] Hornbeck (n 4)403; First Report of Mr Endre Ustor (n 10) [80].

[12] Jurgen Kurtz, 'The MFN Standard and Foreign Investment: An Uneasy Fit?' (2004) 5(6) Journal of World Investment and Trade 861, 863.

with unequal bargaining power, by contrast, the more powerful state typically was the sole beneficiary of an MFN clause.[13] Thus, European imperial trading companies included unilateral MFN clauses in their treaties with the rulers of Asian civilizations.[14] In the case of the imperial power's own colonies, MFN protections were unnecessary or fundamentally undesirable for the management of trading privileges within the empire.[15] Unilateral concessions of trading benefits were also simply imposed as part of capitulation treaties between western powers and 'semi-civilized' states such as the Ottoman Empire, Iran, China, Siam, and Japan.[16] In contrast to the mutually beneficial exchange of MFN clauses among powerful states,[17] then, such clauses served a distinctively exploitative end in the relations between these same states and other societies.[18]

In the first half of the twentieth century, global wars and economic crises largely ruined MFN-based trading relationships.[19] MFN clauses returned only after the Second World War, then becoming a foundation stone, alongside national treatment, for the non-discrimination principle in international trade. MFN treatment is a conceptual pillar of the multilateral trading regime under the WTO. It is captured not only by Article I of the General Agreement on Tariffs and Trade but also by Article II of the General Agreement on Trade in Services and Article 4 of the Agreement on Trade-Related Aspects of Intellectual Property Rights. In turn, MFN treatment was written into investment treaties, and trade agreements with investment chapters, with an ambitious aspiration to embed the ideal of economic non-discrimination into the relatively sprawling field of investor–state relations.

[13] First Report of Mr Endre Ustor (n 10) [13]–[16].

[14] ibid [19].

[15] See Antony Anghie, *Imperialism, Sovereignty and the Making of International Law* (CUP 2004) 250–52; Hornbeck (n 4) 395, 403.

[16] Although initially the Ottoman capitulations were seen as the sovereign's granting of privileges to its trading partners or allies, with the decline of the Empire, they clearly became unilateral concessions granted to western nations particularly after military defeat. See Ozsu (n 4), 129; Anghie (n 15) 84–86; First Report of Mr Endre Ustor (n 10) [20]–[21].

[17] See Ozsu (n 4); Arnulf Becker Lorca, *Mestizo International Law: A Global Intellectual History 1842–1933* (CUP 2015) 81.

[18] See Treaty of Karlowitz (26 January 1699) between the Holy League (Austria, Poland, Venice, and Russia) and the Ottoman Empire; Treaty of Kucuk Kaynarca (21 July 1774) between the Russian Empire and the Ottoman Empire; See Umut Ozsu (n 4); Becker Lorca (n 17) 78–79, 86.

[19] First Report of Mr Endre Ustor (n 10) [30]–[40]; Kurtz (n 12) 864; Trebilcock and others (n 10) 55–56.

3 The Underlying Ideal of Non-discrimination

In essence, non-discrimination in modern international economic law seeks to bar states from discrimination based on nationality without a valid justification. It finds expression in two types of clauses based on relative rather than absolute standards: national treatment and MFN treatment. This root principle of non-discrimination should be the starting point for any application and interpretation of MFN clauses. Yet its promise as an ideal unfortunately has been betrayed in the course of the MFN experience of investment treaty arbitration.

Absent from customary international law, MFN treatment has become standard in economic relations among states by the terms of trade and investment treaties.[20] Undoubtedly, this treaty practice was influenced by the increasing volume, and liberalization, of trade and investment in the post-war era of globalization.[21] Non-discrimination in relation to flows of investment and trade is considered an important contributor to stability in international relations.[22] It is conventionally understood to enable competition in the market for all economic actors and thereby increase efficiency and prosperity.[23]

Such is the ideal of a liberal trading system. Yet this ideal underpinning MFN treatment has not been rigorously tested in the context of investment liberalization and protection under investment treaties, as distinct from the context of trade relations and the WTO framework. Whether it actually translates into better living and working conditions in host states is a complex question and far from legitimate as conventional wisdom.[24] Even so, arbitral tribunals and the surrounding literature of international investment law frequently

[20] Nicholas DiMascio and Joost Pauwelyn, 'Nondiscrimination in Trade and Investment Treaties: Worlds Apart or Two Sides of the Same Coin?' (2008) 102(1) American Journal of International Law 48; Rudolf Dolzer and Christoph Schreuer, *Principles of International Investment Law* (2nd edn, OUP 2012) 206.

[21] Peter Muchlinski, *Multinational Enterprises and the Law* (2nd edn, OUP 2007) 628; Matthias Herdegen, *Principles of International Economic Law* (2nd edn, OUP 2016) 66; UNCTAD Pink Series Sequel: Most Favoured Nation Treatment (2010) 14.

[22] Trebilcock and others (n 10) 58; See also Kurtz (n 12) 864–65 ('MFN treatment … was to play a central remedial role in international efforts to reconstruct the world economy after the Second World War').

[23] DiMascio and Pauwelyn (n 20) 54; Trebilcock and others (n 10) 57, 59 (noting the free-riding challenge of broadly applicable MFN in the multilateral trading regime).

[24] For an overview of the empirical studies on the contribution of IIL to economic development see Jonathan Bonnitcha, Lauge Poulsen, and Michael Waibel, *The Political Economy of the Investment Treaty Regime* (OUP 2017) 155–79. For an analysis of whether investment treaties enhance FDI inflows see Jason Webb Yackee, 'Do Bilateral Investment Treaties Promote Foreign Direct Investment: Some Hints from Alternative Evidence' (2011) 51 Virginia Journal of International Law 397. For an analysis of the 'good governance' effects of investment treaty commitments see Mavluda Sattorova, *The Impact of Investment Treaty Law on Host States: Enabling Good Governance?* (Hart Publishing 2018). See also OECD, 'FDI Qualities Indicators: Measuring the Sustainable Development Impacts of Investment' (2019).

assume greater protections afforded to investors via expansive interpretations of MFN clauses will eventually benefit host states and their populations. When analysing MFN clauses and the resulting arbitral awards, it is important to remember the underlying uncertainty about whether such clauses actually benefit anyone beyond a narrow class of potential claimants and those who service the resolution of their treaty claims.[25]

The non-discrimination principle has developed differently in international investment law as compared to trade law. These differences arise from the different modes of operation,[26] which limit cross-fertilization between the two fields. International trade law is a state-state system. It is largely based on a multilateral regime governed under the WTO umbrella. Even closer trading relationships are established by regional and bilateral agreements.[27] In contrast, international investment law lacks a multilateral arrangement and is based on bilateral and regional arrangements between states. It also has the radical feature of granting direct and enforceable rights for individual foreign investors. Trade law largely deals with flow of trade and market access and therefore focuses on conditions of admission of goods or services and internal conditions for their sale or provision.[28] The non-discrimination principle in this relatively precise context applies to trading conditions for 'like products' and 'like services'.[29] One area of trade law bears more similarities to investment law in terms of breadth of the measures that may affect the beneficiaries. That is provision of services through commercial establishment (Mode 3) in the receiving state under Article I(2)(c) General Agreement on Trade in Services (GATS). Case law emerging from the WTO on the application of MFN treatment to trade in services, particularly through commercial establishment, could provide guidance to arbitral tribunals interpreting MFN in the investment treaty context, particularly on interpretation of the key concepts of 'likeness' and 'treatment'.[30] However, this is of limited guidance to investment law owing to the very small number of WTO cases dealing with the application of MFN under GATS at the time of writing.

[25] See for a general assessment of who benefited from investment treaty arbitration, Gus Van Harten and Pavel Malysheuski, 'Who Has Benefited Financially from Investment Treaty Arbitration? An Evaluation of the Size and Wealth of Claimants' (2016) 12(3) Osgoode Legal Studies Research Paper No 14 1.

[26] DiMascio and Pauwelyn (n 20) 53.

[27] ibid 54.

[28] ibid 53–54.

[29] Kurtz (n 12) 865.

[30] See eg *European Union and its Member States—Certain Measures Relating to the Energy Sector*, Report of the Panel WT/DS476/R (10 August 2018); *Argentina—Measures Relating to Trade in Goods and Services*, Report of the Appellate Body WT/DS453/AB/R (14 April 2016).

Investment law protections are, in contrast to trade law, vast in scope. It pays little attention to regulating the admission of investments (although this issue is increasingly addressed in investment treaties). Rather, it focuses on the treatment of investments after they are admitted to the host state.[31] Once admitted, investors and their assets are subject to the whole range of regulatory relationships with the state at all levels and by all branches. In turn, MFN treatment can affect innumerable sets of rules governing the treatment of investors and their business activities over the entire lifespan of a venture.[32] Moreover, arbitral tribunals have adopted an expansive view of 'treatment' and 'like circumstances' in relation to MFN clauses. Indeed, there is often no discussion in awards of what even constitutes 'treatment' and of whether third party investors used as comparators are in 'like circumstances'. Thus, tribunals dilute the focus of MFN treatment on non-discrimination in order to envision investment treaty norms regardless of the comparative circumstances of economic actors and regardless of the implied objectives of gaps or ambiguities in the basic investment treaty.[33]

DiMascio and Pauwelyn seek to justify the grand normative ambitions of investment law as compared to trade law. They argue that foreign investors and host states take on more risk after an investment is established and operating for a substantial period than importers and exporters do when trading in goods. The latter, it is argued, have less need for each other and more access to alternative partners.[34] Further, investment is argued to be more permanent than trade, meaning that non-discrimination needs to apply to single investments for longer periods to protect them from rules, regulations, or other regulatory conduct that may affect the investment.[35] They argue further that trade disciplines use non-discrimination to create equal competitive opportunities, while investment discipline focus more on the treatment of individual investments.[36] These factors are said to justify more deference to state when interpreting non-discrimination standards in investor–state disputes.[37] Yet the purpose of non-discrimination under investment treaties remains the promise of economic liberalization and its intended benefits for states.[38] The interpretation of MFN treatment in investor–state disputes must therefore emphasize discrimination,

[31] Pre-establishment treatment standards for investments are increasingly adopted in integrated trade and investment agreements eg: EU-Canada Comprehensive Economic and Trade Agreement.
[32] Rodriguez (n 7) 89, 91.
[33] ibid 91–92.
[34] DiMascio and Pauwelyn (n 20) 57–58.
[35] ibid 67–68.
[36] ibid. See also Greenwood (n 9) 557.
[37] DiMascio and Pauwelyn (n 20) 58, 81.
[38] See D Schneiderman, 'National Treatment' ch 2 in this volume); ILC (n 5) [75].

as well as show deference, when reviewing state conduct. Unfortunately, as elaborated below, tribunals generally have done neither.

Another crucial difference is that, while non-discrimination is central to trade governance, it plays a lesser role in the terms of investment treaties.[39] The latter have been built historically on principles of compensation for expropriation and access to fair remedies in the event of disputes. In trade law, non-discrimination in the admission of goods and services is the fundamental standard. Even if the conditions of market access and sale are restrictive, trade standards on goods and services will be satisfied based on non-discrimination by nationality. Put differently, trade law sets no absolute minimum standard of treatment. In contrast, prohibitions against expropriation without compensation and requirements for fair and equitable treatment operate to protect investors even if the host state's conduct affects local and foreign investors alike. Equality of competitive conditions in the marketplace alone does not satisfy the expectations of investment treaties. In addition, investment law goes well beyond trade law in terms of its remedies and disciplinary scope. The remedies under investment treaties typically consist of damages for the investor's losses, while trade law remedies consist of specific performance by the state to re-establish the equality of competitive conditions regardless of nationality.[40] Further, in investment law MFN clauses have been interpreted to give investors direct access to broader substantive standards, or even dispute settlement provisions, in third-country treaties.[41] Thus, tribunals use MFN treatment to expand their power to find a breach of standards contained in a third-country treaty and to award compensation, with little or no analysis of whether there are third-country investors who enjoy competitive advantages over the claimant under the basic investment treaty.[42]

Investment law is also an incredibly diffuse regime based on thousands of treaties interpreted by hundreds of different tribunals. The regime decentralizes decision-making in the extreme. These features exacerbate the instability created by allowing an indeterminate number of private beneficiaries to bring claims and enforce awards.[43] MFN treatment becomes far more complex in

[39] Kurtz (n 12) 866.

[40] Pink Series Sequel (n 20) 5.

[41] See Rodriguez (n 7); see also Section III(B) for an overview of the case law.

[42] This approach was criticized by the US in a letter to the NAFTA Free Trade Commission (Methanex) as transforming the MFN clause as a 'choice of law' clause. It was argued by the US that the MFN clause in NAFTA concerns the actual treatment of investors of third states in like circumstances. See *Methanex* (n 9) [9] (https://2009-2017.state.gov/documents/organization/8252.pdf); Perez-Aznar (n 9).

[43] See for a detailed analysis of the personal scope of investment treaty protections Anil Yilmaz Vastardis, *The Nationality of Corporate Investors under International Investment Law* (Hart Publishing 2020).

this environment than in the relatively ordered, inter-state framework of trade law. Kurtz puts it aptly:

> The transport of the MFN standard from trade into the investment fields seems to have been done without any real analysis as to the implications of this transport. The difficulty with this lack of guidance and forethought is amplified by the potentially broader scope of operation of MFN treatment when applied in the investment context.[44]

The application of MFN clauses under investment treaties cannot be said to have delivered on the underlying promise of improved well-being and prosperity. Investment and trade policies are both just pieces in a complex puzzle of factors contributing to economic well-being. It has been easy to lose sight of this complexity in investment treaty awards and much of the academic literature. Both realms attribute great importance and utility to investment liberalization, highlighting its purported benefits for the rule of law and good governance alongside the promise of development and prosperity.[45] They are light on empirical evidence to test such hypotheses.[46] Yet the claims of utility and benefits serve as convenient justifications for tribunal interpretations and scholarly theories. Arbitral tribunals often justify a chosen interpretation by referring to the ideals of investment promotion and protection.[47] Ultimately, though, they have derailed the MFN standard in investment law from the original ideal of non-discrimination, unlike WTO dispute settlement body which has applied the standard true to this ideal. This divergence of the application of MFN treatment from its purported justification is the subject of the next section.

[44] Kurtz (n 12) 867.

[45] For rule of law and good governance arguments to support the system of IIL see, Susan Franck, 'Foreign Direct Investment, Investment Treaty Arbitration and the Rule of Law' (2007) 19 McGeorge Global Business and Development Law Journal 337; BK Guthrie, 'Beyond Investment Protection: An Examination of the Potential Influence of Investment Treaties on Domestic Rule of Law' (2013) 45 NYU Journal of International Law and Politics 1151; Benedict Kingsbury and Stephan Schill, 'Investor-State Arbitration as Governance: Fair and Equitable Treatment, Proportionality and the Emerging Global Administrative Law' (2009) New York University Public Law and Legal Theory Working Papers 146.

[46] For empirical work challenging the good governance argument see Sattorova (n 24).

[47] See eg *Tokios Tokelés v Ukraine*, ICSID Case No ARB/02/18, Decision on Jurisdiction (29 April 2004) [31].

4 Basic Features of MFN Clauses in Investment Treaties

4.1 Coverage of MFN Clauses

MFN clauses in investment treaties establish a relative rather than an absolute standard of treatment. They promise to afford treatment no less favourable than treatment afforded to investors of third countries. According to the *esjudem generis* principle, the treatments compared as MFN should relate to the same subject matter.[48] In other words, a state may be found in breach of an MFN clause if it 'treats' the investor less favourably than third-country investors concerning the same category of issue. There are usually explicit exclusions from the coverage of MFN clauses. For example, exclusions usually apply to treatment under customs unions, economic unions, free trade agreements and tax treaties.[49] Recently, states have explicitly excluded dispute settlement and fair and equitable treatment clauses in third country treaties from MFN clauses.[50] They have also excluded the content of older investment treaties from MFN clauses in new treaties.[51] This step may help to address the problem of 'importation' of third-country standards to sidestep investment treaty reforms.[52] The most significant departure has come from India, which omitted MFN treatment entirely from its 2015 model investment treaty and its subsequent treaties.[53]

The exact wording of MFN clauses varies widely among investment treaties. The International Law Commission has identified six different formulations.[54] Three are common. These include: (1) clauses that refer broadly to 'treatment' of an investor; (2) clauses that refer to treatment of an investor in relation to specific aspects of the investment process;[55] and (3) clauses that refer to treatment concerning specific or all obligations in the basic treaty,[56] sometimes but not always expressly including dispute

[48] ILC (n 5) [35]; Muchlinski (n 21) 629.

[49] Muchlinski (n 21) 629; Agreement between the Argentine Republic and the Kingdom of Spain on the Reciprocal Promotion and Protection of Investments (signed 3 October 1991, entered into force 28 September 1992), art IV(3) and (4).

[50] See EU-Canada Comprehensive Economic and Trade Agreement (2016); Argentina–Qatar BIT art 4(4); Argentina–Japan BIT art 3(4).

[51] Iran Slovakia BIT art 4(5); Argentina–Japan BIT art 3(5).

[52] UNCTAD, World Investment Report 2015: Reforming International Investment Governance, 120 (UN 2015) 136; C Titi, 'Most-Favoured-Nation Treatment: Survival Clauses and Reform of International Investment Law' (2016) 33(5) Journal of International Arbitration 425–440, 428.

[53] In the subsequent investment treaties signed to date by India, no MFN clause has been included. See India–Belarus, India–Kyrgyzstan, and India–Brazil investment treaties.

[54] ILC (n 5) [59]–[65].

[55] ibid [62] (Such as 'establishment, management, maintenance, use, and disposal' of an investment).

[56] Argentina–Spain BIT 1991, art IV(2).

settlement.[57] Despite variations in the wording of MFN clauses in modern treaties, such clauses are, in formal terms, uniformly reciprocal. The historically concessionary MFN clauses that provided benefits on a unilateral basis have not been adopted. That said, asymmetrical benefits may still ensue where one state is disproportionately importing capital from the other. In these circumstances, the capital-importing state's investors would rarely be in a position to invoke an MFN clause.

Importantly, not all MFN clauses refer explicitly to an obligation to afford the same treatment to investors in 'like circumstances' or 'similar situations'.[58] Yet 'like circumstances' or 'similar situations' lie at the heart of non-discrimination. When tribunals interpret and apply MFN clauses without comparing investors and investments that are in like circumstances, MFN treatment ceases to be a non-discrimination standard. Instead, MFN clauses become a means to pick and choose among the terms of the host state's investment treaties. Tribunals embracing this vision of MFN treatment have left the standard largely devoid of its original justification based on non-discrimination. This detachment from the non-discrimination principle is essential to understanding the emergence of a problematic MFN jurisprudence within investment law.

When arbitral tribunals apply MFN clauses to 'import' standards from third party investment treaties, their analysis does not focus on whether the host state breached the MFN clause by treating third state investors more favourably resulting in losses to the claimant investor. Rather, the analysis focuses directly on whether the host state has breached the external 'imported' standard, without an evaluation that the imported standard does in fact constitute more favourable treatment.[59] Even if a treaty explicitly links MFN treatment to substantive content, there should still be a comparison between, on the one hand, the treatment actually received by investors under the basic treaty and, on the other hand, that received by third-country investors. Otherwise, it is impossible to find a violation of MFN treatment based on a comparison of investors in like circumstances. In turn, a tribunal cannot say that any investor has received less favourable treatment from the host state, putting it at a competitive disadvantage based on nationality.

[57] ILC (n 5) [63] (for instance, fair and equitable treatment standard). Most investment treaties that the UK is a party to include treaty provisions explicitly within the scope of the MFN clause, including dispute settlement. See eg UK–El Salvador BIT, art 3(3).

[58] ILC (n 5) [64].

[59] *Bayindir* (n 8) [153] ff; *Rumeli* (n 8) [575]–[681]; Perez-Aznar (n 9); Rodriguez (n 7) 99; Ishikawa (n 8) 130.

4.2 Enforcement of MFN Clauses in Investment Treaty Arbitration

This section offers a snapshot of MFN clauses and their interpretation by tribunals in order to reveal wider contours of the debate over MFN treatment. In general, claimant investors have invoked MFN clauses in two ways.[60] First, they have used them to challenge the treatment received under internal domestic measures of the host state.[61] Secondly, and more commonly, they have used them to claim the benefit of ostensibly more favourable standards in third-country investment treaties of the host state.[62] This latter usage is particularly controversial.

In the first scenario, tribunals have analysed whether the claimant experienced discrimination by the host state in comparison to third-country investors who are in like circumstances. *Parkerings v Lithuania* offers a good example. In that case, the claimant was a Norwegian investor in Lithuania. It had entered into an agreement with the local government to construct and operate parking structures in the city of Vilnius. It argued, among other things, that the state breached its MFN obligations by treating a Dutch investor more favourably. The Dutch investor was said to have been in like circumstances since it had entered into a similar parking contract with the local government.[63] Article IV of the treaty provided: '[i]nvestments made by investors of one contracting party in the territory of the other contracting party ... shall be accorded treatment no less favourable than that accorded to investments made by investors of any third state'.

The *Parkerings* tribunal decided that an evaluation of the state's MFN obligations required a comparison between the claimant's treatment and that of a third-country investor in like circumstances.[64] The tribunal asked in turn: (1) Is the comparator investor foreign? (2) Are the claimant and the comparator investor in the same economic or business sector? (3) Have the two investors

[60] Perez-Aznar (n 9) 778.

[61] See *Loewen v USA Loewen Group Inc and Raymond L Loewen v United States of America*, ICSID Case No ARB AF/98/3, Award (26 June 2003) [139]–[140]. See also *Parkerings-Compagniet AS v Republic of Lithuania*, ICSID Case No ARB/05/8; *Ioannis Kardassopoulos v Republic of Georgia*, ICSID Case No ARB/05/18; *Cargill Incorporated v United Mexican States*, ICSID Case No ARB AF/05/2; *Apotex Inc v The Government of the United States of America*, ICSID Case No UNCT/10/2; *Vento Motorcycles Inc v United Mexican States*, ICSID Case No ARB AF/17/3.

[62] See *Emilio Agustín Maffezini* (n 8); *Siemens AG v Argentine Republic*, ICSID Case No ARB/02/8, Decision on Jurisdiction (3 August 2004); *Bayindir* (n 8); *Mamidoil Jetoil Greek Petroleum Products Société Anonyme SA v Republic of Albania*, ICSID Case No ARB/11/24.

[63] *Parkerings v Lithuania*, ICSID Case no ARB/05/8 (2005) [202]–[203].

[64] ibid [369] ('The essential condition of the violation of a *MFN* clause is the existence of a different treatment accorded to another foreign investor in a similar situation').

been treated differently by the host state? (4) Was the different treatment justified by a legitimate objective? Having examined these issues, the tribunal decided that the claimant and the Dutch investor were not in like circumstances for several reasons. First, one of the claimant's investments had a more adverse impact on historical and archaeological preservation and the protection of the environment.[65] Such adverse impacts were peculiar to the claimant's investment and justified the different treatment.[66] There was also no evidence, according to the tribunal, that the two investors had been treated differently in terms of administrative requirements and procedures.[67] Secondly, the agreements signed by the local government with each investor were sufficiently different to justify the different treatment.[68] Therefore, it is clear that a thorough evaluation of whether the claimant experienced discrimination in comparison to a third-country investor went to the heart of the MFN analysis.

The second scenario takes the analysis beyond internal domestic measures of the host state. In this scenario, investors have argued that the absence of a standard or clause in the basic treaty itself constitutes less favourable treatment if that standard or clause exists in a third-country treaty. In turn, they have asked the tribunal to import provisions from third-country treaties, whether as a distinct standard from a single treaty or as a desirable mix of standards from several treaties.[69] In this way, all sorts of clauses can purportedly be imported into the basic treaty. They have included for example:

- umbrella clauses for contractual disputes;[70]
- dispute settlement clauses free from wait periods, from requirements to use local courts, or from other preconditions for a claim;[71]
- dispute settlement clauses allowing arbitration as a dispute resolution method where no consent is found at all in the basic treaty;[72]

[65] ibid [392], [396].
[66] ibid [396].
[67] ibid [396].
[68] ibid [420], [428]–[429].
[69] See *MTD Equity Sdn Bhd and MTD Chile SA v Chile*, ICSID Case No ARB/01/7.
[70] *Sergei Paushok, CJSC Golden East Company and CJSC Vostokneftegaz Company v Government of Mongolia*, UNCITRAL (rejected importation of umbrella clause due to specific wording in the applicable basic treaty); *EDF International SA, SAUR International SA and León Participaciones Argentinas SA v Argentine Republic*, ICSID Case No ARB/03/23; *Mr Franck Charles Arif v Republic of Moldova*, ICSID Case No ARB/11/23 (both EDF and Arif awards allowed importation of an umbrella clause contained in a third-party treaty via an MFN clause in the basic treaty).
[71] *Maffezini* (n 8); *Daimler Financial Services AG v Argentine Republic*, ICSID Case No ARB/05/01, Award (22 August 2012); *Hochtief AG v Argentine Republic*, ICSID Case No ARB/07/31, Decision on Jurisdiction (24 October 2011).
[72] *Hochtief* (n 71) [79]–[82]; *European American Investment Bank AG (EURAM) v Slovak Republic, UNCITRAL*, Award on Jurisdiction (22 October 2012) [447]; See also *Venezuela US, SRL (Barbados)* v *Bolivarian Republic of Venezuela*, PCA Case No 2013-34 (26 July 2016); *Menzies Middle East and Africa*

- dispute settlement clauses allowing access to a different arbitral institution than in the basic treaty;[73]
- clauses on the material, temporal, or personal scope of a third-country treaty;[74]
- dispute settlement clauses covering a wider set of disputes than the basic treaty;[75]
- clauses on damages that allow for more generous compensation;[76]
- substantive standards that are completely absent from the basic treaty or worded more beneficially in the third-state treaty.[77]

Further, investors have tried to import clauses from treaties that did not deal with investment protection at all, albeit, in this respect, without success.[78] Overall, the use of MFN clauses to impugn the favourability of different treaties of the host state has been extraordinary.

The first instance of an MFN clause being invoked by an investor arose in the very first known claim under investment treaties. Perhaps revealing the novelty of the argument, it was unsuccessful. In *AAPL v Sri Lanka*, the tribunal held that the liability standard in a third-country treaty (between Sri Lanka and

SA and Aviation Handling Services International Ltd v *Republic of Senegal*, ICSID Case No ARB/15/21 (5 August 2016).

[73] *Plama Consortium Limited v Republic of Bulgaria*, ICSID Case No ARB/03/24, Decision on Jurisdiction (8 February 2005) [40]; *Garanti Koza LLP v Turkmenistan*, ICSID Case No ARB/11/20, Decision on Jurisdiction (3 July 2013) [38].

[74] *Yaung Chi OO Trading Pte Ltd v Government of the Union of Myanmar*, ASEAN ID Case No ARB/01/1; *Société Générale in respect of DR Energy Holdings Limited and Empresa Distribuidora de Electricidad del Este SA v Dominican Republic*, LCIA Case No UN 7927, IIC 366 (2008) (Award on Preliminary Objections to Jurisdiction); *Vannessa Ventures Ltd v Bolivarian Republic of Venezuela*, ICSID Case No ARB AF/04/6; *Metal-Tech Ltd v Republic of Uzbekistan*, ICSID Case No ARB/10/3; *The Canadian Cattlemen for Fair Trade v United States of America*, UNCITRAL; on retroactive application of treaties *Técnicas Medioambientales Tecmed SA v The United Mexican States*, ICSID Case No ARB AF/00/2 and *MCI Power Group LC and New Turbine Inc v Republic of Ecuador*, ICSID Case No ARB/03/6.

[75] *Salini Costruttori SpA and Italstrade SpA v The Hashemite Kingdom of Jordan*, ICSID Case No ARB/02/13; *RosInvestCo UK Ltd v Russian Federation*, SCC Case No V079/2005; *Telenor Mobile Communications AS v Republic of Hungary*, ICSID Case No ARB/04/15; *Renta 4 SVSA Ahorro Corporacionemergentes FI Quasar de Valores SICAV SA Orgor de Valores SICAV SA GBI 9000 SICAV SA and ALOS 34 SL v Russian Federation* SCC CASE NO ARBITRATION V (024/2007); *Señor Tza Yap Shum v The Republic of Peru*, ICSID Case No ARB/07/6; *Beijing Urban Construction Group Co Ltd v Republic of Yemen*, ICSID Case No ARB/14/30.

[76] *CME Czech Republic BV v Czech Republic*, UNCITRAL, Final Award (14 March 2003) [500]—and see separate opinion of Ian Brownlie.

[77] *Hesham T M Al Warraq v Republic of Indonesia*, UNCITRAL; *Pope & Talbot Inc v The Government of Canada*, UNCITRAL; *Rumeli* (n 8); *Mamidoil* (n 62).

[78] *Romak SA (Switzerland) v Republic of Uzbekistan*, UNCITRAL, PCA Case No AA280 (Investor invoked the New York Convention); *Frontier Petroleum Services Ltd v Czech Republic*, UNCITRAL (Investor invoked European Convention on Human Rights).

Switzerland) was not shown by the claimant to be more favourable.[79] However, the tribunal described the MFN clause as 'incorporating' standards from other investment treaties, signalling an openness to MFN clause being interpreted as importing standards from third-country treaties. Moreover, claimant's counsel had at this early stage explicitly argued that the MFN clause served to improve the basic treaty by incorporating standards from other investment treaties of Sri Lanka.[80]

The pivotal turn came with the well-known and controversial case of *Maffezini v Spain*. For the first time in that case, a tribunal allowed the importation of procedural rules under an MFN clause. Thus, it began the abandonment of MFN's origins in non-discrimination. The MFN clause in *Maffezini* was Article IV of the Argentina–Spain BIT, which stated: 'In all matters subject to this Agreement, this treatment shall not be less favorable than that extended by each Party to the investments made in its territory by investors of a third country.' The same BIT required under its Article X that, before submitting an arbitration claim, investors should first apply to the domestic courts to seek a remedy. If a satisfactory resolution was not obtained within eighteen months, the investor could file for arbitration. Arguing MFN treatment, the claimant in *Maffezini* pointed to Spain's investment treaty with Chile, which did not require recourse to domestic courts. Thus, Chilean investors were said to be treated more favourably in Spain than Argentinean investors.[81]

In examining this MFN argument, neither the claimant nor the tribunal addressed whether there was any actual Chilean investor in like circumstances to the claimant. That is, they did not identify a comparator investor that had resorted to arbitration and whether this step put the claimant at a disadvantage. Spain argued that the

> [p]urpose of the most favoured nation clause [is] to avoid discrimination, [and] such discrimination can only take place in connection with material economic treatment and not with regard to procedural matters. Only if it could be established that resort to domestic tribunals would produce objective disadvantages for the investor would it be possible to argue material effects on the treatment owed.[82]

[79] *Asian Agricultural Products Ltd v Republic of* Sri Lanka, ICSID Case No ARB/87/3, Final Award (27 June 1990).
[80] *AAPL v Sri Lanka* (n 79) [30], [54].
[81] *Maffezini* (n 8) [40].
[82] ibid [42].

In response, the tribunal made two key findings. First, it asserted that, if a third-country treaty has more advantageous standards, they can be extended to a claimant simply by the operation of the MFN clause in the basic treaty.[83] Secondly, it asserted that the method of dispute settlement is crucial to investor protection and to an investor's treatment.[84] To support this position, the tribunal relied on the analysis of the arbitration commission in the historical *Ambatielos case*, where the commission found that 'administration of justice' mechanisms available to traders are a matter concerning the treatment of traders.[85] Further, the *Maffezini* tribunal referred to instances of consular jurisdiction used by colonial powers to secure the rights of their investors in states that were not their colonies, but rather 'semi-civilized' states.[86] Notably, this unequal structure inherent to imperialism was relied on in *Maffezini* in spite of its incompatibility with international law principles of sovereignty, equality of states, and self-determination.[87]

With a view to the treaty regime in general, the *Maffezini* tribunal also endorsed the 'importation' of standards via MFN clauses as a means to harmonize investment treaty standards and expand investor protection. Even so, it acknowledged limits to the importation of dispute settlement standards, referring vaguely to public policy considerations.[88] According to the tribunal, MFN clauses could not be used to override such requirements as exhaustion of local remedies or fork-in-the-road clauses. Avoidance of these requirements based on MFN clauses was said to give rise to 'disruptive treaty-shopping'.[89] How these exceptions could be said to differ from the express precondition in the Spain-Argentina BIT itself—requiring recourse to courts for a set period—was not explained by the tribunal.

Since *Maffezini*, tribunals have disagreed for years over whether MFN treatment allows for the evasion of dispute settlement arrangements in the basic treaty.[90] Some have argued that MFN clauses only cover substantive standards

[83] ibid [45].
[84] ibid [46], [54].
[85] In *Plama v Bulgaria* (n 73) it was held that *Maffezini* (n 8) misconstrued the *Ambatielos* finding on 'administration of justice' because that ruling relates to provisions concerning substantive protection in the sense of denial of justice in the domestic courts. It does not relate to the import of dispute resolution provisions of another treaty into the basic treaty.
[86] *Plama v Bulgaria* (n 73) [54]. See also Becker Lorca (n 17) 136.
[87] See for an overview of consular jurisdiction Pawel Czubik and Piotr Szwedo, 'Consular Jurisdiction' Max Planck Encyclopaedia of Public International Law. See also Antony Anghie (n 15) 84–86; Becker Lorca (n 17) 94–95. For a discussion of racism in international investment law see T Van Ho, 'Angels, Virgins, Demons, Whores: Moving Towards an Antiracist Praxis by Confronting Modern Investment Law Scholarship' (2022) 23(2) Journal of World Investment and Trade 347.
[88] *Maffezini* (n 8) [62]–[63].
[89] ibid [63].
[90] *Plama v Bulgaria* (n 73); *Salini v Jordan* (n 75); *Renta 4 v Russia* (n 75). See for a detailed analysis of awards considering the application of MFN clauses to jurisdiction Julie A Maupin, 'MFN-Based

of treatment and that they do not extend to procedural standards, unless expressly permitted otherwise in the treaty.[91] Others have argued that procedural rights go to the heart of investors' treatment and MFN clauses can import procedural standards, unless expressly excluded by the applicable treaty.[92] Several tribunals reached opposite conclusions on the issue even for the same MFN clause in the Argentina-Germany BIT.[93] Arbitrators have frequently dissented just as international law experts have completely disagreed on the issue.[94]

Arbitral awards contrary to the *Maffezini* approach focus on two concerns:[95] (1) dispute settlement requirements cannot be framed as an issue of treatment of investors under the MFN standard and (2) a state's consent to dispute settlement cannot be manufactured or modified by the operation of an MFN clause (unless expressly allowed by the clause itself).[96] Maupin's analysis

Jurisdiction in Investor-State Arbitration: Is There Any Hope for a Consistent Approach?' (2011) 14(1) Journal of International Economic Law 157, 160 (Analyses the diverse awards under categories relating to the 'the type of MFN clause interpreted, the MFN question addressed, the outcome of the award and the major reasons given for the outcome').

[91] *Plama v Bulgaria* (n 73) [223]; Zachary Douglas, 'The MFN Clause in Investment Arbitration: Treaty Interpretation Off the Rails' (2011) 2(1) Journal of International Dispute Settlement 97.

[92] *Renta 4 SVSA and Others v Russian Federation*, SCC Case No V24/2007, Separate Opinion of Charles Brower, para 10 (20 March 2009) ('I see no reason why an issue of the incorporation of broader consent to arbitration under the host State's third-country investment treaties should be treated differently from the consistently accepted application of MFN clauses to substantive standards of treatment ...'); Stephan W Schill, 'Most-Favored-Nation Clauses as a Basis of Jurisdiction in Investment Treaty Arbitration: Arbitral Jurisprudence at a Crossroads' (2009) 10 Journal of World Investment and Trade 189, 210–14.

[93] *Daimler v Argentina* (n 71); *Hochtief v Argentina* (n 71); *Wintershall AG v Argentine Republic*, ICSID Case No ARB/04/14, Award (8 December 2008); *Siemens v Argentina* (n 62).

[94] I Brownlie Dissent in *CME Czech Republic BV v Czech Republic* (n 76)para 11 ('The application of the most-favoured nation clause ... to the compensation provisions of the Dutch Treaty in order to incorporate the substantially different formulation in the U.S. Treaty is an unattractive hypothesis. The presumption must be that the clause promises MFN treatment only in matters of treatment of an investment, and not to the process of dispute settlement'); C Brower Dissent in *Daimler v Argentina* (n 71) (arguing that 'the Award's view on the manner in which the MFN clause affects the 18-month domestic courts requirement is misplaced'. In his view, the MFN clause allows the investor to side-step the domestic recourse requirement and that the 18-month period is a question of admissibility and not jurisdiction). Brower also dissented to the *Renta 4* award's rejection of applying an MFN clause to the issue of dispute settlement; see J Christopher Thomas QC Dissent in *Hochtief v Argentina* Award (where one of the arbitrators was C Brower) (dissenting to the Award's interpretation of the MFN clause to allow the investor to sidestep the domestic recourse requirement in Argentina-Germany BIT). See also L Boisson de Chazournes' Dissenting Opinion in *Garanti Koza LLP v Turkmenistan*, ICSID Case No ARB/11/20, Decision on the Objection to Jurisdiction for Lack of Consent (3 July 2013) paras 40 ff.

[95] See *Daimler v Argentina* (n 71) 63–119; *Plama v Bulgaria* (n 73). See Douglas (n 91) 113 ('The *Maffezini* doctrine ... permits the jurisdictional mandate of the tribunal to be modified *after* a dispute has arisen at the suit of one of the disputing parties at a time when the claimant investor and respondent host state have already concluded a binding arbitration agreement and have entered into a relationship of procedural equality ... It leads to a mass of wasteful litigation about how to litigate.'; Schill disagrees with Douglas on MFN clauses' ability to apply to jurisdictional provisions in SW Schill, 'Allocating Adjudicatory Authority: Most-Favoured-Nation Clauses as a Basis of Jurisdiction - A Reply to Zachary Douglas' (2011) 2(2) Journal of International Settlement 353.

[96] See eg the UK–Mozambique BIT, which explicitly extends the coverage of the MFN clause to dispute resolution matters in art 3(3).

of the divergent views found no other explanation for disagreements than the interpretative expansive or restrictive approach of each tribunal.[97] Similarly, Muchlinski has observed that the cases following *Maffezini* 'assume that dispute settlement clauses are included unless explicitly excluded',[98] whereas those that do not adopt the opposite presumption. Thus, the starting point for treaty interpretation governs the outcome. In essence, these different approaches reflect a debate over whether MFN treatment should be transformed into a tool of multilateralism offering the broadest protection possible to investors.[99]

5 MFN Clauses and Treaty Interpretation: Unpacking the Misconceptions and Recalling the Non-discrimination Rationale

There is no single MFN standard in investment treaties. MFN language has evolved since the first modern investment treaty in 1959.[100] Differences of wording may give rise to variations in coverage and justify diverse interpretations. Yet, diversity in interpretation is also often not a consequence of different wording but of different interpretative presumptions.[101] Recognizing this dynamic, reform of MFN clauses has been part of a wider recalibration that aims to scale back the unforeseen and undesirable reach of arbitral tribunals and investment treaty protections.[102] As states renegotiate their treaties or sign new ones, they seek to limit the discretion of tribunals by stipulating detailed descriptions and clearer boundaries for MFN treatment.[103] Against this background, in this section I trace the key debates over the interpretation of MFN clauses, following *Maffezini*, where the regime took a particularly

[97] Maupin (n 90), 179–80. See also Relja Radovic, 'Between Rights and Remedies: The Access to Investment Treaty Arbitration as a Substantive Right of Foreign Investors' (2019) 10(1) Journal of International Dispute Settlement 42.

[98] Muchlinski (n 21) 634.

[99] For the different positions in this debate see SW Schill, *The Multilateralization of International Investment Law* (CUP 2009) (arguing that MFN is a tool for multilateralising investment treaties); Perez-Aznar (n 9) (arguing that multilateralism emerges from state cooperation not from arbitral decisions).

[100] Germany–Pakistan BIT.

[101] See *Daimler v Argentina* (n 71); *Hochtief v Argentina* (n 71); *Wintershall v Argentina* (n 93); *Siemens v Argentina* (n 62).

[102] UNCITRAL WG III identified MFN clauses as one of the areas calling for reform, see n 1; CETA art 8.7(4) explicitly states that MFN clause does not operate to import standards in the abstract—'MFN clause will be breached if measures adopted result in less favourable treatment'.

[103] CETA art 8.7(4); Netherlands Draft Model BIT 2018, art 3(3); EU–Vietnam FTA art 2.4 (5); China–UEA BIT, art 4(8); Australia–Uruguay BIT, art 5(1) and (2); Argentina–Japan BIT, art 3(2) and (3); Japan–Jordan BIT, art 4; CPTPP, art 9.5(3).

unfortunate turn, and explain the misconceptions largely caused by the detachment of MFN treatment from its non-discrimination origins.

After the *Maffezini* award was rendered, the main debate on the interpretation of MFN clauses revolved around whether they allowed investors who were protected by the basic treaty to benefit also from dispute resolution clauses in third-country treaties. While this debate has been fierce,[104] it was mostly and long accepted as 'conventional wisdom' that MFN clauses allowed investors to benefit from more favourable substantive standards in third-country treaties.[105] This position has since been questioned. Another key moment was marked by the decision of the arbitral tribunal in *Ickale v Turkmenistan*, challenging the accepted wisdom that MFN clauses automatically allow investors protected under the basic treaty access to more favourable substantive standards in third-party treaties without engaging in a comparison of treatments received by investors.[106] In a much-debated article about the decision in *Ickale v Turkmenistan*, Batifort and Heath have argued for a bottom-up approach in interpreting MFN clauses. Such an approach would mean that the scope of each MFN clause should be evaluated on its merits, instead of assuming that all MFN clauses cover substantive standards regardless of their formulation.[107] Thus, there is a fresh debate about the wisdom of automatically allowing investors to access more favourable substantive standards in third-country treaties.

In the investment law community, there is broad consensus that there is no such thing as a standard MFN clause. Such clauses vary in their wording from one treaty to another.[108] Differently drafted clauses will be interpreted on their own terms under Articles 31 and 32 of the Vienna Convention on the Law of Treaties standards of treaty interpretation. Their scope of application may in turn vary.[109] Yet, diversity in the formulation of MFN clauses does not mean that an interpretation can be detached from the understanding and purpose

[104] See for contrasting interpretations of the Argentina–Germany BIT's MFN clause *Siemens v Argentina* (n 62); and *Hochtief v Argentina* (n 71) (finding in favour of applying MFN clause to benefit the investor from 'more favourable' dispute settlement clause in third party treaty); *Wintershall v Argentina* (n 93); *Daimler v Argentina* (n 71) (finding against applying the MFN clause to benefit the investor from 'more favourable' dispute settlement clause in third party treaty). See also nn 15 and 16 above.

[105] Batifort and Heath (n 8) 873, 877; Paparinskis (n 6) (arguing the presence of state practice on importation of substantive standards). For an argument to the contrary see Rodriguez (n 9).

[106] *İçkale İnşaat Limited Şirketi v Turkmenistan* (n 9).

[107] Batifort and Heath (n 8).

[108] Michael Waibel, 'Putting the MFN Genie Back in the Bottle' (2018) 112 American Journal of International Law Unbound 60, 61; Donald McRae, 'Introduction to the Symposium on Simon Batifort' (2018) 114 American Journal of International Law Unbound 192; and Batifort and Heath (n 8) 40.

[109] Batifort and Heath (n 8) 40.

of MFN treatment under international law.[110] Paparinskis argues that state practice on MFN clauses, expressed through submissions to the International Law Commission and through their pleadings before arbitral tribunals, reveal a wide consensus that MFN clauses allow access to more favourable substantive protections found in third-country treaties.[111] However, some of recent treaties demonstrate that state practice is evolving, with some states moving away from this position by stipulating in new treaties that substantive standards in other treaties do not in themselves constitute 'treatment'.[112]

At this juncture, it may be helpful to step back from these debates. The procedure-substance question narrows the contours of interpretation of MFN clauses. It also limits the extent to which investment law practice has deviated from the general international law of non-discrimination and of treaties. In the next two sections, the departure of MFN treatment in investment law is unpacked in two ways. First, it is shown how MFN treatment has been divorced from core principle of non-discrimination. Secondly, it is demonstrated that the practice of 'importation' from third-country treaties, using MFN clauses, itself deviates from principles of treaty law.

5.1 Misconceptions about the Meaning of 'More Favourable Treatment'

A peculiar feature of investment treaty law and scholarship is that the idea of 'more favourable treatment' has been extended to investment treaty standards in third-country treaties where they are absent from (or narrower than in) the basic treaty. It is true that the use of MFN clauses to determine a state's obligations by referring to another treaty is not unique to investment law.[113] But the latter is unique in another way. When interpretating MFN clauses, arbitral tribunals rarely consider whether the presence of a third-country treaty standard has led to any less favourable treatment for a claimant in real terms.[114] They also do not consider whether a similarly situated investor, protected by the third-country treaty, has actually benefited from the relevant standard,

110 Waibel (n 108) 61.
111 Paparinskis (n 6) 51–52.
112 CETA and Dutch Model Investment treaty.
113 Paparinskis (n 6) 50.
114 Exceptions to this include *ADF Group Inc v United States of America*, ICSID Case No ARB AF/00/1; *Crompton (Chemtura) Corp v Government of Canada*, UNCITRAL, PCA Case No 2008-1, Award (2 August 2010); *İçkale v Turkmenistan* (n 9)—although not exactly formulated in this way.

such that it is given a distinct competitive advantage over the claimant. Arbitral awards and scholarship instead concentrate on MFN in the abstract.

This impractical approach has two consequences for MFN clauses in investment law. The first is that there is broad acceptance that the absence of a particular word or phrase in a third-country treaty automatically amounts to less favourable treatment of an investor.[115] While an undertaking of, for example, fair and equitable treatment in another treaty may signal a promise of more favourable treatment of other investors, its mere existence does not automatically establish a breach of the MFN clause in the basic treaty. More is needed. At least it must be shown that some comparator investor received and benefited from FET in the host state in ways putting the claimant at an economic disadvantage.

Besides this lack of attention to the necessary factual comparison of investors, some tribunals have applied an MFN clause without even finding a breach of that clause by the host state. For instance, in *Rumeli v Kazakhstan*[116] the tribunal's entire analysis of the MFN clause was to state that the parties agreed that the clause allowed for the importation of standards from third-country treaties.[117] It then applied the imported standards and simply assessed whether the state breached 'the BIT'. No reasoning was offered on whether the breach was of the basic treaty's MFN clause or of an imported standard. In all, the tribunal imported four substantive standards from a third-country treaty. These included FET, protection against denial of justice, full protection and security, and an obligation not to impair by unreasonable, arbitrary, or discriminatory measures the management, maintenance, use, enjoyment, or disposal of the investment. From this loot bag of imported standards, the tribunal found a violation only of FET. Nowhere did it consider whether the claimant was treated less favourably than similarly situated investors under the third-country treaty.

Similarly, where a dispute settlement clause in the basic treaty is compared to a clause in a third-state treaty that does not require waiting periods before dispute settlement, the existence of the latter does not automatically establish more favourable treatment. To jump in the abstract to this conclusion, as was done in *Maffezini*, exposes an underlying assumption that courts are always

[115] In *ADF v US* (n 114) [194]–[197]. The tribunal challenged this broadly accepted understanding of MFN clauses—'investor must demonstrate the more favourable nature of the invoked treaty provisions via MFN'.
[116] *Rumeli v Kazakhstan* (n 8) [615], [618].
[117] ibid [575].

inferior to investment treaty arbitrators.[118] Yet, a precondition of recourse to local remedies does not necessarily disadvantage an investor. Moreover, the necessary analysis cannot be done in the abstract. Under a dispute settlement clause with a wait period, the parties may be encouraged to find an amicable settlement. Doing so can save time and money. It can maintain good will. Both outcomes are more favourable for the investor. Without facts, it cannot be assumed that the different wording of a provision in one treaty is necessarily more favourable than that in another.

There is a related consequence of assessing treaties in the abstract when applying an MFN clause. This approach leaves no room to evaluate whether the investor and its investment actually received less favourable treatment than third-country investors. One study found no investment treaty award that premised a breach of MFN treatment on the investor receiving discriminatory treatment as compared to investors of other states in the host state.[119] That suggests a lack of realism in investment law. A minority of awards did engage in such an analysis where the wording of an MFN clause explicitly applied it to investors who were in 'like circumstances' or 'similar situations'.[120] Tribunals have also engaged in close comparisons of the treatment received by different investors when the alleged MFN breach was based on internal domestic measures of the host state.[121] However, MFN treatment is always a non-discrimination standard. It is therefore crucial to interpret an MFN clause, regardless of its exact wording, by examining actual circumstances of alleged discrimination. Most investor claimants invoke MFN clauses to benefit from third-country treaty standards. Thus, they treat MFN clauses not as safeguards against discrimination but as 'choice of law' clauses.[122] In *Rumeli v Kazakhstan*,

[118] This view is widely held by mainstream IIL practitioners and academics. See Charles Brower Dissenting opinion in *Daimler v Argentina* (n 71) [36]–[38]; Francisco Orrego Vicuña, 'Reports of [Maffezini's] Demise Have Been Greatly Exaggerated' (2012) 3(2) Journal of International Dispute Settlement 299, 306–308.

[119] Bonnitcha, Poulsen, and Waibel (n 24) 94, table 4.2; See also UNCTAD Pink Series Sequel: Most-favoured Nation Treatment 17 'MFN treatment has rarely been invoked to challenge the actual level of material treatment given to foreign investors as regards establishment, access or competitive conditions in host states.'

[120] See *İçkale v Turkmenistan* (n 9); for an application of the like circumstances analysis in this way in the context of national treatment clauses see *SD Myers Inc v Government of Canada*, UNCITRAL, Partial Award (13 November 2000) [250].

[121] See *Parkerings v Lithuania* (n 61).

[122] In a submission made to the NAFTA Free Trade Commission in relation to the interpretation of certain provisions of NAFTA arising from the *Methanex v USA* (n 9) dispute, the USA submitted that 'art 1103 [MFN Clause] is not a choice-of-law clause' 9; UNCTAD Pink Series Sequel MFN 5 ('In the context of international investment, the current debate is not centered on alleged violation or breaches of the MFN treatment *per se*. Instead it focuses on the possibility for claimants to pick from third treaties allegedly more favourable provisions relating to protection standards or ISDS and thereby derogate from or modify provisions of the basic treaty').

for example, the tribunal did not discuss whether the imported treaty standards offered more favourable treatment than those in the basic treaty. It also neglected to discuss whether the investor was competitively disadvantaged and suffered loss as a result of the absence of imported standards in the basic treaty. The wording of an MFN clause is crucial to its interpretation. Yet it is equally important to apply the clause compatibly with the non-discrimination foundation of MFN treatment in international economic law.[123]

5.2 Misconceptions about the Operation of MFN Clauses

A key challenge for interpreters of MFN clauses is to pin down their effect and function based on the international law of treaty interpretation. What rights and obligations do MFN clauses create? The answer is relatively straightforward when considering the effect of MFN clauses on trade tariffs and quotas. In such cases, an MFN clause in the basic treaty obliges the state to grant no less favourable market access to traders of different third-country nationalities. If state B, under a treaty with state C, gives cotton traders from state C lower tariffs than traders from state A, then state A can invoke an MFN clause in the basic treaty to obtain the same tariffs for its cotton traders. Here, MFN clauses are easy to apply. It is relatively simple to pin down the discriminatory act giving rise to an MFN breach. The situation is different in investment law, especially when allegedly more favourable treatment is found in the third-country treaty itself.

It is largely assumed in investment law that MFN clauses import standards from third-country treaties.[124] There is no explicit finding that the MFN clause itself was breached. Likewise, there is no discussion of what led to the breach and what loss was suffered by the investor as a result. Ziegler explains that the MFN clause transforms the basic treaty into 'a dynamic source of law'.[125] By extension, rights and obligations under the basic treaty may fluctuate widely and unpredictably. This has been a widely accepted view among IIL tribunals as to the operation of MFN clauses. But this mode of operation is not compatible with the general principles of international law on MFN clauses.[126]

[123] McRae (n 108) 40; Waibel (n 108) 61.

[124] Christoph Schreuer, 'Introduction: Interrelationship of Standards' in A Reinisch (ed), *Standards of Investment Protection* (OUP 2008) 6; Schill (n 99) 126, 127, 140 ('The use of MFN clauses to import more favourable conditions from third-country BITs is largely uncontested').

[125] Andreas R Ziegler, 'Most-Favoured-Nation (MFN) Treatment' in A Reinisch (ed), *Standards of Investment Protection* (OUP 2008) 65.

[126] *Anglo-Iranian Oil Co (United Kingdom v Iran)* [1952] ICJ Rep 2, 533 ('The ICJ in the Anglo–Iranian Oil company case has rejected the notion that an MFN clause "acquires its content only when

Schill argues that importation does not conflict with the *inter partes* effect of treaties. He does so on the basis that importation does not modify the relationship between the parties of the basic treaty. Rather, the content of the third-country treaty 'becomes operative by means of the basic treaty's MFN clause'.[127] Schill continues by describing the operation of MFN clauses as an 'automatic treaty adaptation mechanism without the need for the State parties to the basic treaty to negotiate anew'.[128] It is difficult to reconcile the latter part of this approach with the former. Schill's broader rationale for supporting importation of standards is that MFN clauses operate to multilateralize investment treaty law.[129] That approach conflicts directly with principles of party-based intent in treaty negotiation. It has been criticized by Perez-Aznar as pushing an agenda of multilateralization through arbitral awards instead of state cooperation.[130] It puts the policy choices of tribunals ahead of the written agreements of states parties.

Greenwood and Perez-Aznar argue that tribunals should abandon the importation approach and focus instead on whether the MFN clause itself was breached. The mechanics of the operation of MFN clauses are essential, regardless of their wording. Unless the basic treaty explicitly says that it 'incorporates' more favourable standards in third-country treaties, MFN clauses should not be read to do so. Otherwise, arbitral tribunals obtain an unauthorized power to decide on violations of an external standard, rather than the MFN commitment in the basic treaty. An investor may be able to demand access to a more favourable standard based on an MFN clause, but that does not incorporate the external standard itself into the basic treaty.[131] The proper focus lies in whether

the grantor State enters into relations with a third State, and its content increases whenever fresh favours are granted to third States"'. The position of the ICJ was adopted in the ILC Draft Articles on MFN with commentaries, Commentary, art 8(3): 'The view that the third-party treaty (the treaty by which the granting State extends favours to a third State) is the origin of the rights of the beneficiary State (a State not party to the third-party treaty) runs counter to the rule embodied in article 36, paragraph 1, of the Vienna Convention'; para 5: 'Article 8 reflects the view that the basic act [*acte regie*] is the agreement between the granting State and the beneficiary State. Under this agreement, i.e. under the most-favoured-nation clause, the beneficiary State will benefit from the favours extended by the granting State to the third State, but only because this is the common wish of the granting State and the beneficiary State. The agreement between the granting State and a third State creating obligations in their mutual relations does not create obligations in the relations between the granting State and the beneficiary State. It is nothing more than an act creating a condition (*acte condition*)'. For an analysis of the Anglo–Iranian case in its broader political and historical context see Sundhya Pahuja and Cait Storr, 'Rethinking Iran and International Law: The Anglo-Iranian Oil Company Case Revisited' in James Crawford and others (eds), *The International Legal Order: Current Needs and Possible Responses, Essays in Honour of Djamchid Momtaz* (Brill 2017) 53–74.

[127] Schill (n 99) 127.
[128] ibid.
[129] ibid 121.
[130] Perez-Aznar (n 9).
[131] Greenwood (n 9) 560–61.

or not the investor was disadvantaged in comparison to a third-country investor in a competitive relationship with the claimant investor. This approach to analysing MFN has guided the application of the standard in the context of trade in services under WTO case law where the presence of a competitive relationship is a precondition of moving on to analysing whether a service provider has been subjected to less favourable treatment.[132] Following this approach, if two foreign investors in the same sector were subjected to different performance requirements based on their nationality, resulting in one gaining more profits compared to the other, the losing investor could invoke an MFN clause to be compensated for losses arising from less favourable treatment. This approach allows for a departure from the negotiated bargain on performance requirements found in the original treaty where the claimant is otherwise in a competitive disadvantage vis-à-vis an actual third country investor operating in the same sector. It does not, however, allow the rewriting of terms of the basic treaty by importing external standards from a third-country treaty where no actual discrimination has been experienced by the claimant.

6 Conclusion

The interpretation of MFN treatment in investment law has taken several unfortunate turns. At the heart of these is the deviation from the non-discrimination origins of MFN treatment. Tribunals and scholars often invoke Articles 31 and 32 of the Vienna Convention on the Law of Treaties to support their interpretative approaches for MFN clauses. Yet, they come to radically different conclusions about the meaning and operation of similarly or identically worded clauses. Whose interpretation is correct? Largely missing from the awards, whether they resolve issues of dispute settlement or substantive standards, is a granular analysis of the concepts of 'treatment' and 'like circumstances'. Also lacking is the application of these elements of MFN treatment to concrete facts relevant to the specific circumstances of the claimant and its investment.

Meanwhile, states have gradually responded to their experience with MFN clauses by refining the language of new treaties. Increasingly, MFN clauses explicitly exclude dispute settlement from their scope.[133] They also use explicit language to limit 'importation' of standards from other treaties.[134] Newer

[132] *Argentina—Measures Relating to Trade in Goods and Services* (n 30) [6.34].
[133] UK–Australia FTA 2021, art 13.6(3); Georgia–Japan BIT 2021, art 3(2).
[134] See EU and the Netherlands recent treaty practice.

treaties state that substantive obligations in third-country treaties do not automatically constitute 'more favourable treatment'.[135] These limitations on what can be called treatment in the application of MFN clauses will likely limit the radius of power of the tribunals. Yet, it remains uncertain how such clauses will be used creatively by claimants or tribunals. If the reformed versions of MFN treatment do not return tribunals to the underlying goal of non-discrimination, this will justify even greater rejection by states, whether by completely excluding MFN clauses from investment treaties[136] or by completely excluding arbitral tribunals from the resolution of investor–state disputes.

135 CETA 8.7(4). See also Iran–Slovakia BIT; Hungary–Kyrgyzstan BIT (2020), art 4(3).
136 See Model Indian BIT.

4

Expropriation

Nicolás M. Perrone

1 Introduction

This chapter examines the expropriation standard under international law and investment treaties through the lens of a pluralistic and relational approach to property rights.[1] The objective is twofold. The chapter discusses canonical issues, while also uncovering interpretative aspects that have been overlooked when resolving claims of direct and indirect expropriation. Some investment disputes reveal that states can behave in an arbitrary and discriminatory manner. But others show that conflict can centre on democratically decided social transformations, implementing a plurality of property arrangements or new public regulation. In this regard, it is worth observing two things. First, the economics literature has shown that private property rights are not always the most efficient form of property arrangement. Elinor Ostrom has observed that commons fare better than private property rights in certain situations.[2] To assume that private property represents a benchmark of economic efficiency is, in other words, incorrect. Secondly, property serves a plurality of purposes, not only the maximization of economic benefits. Legal orders include principles and rules—sometimes in the form of ownership obligations—that respond to the social functions served by property.[3]

The chapter is organized as follows. The first section briefly introduces the notions of direct and indirect expropriation. Later, this chapter examines how international investment law has approached the question of what the object of expropriation can be. This is important because there is no reason to assume that investors always have a right—let alone an absolute right—against other

[1] See eg Gregory S Alexander and Eduardo M Peñalver, *An Introduction to Property Theory* (CUP 2012) 94–101.

[2] See Elinor Ostrom, *Governing the Commons: The Evolution of Institutions for Collective Action* (CUP 2016).

[3] See Léon Duguit, *Autour de la fonction sociale de la propriété* (Dalloz, 1901); Gregory Alexander, 'The Social-Obligation Norm in American Property Law' (2008) 94 Cornell Law Review745.

Nicolás M. Perrone, *Expropriation* In: *Rethinking Investment Law*. Edited by: David Schneiderman and Gus Van Harten, Oxford University Press. © Nicolás M. Perrone 2023. DOI: 10.1093/oso/9780192871084.003.0004

actors. The third section examines the expropriation of contracts. Contracts are a central piece of many foreign investment projects but the investment regime has struggled to draw a line between contractual and treaty claims. The fourth and fifth sections examine direct and indirect expropriations. They critically discuss the premise that these two scenarios are comparable, and pose questions about key issues like compensation and the relationship between the effects of public measures and the right to regulate. In so doing, this chapter discusses only those key awards that have informed the debate in the last decades. For an external point of reference, the different sections rely on property cases and literature from the United States. The reasons for this are that this country has a long tradition of constitutional property protection and that international investment law, and in particular the expropriation standard, has borrowed heavily from United States constitutional law and the notion of regulatory takings.[4]

2 Two Basic Notions: Direct and Indirect Expropriation

According to investment treaties, states can annihilate a foreign investment in either a direct or an indirect manner. Direct expropriations are forced transfers of ownership from a private actor to the state. Most constitutions recognize a state's right to expropriate property. In the United States, this right is known as eminent domain. Forced transfers of property can be carried out in different ways. Governments can follow the procedure previously determined by law (ie due process), or take control of the investment project in an unexpected manner. The political context of these forced transfers of property can also vary, ranging from a large-scale social transformation to the creation of a national park. International law and investment treaties permit direct expropriations. But these measures are permissible only if states comply with specific legal requirements. States' right to expropriate derives from the sovereign right to define their economic system, while the requirements for a lawful expropriation—particularly the obligation to compensate—limit this

[4] See David Schneiderman, *Constitutionalizing Economic Globalization. Investment Rules and Democracy's Promise* (CUP 2008); Parvan Parvanov and Mark Kantor, 'Comparing U.S. Law and Recent U.S. Investment Agreements: Much More Similar than you Might Expect' in Karl Sauvant (ed), *The Yearbook on International Investment Law and Policy 2010/2011* (OUP 2012) 741. This does not imply that international investment law and constitutional property in the United States are quite the same. See Vicki Been and Joel C Beauvais, 'The Global Fifth Amendment-NAFTA's Investment Protections and the Misguided Quest for an International Regulatory Takings Doctrine' (2003) 78 New York University Law Review 30.

sovereign right and serves to adjust states' behaviour to the expectation of the international community of foreign investors.[5]

Indirect expropriations, on the other hand, are according to most investment treaties public measures 'having the effects of' or 'tantamount to' a direct expropriation.[6] A crucial distinction between a direct and an indirect expropriation is the lack of transfer of ownership. Whereas direct expropriations redistribute the rights and entitlements that make the investment project, an indirect expropriation makes the economic activity legally impossible or simply uneconomic. This may or may not benefit the state finances.[7] Regulating an activity, such as smoking tobacco, may reduce the cost of public health but also lower public revenue. Most investment treaties include no reference to states' right to regulate, but decisions and awards have acknowledged that states have the sovereign authority to impose taxes and regulate economic activities. In *Oscar Chinn*, the Permanent Court of International Justice recognized police powers as the normal exercise of governmental functions.[8] Several investment awards have reasoned similarly.[9] In this way, the legal issue in a case of indirect expropriation is not whether states can implement or modify regulations, but if the controversial regulations have gone 'too far'.[10] Resolving claims of direct and indirect expropriation open difficult interpretative challenges, some of which are examined below.

3 What Can Be the Object of an Expropriation?

Not everything can be expropriated under international law. According to the *Oscar Chinn* decision, 'favourable business conditions' and 'goodwill' cannot be expropriated.[11] Determining *what* can be the object of expropriation has important implications. What is left outside cannot give rise to states' liability

[5] International law does not establish a fundamental right to be free from economic coercion. See Antonios Tzanakopoulos, 'The Right to Be Free from Economic Coercion' (2015) 4 Cambridge Journal of International and Comparative Law 616.

[6] Rudolf Dolzer and Christoph Schreuer, *Principles of International Investment Law* (OUP 2012) 102.

[7] August Reinisch, 'Expropriation' in Peter Muchlinski, Federico Ortino, and Christoph Schreuer (eds), *The Oxford Handbook of International Investment Law* (OUP 2008) 442.

[8] *Oscar Chinn (Britain v Belgium)* [1934] PCIJ (Ser A/B) No 63, 99.

[9] *Tecmed v Mexico*, ICSID Case No ARB AF/00/2, Award (29 May 2003) 115; *Philip Morris v Uruguay* (n 9) 295.

[10] See *Mahon v Pennsylvania Coal* 260 US 393 (1922). This case was decided in 1922 by the United States Supreme Court. See also Carol Rose, 'Mahon Reconstructed: Why the Takings Issue Is Still a Muddle' (1984) 57 Southern California Law Review561.

[11] *Oscar Chinn Case* (n 8) 99. For a good review of early twentieth century cases, decided based on the notion of acquired rights see Pierre A Lalive, 'The Doctrine of Acquired Rights' in Southwestern Legal Foundation, *Rights and Duties of Private Investors Abroad* (M Bender 1965) 145.

under this standard. Most investment treaties in force have a broad definition of investment, including tangible and intangible rights.[12] They protect 'every asset', from sovereign debt to an arbitral award.[13] But recent treaties have adopted a narrower approach. They do not include a broad definition of investment and explicitly exclude some assets or industries, such as sovereign debt or tobacco.[14] This evolution in treaty drafting indicates that states are willing to reduce the scope of foreign investment protection. In this as in other areas of international investment law, however, states have reacted to, rather than anticipated, investment awards.[15] For this reason, it is necessary to examine the reasoning employed by arbitrators to understand fully *what* can be the object of expropriation.

Most awards describe the assets covered by investment treaties having in mind the investment project. Focusing on the position of investors, arbitrators observe that their projects rely on licences, permits, contracts, and other entitlements to carry out a business. As the *Methanex* tribunal reasons, the object of protection is a 'contemporary conception [of property] which includes managerial control over components of a process that is wealth producing'.[16] This interpretation corresponds to the object and purpose of investment treaties (ie to 'maximize effective utilization of the community and individuals economic resources'[17]) and is also consistent with the definition of investment adopted by most tribunals when deciding their jurisdiction *ratione materiae* (ie a contribution of capital, for a period of time, assuming a risk, and with the expectation of making economic returns).[18]

[12] *SPP v Egypt*, ICSID Case No ARB/84/3, Award (20 May 1992) 164; *Wena Hotels v Egypt*, ICSID Case No ARB/98/4, Award (8 December 2000) 98; *Pope & Talbot v Canada*, UNCITRAL–NAFTA, Interim Award (26 June 2000) 96; *SD Myers v Canada*, NAFTA–UNCITRAL, Partial Award (13 November 2000) 281.

[13] According to the UNCTAD Investment Policy Hub Website, 2,499 out of 2,577 mapped treaties have an asset-based definition. Based on this broad definition of investment, investment tribunals have decided, eg that an arbitral award is an asset that can be object of an expropriation. See *Saipem v Bangladesh*, ICSID Case No ARB/05/07, Award (30 June 2009); *ATA v Jordan*, ICSID Case No ARB/08/2, Award (18 May 2012).

[14] According to the UNCTAD Investment Policy Hub Website, 136 out of 2,577 mapped treaties exclude some specific assets (eg sovereign debt, ordinary commercial transactions, etc.). The Comprehensive and Progressive Agreement for Trans-Pacific Partnership contains a broad tobacco carve-out, whereby 'if a Party elects to deny benefits with respect to such claims, any such claim shall be dismissed' (Article 29.5).

[15] José E Alvarez, 'Why are We "Re-Calibrating" Our Investment Treaties?' (2010) 4 World Arbitration and Mediation Review 143.

[16] *Methanex v USA*, UNCITRAL–NAFTA, Final Award of the Tribunal on Jurisdiction and Merits (3 August 2005) Part IV, Ch D, 17.

[17] US Model Bilateral Investment Treaties 1984, 2002, and 2012.

[18] *Fedax v Venezuela*, ICSID Case No ARB/96/3, Decision on Jurisdiction (11 July 1997) 43; *Pey Casado v Chile*, ICSID Case No ARB/98/2, Award (8 May 2008) 232; *Romak v Uzbekistan*, UNCITRAL, PCA Case No AA280, Award (26 November 2009) 207. For a more detailed analysis of the implications of this interpretation for the merits of an investment dispute, see Nicolás M Perrone, 'The Emerging

On the other hand, this interpretation downplays the distributive and normative tensions intrinsic to the concept of property. The *Methanex* tribunal suggests there is a tension between a *contemporary* vs. an alleged *out-dated* conception of property when property, in reality, is normatively pluralistic. Property facilitates wealth maximization, is part of individual personhood and shapes and enables community life.[19]

The 'wealth producing' conception of foreign investor rights has shaped some arbitral decision-making. Some tribunals have concentrated on the economic benefits instead of the tangible and intangible rights involved in a foreign investment. The *CME* tribunal notes that in this case '[w]hat was destroyed was the commercial value of the investment'.[20] These arbitrators conflate the expectation of economic returns with foreign investor rights, protecting value instead of ownership rights. A problem with this reasoning is that markets actors define economic value after assessing large flows of information. For them, laws are just a piece of information.[21] Legally protecting economic value distorts this relationship. It elevates the purposes of wealth maximization and profit-making over other social norms and preferences, 'underwrit[ing] the investor-profits of predatory and extractive enterprises'.[22]

Other awards, however, have focused on the control and enjoyment of a foreign investment as the object of protection.[23] This reasoning relies on Honoré's description of ownership as a bundle of rights.[24] The bundle serves as a framework to assess the impact of the measure on private property rights.[25]

Global Right to Investment: Understanding the Reasoning Behind Foreign Investor Rights' (2017) 8 Journal of International Dispute Settlement 673, 682–83.

[19] Margaret Radin, 'Property and Personhood' (1981) 34 Stanford Law Review 957, 959; Carol Rose, 'Takings and the Practices of Property: Property as Wealth, Property as Propriety' in Carol Rose, *Property and Persuasion: Essays on the History, Theory, and Rhetoric of Ownership* (Westview Press 1994) 49; Gregory S Alexander and others, 'A Statement of Progressive Property' (2008) 94 Cornell Law Review 743, 748.

[20] See *CME v Czech Republic*, UNCITRAL, Partial Award (13 September 2001) 591. See also *Metalclad v Mexico*, ICSID Case No ARB AF/97/1, Award (30 August 2000) 103; *Burlington v Ecuador*, ICSID Case No ARB/08/5, Decision on Liability (14 December 2012) 397 ('The loss of viability does not necessarily imply a loss of management or control. What matters is the capacity to earn a commercial return. After all, investors make investments to earn a return').

[21] James Penner, *The Idea of Property in Law* (OUP 2000) 15–16; Christian Barrère, 'Judicial System and Property Rights' in Enrico Colombatto (ed), *The Elgar Companion to the Economics of Property Rights* (Edward Elgar Publishing 2006) 129, 150–51.

[22] Jeremy Waldron, *The Rule of Law and the Measure of Property* (CUP 2012) 73.

[23] *El Paso v Argentina*, ICSID Case No ARB/03/15, Award (31 October 2011) 252.

[24] AM Honoré, 'Ownership' in AG Guest (ed), *Oxford Essays in Jurisprudence* (OUP 1961) 107, 112–24.

[25] See Henry Smith, 'Property as the Law of Things' (2012) 125 Harvard Law Review 1691. Smith criticizes the idea of bundle of rights but concedes that 'as an analytical device, the bundle picture can be very useful' 1696.

Arbitrators examine whether the investors are still in control of the investment, continue with the same economic activity, and enjoy the benefits of the project.[26] They have noted, in this regard, that some public interference with the control or enjoyment of the investment is not equivalent to expropriation. Something more serious is required to annihilate the bundle of rights. The situation is less clear, on the other hand, when the public measure prohibits the activity or renders the project uneconomical. These scenarios will be considered below in Section 5. Here, it suffices to say that state actions rarely annihilate the overall control and enjoyment of a business project—except in the case of a direct expropriation (ie a forced transfer of ownership).[27] Tribunals have decided that there is no expropriation if an investor is unable to export production[28] or earn the tariffs in a particular currency.[29]

The situation changes if arbitrators accept partial expropriations.[30] As Singer has shown, legal realists relied on the bundle of rights to justify limitations to private property, but later the bundle of rights was appropriated by others scholars who privileged wealth maximization over distributive concerns.[31] The latter argue that states should also compensate for the destruction of any stick in the bundle of rights. This issue arises, as the *Gami* tribunal explains, when the public measure only takes a fraction of the investment.[32] In these cases, arbitrators can decide that the measure did not affect the investment project too seriously, or conclude instead that a specific stick in the bundle was annihilated and requires compensation—even if the investment remains profitable and under the control of the investor.[33] What has been expropriated is not the entire investment—and this would be reflected when calculating compensation—but the state would still be found liable and incur international responsibility. In comparative property law, this issue is known as the problem of the denominator.[34]

Closely related to partial expropriations is how arbitrators define the scope of ownership. If the standard of expropriation protects something more specific than overall control and enjoyment, the action moves to how adjudicators

[26] *Azurix v Argentina*, ICSID Case No ARB/01/12, Award (14 July 2006) 322; *LG&E v Argentina*, ICSID Case No ARB/02/1, Decision on Liability (3 October 2006) 36.

[27] *SD Myers v Canada* (n 12) 282.

[28] *Pope & Talbot v Canada* (n 12) 96.

[29] *El Paso v Argentina* (n 23).

[30] Dolzer and Schreuer (n 6) note that 'an approach that looks exclusively at control over the overall investment is unable to contemplate the expropriation of specific rights enjoyed by the investor' 118.

[31] Joseph William Singer, *Entitlement: The Paradoxes of Property* (YUP 2000) 12–13.

[32] *GAMI v Mexico*, UNCITRAL-NAFTA, Award (15 November 2004) 126.

[33] See Dolzer and Schreuer (n 6) 119.

[34] John Fee, 'Unearthing the Denominator in Regulatory Taking Claims' (1994) 61 The University of Chicago Law Review 1538.

define each stick in the bundle of rights. Investment tribunals have adopted different approaches to defining the scope of ownership. One is to look at the applicable domestic laws.[35] In the case of *Philip Morris v Uruguay*, the arbitrators framed this issue as to whether Philip Morris had under Uruguayan law a right to use the trademark or to exclude competitors from using it.[36] The advantage of applying domestic law is that this should aid the tribunal to respect the plurality of norms and preferences that a host society has embedded in the concept of property. The problem is that the concept of property remains indeterminate, precisely because of this normative complexity, and therefore it always requires interpretation.[37] In investor–state dispute settlement (ISDS), as there is no need to exhaust local remedies, this interpretation is the job of international arbitrators (assisted by the parties and their experts).

An alternative approach to defining the scope of ownership focuses on foreign investor legitimate expectations.[38] The arbitrators in *Metalclad* and *CME*, as Gaillard explains, replaced the notion of acquired or vested right, which was relied on by earlier international tribunals such as *Oscar Chinn*, for the notion of legitimate expectations.[39] The violation of one of these expectations—which resemble, for instance, investment-backed expectations in US constitutional property law—could then constitute an expropriation. In *Metalclad*, the tribunal decided that the investor had a right to carry out a waste-disposal project based on the principle of transparency and Mexico's representations.[40] The arbitrators in *CME* found that the investor was entitled to rely on the original structure of a media project, and that a forced restructuring and other subsequent events destroyed this right.[41] In both cases, the annihilation of these expectations amounted to expropriation.

Subsequent to these disputes, however, tribunals have not, for the most part, drawn on the doctrine of legitimate expectations when deciding claims of expropriation, reducing the number of awards against states under this standard

[35] See Zachary Douglas, *International Investment Claims* (CUP 2009) 41–42, 52–71, 81–90. Tribunals have also relied on domestic law to decide whether a resource can be commodified and privately allocated; See *Bayview Irrigation v Mexico*, ICSID Case No ARB AF/05/1, Award (19 June 2007) 118.

[36] *Philip Morris v Uruguay* (n 9) 243.

[37] Alexander refers to this problem as 'the Formalist trap'. Gregory Alexander, *The Global Debate Over Constitutional Property: Lessons for American Takings Jurisprudence* (University of Chicago Press 2006) 1.

[38] Stephen Fietta, 'Expropriation and the "Fair and Equitable" Standard' (2006) 23 Journal of International Arbitration 375, 379–81; Dolzer and Schreuer (n 6) 115–57.

[39] Emmanuelle Gaillard, 'Chronique des sentences arbitrales: Centre International pour le Règlement des Différends Relatifs aux Investissements (CIRDI)' (2008) 1 Journal du droit international 311, 332–34.

[40] *Metalclad v Mexico* (n 20) 76, 104, 107.

[41] *CME v Czech Republic* (n 20) 98–102.

of treatment. This does not mean that disappointing legitimate expectations cannot constitute a treaty breach under other standards.[42]

4 Can Contracts Be Expropriated?

Whether states can expropriate contracts under international investment law is a significant question for foreign investors and states. International courts and tribunals as well as many commentators accept that contracts can be expropriated under international law.[43] Indeed, the expropriation of concession contracts gave rise to several investment disputes during the 1960s and 1970s. According to international investment treaties, the expropriation of contracts are a corollary to the broad definition of investment, which includes intangible property and contractual rights. The protection of contractual rights, it could be said, goes to the core of international investment law. Investment arbitrators underscore that the underlying rationale of this legal regime is to enable states' to make meaningful promises[44] to enforce these promises (*pacta sunt servanda*).[45] Functionally speaking, however, distinguishing between property and contracts can be difficult. Contractual obligations can create a special kind of ownership framework—as in a concession—or adjust the scope of ownership—as in stabilization agreements whereby investors are shielded from tax or other regulatory changes.[46]

Investment tribunals have accepted that contracts can be expropriated under investment treaties. Arbitrators have reasoned that states can use their sovereign powers to terminate a concession or to disregard a stabilization clause without paying compensation.[47] There are, however, certain issues that are specific to the expropriation of contracts. One is to determine whether the state has acted using its sovereign or its commercial powers. Tribunals have decided that they only have jurisdiction when states have exercised sovereign authority.

[42] Fietta (n 38); See also David Schneiderman, 'Legitimacy and Reflexivity in International Investment Arbitration: A New Self-Restraint?' (2011) 4 Journal of International Dispute Settlement 471, 494.

[43] See Dolzer and Schreuer (n 6) 126–29; Reinisch (n 7) 407, 417–18.

[44] Jan Paulsson, 'The Power of States to Make Meaningful Promises to Foreigners' (2010) 1(2) Journal of International Dispute Settlement 341.

[45] Michael W Reisman, '"Case Specific Mandates" versus "Systemic Implications": How Should Investment Tribunals Decide?' (2013) 29 Arbitration International 131, 151.

[46] Nicolás M Perrone, 'Neoliberalism and economic sovereignty: property, contracts, and foreign investment relations' in Honor Brabazon (ed), *Neoliberal Legality: Understanding the Role of Law in the Neoliberal Project* (Routledge 2016) 43, 45.

[47] *Eureko v Republic of Poland*, UNCITRAL, Partial Award (19 August 2005) 241; *Impreglio v Pakistan*, ICSID Case No ARB/03/3, Decision on Jurisdiction (22 April 2005) 281.

Investment treaties do not protect investors from 'normal commercial risks'.[48] Those risks remain allocated to foreign investors. When states act like any other business actor, investment treaties provide no protection to foreign investors. In *Waste Management 2*, for instance, the tribunal reasoned that non-payment is a typical commercial risk not covered by an investment treaty.[49]

While the distinction between sovereign and commercial activity is hardly clear, further problems arise in interpreting (1) the contractual dispute resolution clause and (2) treaty standards and applicable laws to the contract. The first question was discussed in the *Vivendi* case. The tribunal initially declined jurisdiction because the concession contract included a dispute resolution clause granting exclusive jurisdiction to the courts of Tucumán (an Argentine province). The Annulment Committee annulled this award, however, clarifying that tribunals have jurisdiction over treaty claims despite the existence of a contractual dispute resolution clause.[50] Commercial issues, on the other hand, remain within the remit of the court or tribunal defined by the contract or the applicable laws. The rationale for this conclusion is that arbitral tribunals constituted according to the applicable treaty are the right fora to hear treaty claims. ISDS is defined as a mandatory—or a sticky-default—jurisdiction for treaty claims.[51]

Separating treaty and contracts claims, secondly, raises problems when deciding the merits of a case. Contracts involving the state—in some jurisdictions explicitly recognized as administrative contracts—are governed by rules that implicitly or explicitly recognize the role of the state to pursue the public interest. The question, then, is how tribunals can separate contract from treaty claims if the applicable contractual law responds to the regulatory personality of the state, as opposed to an alleged business personality. The existence of the latter, in fact, can be questioned as states should always act for the public good. The problem of artificially separating the contractual and treaty dimensions of an investment dispute is the risk of *rewriting* the contract.

This rewriting occurred in *Occidental 2*.[52] This case originated when Occidental transferred an interest in the investment project without the approval of the Ecuadorian government, which was mandatory according to the

48 *Waste Management v Mexico 2*, ICSID Case No ARB AF/00/3, Award (30 April 2004) 177.

49 ibid 160, 174.

50 *Vivendi v Argentina*, ICSID Case No ARB/97/3, Decision on Annulment (3 July 2002) 96.

51 See Julian Arato, 'The Private Law Critique of International Investment Law' (2019) 113 American Journal of International Law 1, 29.

52 *Occidental Petroleum v Ecuador*, ICSID Case No ARB/06/11, Award (5 October 2012); Another example of contract rewriting is *Eureko v Republic of Poland* (n 47). See Zachary Douglas, 'Nothing if Not Critical for Investment Treaty Arbitration: Occidental, Eureko and Methanex' (2006) 22 Arbitration International 27.

concession agreement. Ecuador, then, terminated the concession under the assumption that the breach was appropriately documented and the terms of the contract were sufficiently clear. The penalty for this sort of breach was termination. The *Occidental 2* tribunal acknowledged both Occidental's breach and the terms of the contract, but disagreed about the applicable law to this question. Notwithstanding the contract, these arbitrators decided that Ecuador had an obligation to act in a proportionate manner according to the US-Ecuador investment treaty and Ecuadorian law. Considering not only the contractual breach, but also the lack of economic damage to Ecuador, the tribunal decided that the termination of the contract was disproportionate and equivalent to expropriation.[53] While so doing, notably, the tribunal also dismissed the public rationales that Ecuador put forward to include and utilize the termination clause.[54]

The expropriation of contracts opens up sensitive issues for foreign investors and states. For foreign investors, investment contracts—together with investment treaties and ISDS—amount to a high level of rights protection. For states, the situation is quite the opposite. Under international law, no standards govern the content of investment contracts. There are strict rules about how states can use their sovereign and contractual powers, but no limitations to the incentives that states can offer in these contracts to entice foreign investors. For countries without much bargaining power, this situation may lead to an unbalanced distribution of benefits, costs, and risks. Further, an important issue is whether foreign investors could contractually waive their substantive and procedural rights under investment treaties. The few awards on this question, regrettably, have reached inconsistent conclusions.[55]

5 Direct Expropriation

The primary sources of international law recognize states' right to expropriate. International treaties, international customary law, and the general principles of laws accept states' right to expropriate property or exercise the power of eminent domain.[56] But the state of international law was not always so clear. During the post-colonial period, some scholars argued that certain direct

[53] *Occidental Petroleum v Ecuador* (n 52) 416–50.
[54] ibid 434, 448–50.
[55] See *Aguas del Tunari v Bolivia*, ICSID Case No ARB/02/3, Decision on Jurisdiction (21 October 2005) 119; *SGS v Philippines*, ICSID Case No ARB/02/6, Decision on Jurisdiction (29 January 2004) 154.
[56] Dolzer and Schreuer (n 6) 98–99.

expropriations were unlawful under international law, for instance, when the underlying rights emerged from a concession contract or the host state had given a specific commitment against expropriation.[57] Essentially, these two cases would fall under the *pacta sunt servanda* principle. States have a sovereign power to expropriate, but they can give it up through consent.[58] The challenges created by the post-colonial period, however, made this position untenable in that political context. Not only were Global South countries not in control of their economic affairs but the conditions attached to these concessions were openly imbalanced.[59] To clarify the situation, newly independent countries promoted the United Nations General Assembly Resolution on Permanent Sovereignty over Natural Resources (PSNR), which was approved by both capital importing and exporting countries.[60]

But a state's right to expropriate is not unlimited. Under international law and investment treaties, a state must comply with four requirements to expropriate lawfully. A lawful expropriation needs to be (1) done for a public purpose, (2) cannot be discriminatory, (3) should be carried out according to the due process of law, and (4) needs to be followed by appropriate compensation.[61]

Before discussing these requirements, it is worth distinguishing an expropriation that meets these requirements, ie a lawful expropriation, from an illegal expropriation. According to the principles set in the *Chorzow Factory* case, a foreign investor whose property has been illegally expropriated could, theoretically at least, demand the restitution of the property.[62] Tribunals and investors, however, have hesitated to order or request this remedy. Instead, when deciding that an expropriation is unlawful, some arbitrators have chosen to impose a higher amount of compensation.[63]

The first requirement to make a lawful expropriation is public purpose. An expropriation must be for a public purpose as opposed to a specific private interest. In practice, arbitrators have not questioned a declaration of public

[57] Hartley Shawcross, 'Problems of Foreign Investment' (1961) 102 Recueil des Cours 339, 353.

[58] See Paulsson (n 44).

[59] Muthucumaraswamy Sornarajah, *The International Law on Foreign Investment* (CUP 2017) 48–52; Anthony Anghie, *Imperialism, Sovereignty and the Making of International Law* (CUP 2007) 211–13.

[60] UNGA Res 1803 (XVII) (14 December 1962) 'Permanent sovereignty over natural resources' UN Doc A/RES/1803. The hard cases, ie a case in which a host state grants a specific commitment against expropriation, have not arisen in practice. While it is unlikely that such a commitment would prevent an expropriation, it could still open a discussion over the legality of the expropriation and the amount of compensation.

[61] Dolzer and Schreuer (n 6) 99–100.

[62] See *Chorzów Factory Case* [1929] PCIJ, Series A, No 9 (26 July 1927).

[63] See *ConocoPhillips v Venezuela*, ICSID Case No ARB/07/30, Decision on Jurisdiction and Merits (3 September 2013) and Award (8 March 2019); *Guaracachi v Bolivia*, UNCITRAL, PCA Case No 2011-17, Award (31 January 2014).

interest.[64] In comparative constitutional property law, similarly, the public purpose of an expropriation has rarely been challenged.[65] One of those few instances is the *Kelo v City of New London* case in the United States.[66] In this case, the claimant argued that expropriating residential property to facilitate a private investment was not in the public interest. The United States Supreme Court, however, sided with the state defining private redevelopment plans as a 'public use' under the Constitution. This decision privileged the utility derived from this investment plan over the importance of property for individual personhood and community life. Interestingly, both conservative and progressive camps criticized the result.[67]

A lawful expropriation also needs to be non-discriminatory. States need to treat foreign investors like domestic and other foreign investors in similar circumstances.[68] The chapter discussing the national treatment and most-favoured standards examines the notion of similar circumstances. Here, it suffices to say that expropriating a foreign investor to favour a domestic or another foreign investor could render these measures illegal under international law and investment treaties. The issue would not be the public purpose per se but the benefit created for a domestic or foreign competitor in similar circumstances.

When expropriating, moreover, states have to follow the due process of law. Governments have to obey their respective laws and regulations before taking control of a foreign investment project.[69] This requirement has not given rise to specific issues, but due process is a broad concept that could lead to controversy in the future.[70] Recent awards have reasoned that there are minimum due process requirements when discussing other treaty standards, namely an obligation to consult or allow the participation of foreign investors in the domestic decision-making process.[71] Arbitrators could interpret that these requirements are in addition to domestic rules.

Lastly, the most controversial requirement is the need to pay appropriate compensation. State practice confirms that countries have to pay compensation

[64] Dolzer and Schreuer (n 6) 99.
[65] Alexander and Peñalver (n 1) 161.
[66] *Kelo v City of New London* 545 US 469 (2005).
[67] 'The opposition cut across conventional partisan, ideological, racial, and gender divisions.' See Ilya Somin, 'The Political and Judicial Reaction to *Kelo*' *The Washington Post* (4 June 2015).
[68] Dolzer and Schreuer (n 6) 100.
[69] ibid.
[70] ibid.
[71] See *Bear Creek v Peru*, ICSID Case No ARB/14/2, Award (30 November 2017) 403–407; *Electrabel v Hungary*, ICSID Case No ARB/07/19, Decision on Jurisdiction, Applicable Law and Liability (30 November 2012) 7.79; *Franck Charles Arif v Moldova*, ICSID Case No ARB/11/23, Award (8 April 2013) 537–38.

when taking foreign property. Except for expropriations in Russia and few other communist countries or in the case of enemy property taken during wartime, governments pay compensation when expropriating foreign-owned assets.[72] Notably, this includes Mexico in the 1930s, with some exceptions Czechoslovakia and Poland in the 1940s, and Egypt in the 1950s (the nationalization of the Suez Canal Company).[73] Similarly, the PSNR recognizes states' right to expropriate and requires states to pay 'appropriate compensation, in accordance with the rules in force in the state taking such measures in the exercise of its sovereignty and in accordance with international law'.[74]

The consensus in favour of paying compensation, however, contrasts with the plurality of compensation practices. While the United States and European countries have indeed claimed that states must pay 'prompt, adequate and effective compensation', state practice before and right after the Second World War shows a different trend. Most expropriations were followed by partial compensation only, ie below market price, and it was not necessarily prompt or effective.[75] Influential international law scholars defended this practice. Fischer Williams, Lauterpacht, and Oppenheim argued that partial compensation was legal under international law as long as nationals and foreigners were treated equally.[76] A more restrictive position on the issue of compensation, they observed, would impose unacceptable limits on states' right to change their social and economic organization. These authors distinguished between individual expropriations and large-scale nationalization, whereby the latter should be subject to a different and lesser standard of compensation.

During the post-colonial period, newly independent countries defended the practice of partial compensation, asserting that compensation should consider previous colonial injustices and the compensating state's finances.[77] Political independence in Africa and Asia was not accompanied by sovereignty over natural resources, which in many instances remained under foreign-control thanks to previously signed concession contracts. According to the former metropolis, these concessions had created vested rights that could not be terminated without providing full compensation.[78] The PSNR

[72] Georg Schwarzenberger, *Foreign Investments and International Law* (Stevens & Sons 1969) 23–26, 30–89.

[73] ibid.

[74] UNGA Res 1803 (n 60).

[75] See Schwarzenberger (n 72) 23–26, 30–89. See also Sornarajah (n 59) 528–29.

[76] John Fischer Williams, 'International Law and the Property of Aliens' (1928) 9 British Yearbook of International Law 1; Lassa Oppenheim and Hersch Lauterpacht, *International Law: A Treatise* (Longmans, Green and Co 1948) 317–18; See further Sornarajah (n 59) 495, 516.

[77] Anghie (n 59) 213.

[78] ibid.

was meant to recognize decolonization as a large-scale process of social transformation, which required not only redistributing wealth but also redefining the purposes of property. As centre-periphery theorists observed, the economic use of natural resources in the Global South continued to serve the colonial division of labour and perpetuated economic inequality between centre and periphery.[79] But the PSNR did not fulfil this ambitious goal. Broad support in the General Assembly of the United Nations was only possible thanks to language that allowed capital importing and exporting countries to maintain their differing views on compensation.[80] The Charter of Economic Rights and Duties of States, which explicitly stated that compensation should be determined according to domestic laws, was opposed by most capital-exporting countries.[81]

Investment treaties settled this controversy in favour of the 'prompt, adequate and effective' formula, but the question remains unresolved under general international law. Customary law, as explained above, and general principles in most countries do not show a consensus about whether and to what extent the law should be responsive to the social and political context in determining the amount of compensation due.[82] Neither was this issue resolved multilaterally. The World Bank Guidelines on the Treatment of Foreign Investment recognize a difference between 'takings of specific investments' and 'comprehensive non-discriminatory nationalizations of the kinds that take place in the context of large scale social reforms'.[83] According to these guidelines, the latter may require states to pay partial compensation only. Investment treaties, it is true, have changed this picture dramatically after capital importing countries signed thousands of treaties that require full compensation and provide no exception for large social transformations.[84] But it is unclear whether these bilateral, regional, or sectoral treaties have changed customary international law or

[79] Prebisch explained this divergence using the idea of 'unequal exchange'. See Raúl Prebisch, 'Economic Survey of Latin America 1949' (United Nations 1951).

[80] GW Haight, 'The New International Economic Order and the Charter of Economic Rights and Duties of States' (1975) 9 International Lawyer 591, 601–603.

[81] ibid.

[82] For instance, the original 1991 Colombian Constitution permitted expropriation without compensation, although this provision was later reformed in 1999 (1991 Colombian Constitution, Article 58). Similarly, the 1996 South African Constitution authorizes the judiciary to take into account the historical injustice created by the Apartheid (Constitution of South Africa, s 25).

[83] World Bank, 'Guidelines on the Treatment of Foreign Direct Investment' (The World Bank Group 1992) 28–29.

[84] As Salacuse explains, the international investment regime suffered a process of 'treatification'. Jeswald Salacuse, 'The Treatification of International Investment Law' (2007) 13 Law & Business Review of the Americas 155.

if they reflect the general principles of law as per Article 38 of the Statute of the International Court of Justice.[85]

In line with the text of investment treaties, ISDS practice has rejected the partial compensation thesis. Some awards, actually, have supplied reasons directly opposed to it. In *Tecmed*, the arbitrators relied on a decision of the European Convention of Human Rights to conclude that it would be unfair to distribute the burden of a social transformation between foreigners and nationals equally.[86] The reasoning is that foreigners do not participate in the domestic decision-making process and will not benefit from these reforms. Other tribunals, similarly, have underscored the weak position of foreign investors vis-à-vis host states and other local actors who participate in domestic politics and understand better the local context.[87] This position is problematic, however. For one, empirical evidence shows that foreign investors are treated the same or better than domestic firms.[88] For another, this rigid approach to the amount of compensation makes international investment law unresponsive to the local context. Arbitrators have not discussed whether treating foreign investors better than their domestic counterparts may encourage the former to behave as an 'outsider', who is interested neither in the well-being of locals nor in the resolution of social crises.[89]

6 Indirect Expropriation

International law recognizes states' right to regulate economic activity subject to the limits imposed by international law and investment treaties. States can capture a higher share of the benefits through taxation or can curb the costs and risks of an investment by imposing higher health, safety, or environmental standards.[90] This regulation, however, has to remain within certain boundaries. One of these limits is that regulations shall not constitute indirect

[85] See eg José E Alvarez, 'A BIT on Custom' (2009) 42 New York University Journal of International Law and Policy 17; Martins Paparinskis, *The International Minimum Standard and Fair and Equitable Treatment* (OUP 2013).

[86] *Tecmed v Mexico* (n 9) 122 (relying on *James and Others v United Kingdom* App no 8793/79 (ECHR, 21 February 1986) para 63.

[87] *Azurix v Argentina* (n 26) 310–11; Separate Opinion of Thomas Wälde in *Thunderbird v Mexico*, UNCITRAL-NAFTA, Award (1 December 2005) 4, 12, 33, 57; *Joseph Lemire v Ukraine*, ICSID Case No ARB/06/18, Award (28 March 2011) 57.

[88] Jonathan Bonnitcha, Lauge N. Skovgaard Poulsen, and Michael Waibel, *The Political Economy of the Investment Treaty Regime* (OUP 2017) 150.

[89] See Waldron (n 22) 105.

[90] See eg OECD, '"Indirect Expropriation" and the "Right to Regulate" in International Investment Law' (2004) OECD Working Papers on International Investment 2004/04, 7–9.

expropriations, ie they shall not be 'equivalent to' or 'tantamount to' a direct expropriation.

Unfortunately, likening indirect to direct expropriations does not provide a precise formula to distinguish between legitimate regulations and expropriatory measures. First, regulations do not imply a transfer of ownership and rarely create large economic benefits for states. Tribunals have admitted that 'expropriation can exist despite there being no obvious benefit to the State concerned'.[91] The effects of direct and indirect expropriation, in other words, are rarely quite the same. Secondly, the state may seek different public goals. Direct expropriations redistribute resources or seek to establish a different balance between common, communal, and private property. Regulations that radically affect the control or enjoyment of a resource may seek similar objectives, but may also aim to curb the costs and risks that the foreign investment itself has introduced into the host country and community.[92] The most controversial indirect expropriation cases, in ISDS practice, fall within this second category.

Before turning to discuss how arbitrators draw a line between legitimate regulations and indirect expropriations, it is worth examining what kind of state measures can amount to indirect expropriation. Customary and treaty law are quite broad in this regard. Any state measure can constitute an indirect expropriation.[93] These measures may be executive and legislative acts, such as the denial of a permit or a general law. Whether judicial decisions can amount to expropriation, however, has created some controversy. Tribunals have concluded that judicial decisions, like any other state measure, can constitute an expropriation.[94] But another position contends that judicial decisions should be analysed through the lens of denial of justice.[95] Moreover, tribunals accept that an indirect expropriation may result from one or the cumulative effects of different public measures. This kind of indirect expropriation is known as creeping expropriation and is not uncommon in ISDS practice.[96]

Claims of indirect expropriations are likely to be *hard* cases. Arbitrators and investment law scholars recognize that developing a precise formula to distinguish between legitimate regulation and indirect expropriation is a difficult task. In *Generation Ukraine*, the arbitrators explained that '[t]he decisive considerations vary from case to case, depending not only on the specific facts of

[91] *Rumeli v Kazakhstan*, ICSID Case No ARB/05/16, Award (29 July 2008) 707.

[92] See *Feldman v Mexico*, ICSID Case No ARB AF/99/1, Award (16 December 2002) 103–106.

[93] *Tecmed v Mexico* (n 9) 114.

[94] *Saipem v Bangladesh* (n 13) 133; *Eli Lilly v Canada*, UNCITRAL–ICSID Case No UNCT/14/2, Award (16 March 2017) 221.

[95] See Paparinskis (n 87) 208; Sattorova in this volume.

[96] Reinisch (n 7) 426; Dolzer and Schreuer (n 6) 125.

a grievance but also on the way the evidence is presented, and the legal bases pleaded'.[97] In *Saluka*, the tribunal similarly noted that international law 'has yet to draw a bright and easily distinguishable line' between legitimate regulation and indirect expropriation.[98] But the problem is, as Dolzer and Schreuer have noted, that drawing this line may not be possible at all.[99] These authors observe that domestic tribunals have also failed to elaborate a definitive formula.[100] Property scholarship confirms this.[101] Trying to explain why it is so difficult to draw a precise line in cases of indirect expropriation, Rose has argued that the problem is not that judges follow different formulas but that in so doing they show their different normative preferences.[102] Because of the plurality of purposes that can be embedded in the concept of property, this is mostly unsurprising.

This conclusion suggests not only that comparative law may not be helpful to resolve the issue, but also that the task itself may be problematic. Introducing domestic standards in investment treaties may contribute to clarifying some questions but would not solve the problem. The American doctrine of balancing (*Penn Central v New York*) has been incorporated into several investment treaties, in special annexes dealing with expropriation,[103] but scholars in the United States have criticized it for being a form of 'ad hocery' and 'open-ended balancing'.[104]

In ISDS practice, arbitrators have made their normative preferences explicit when linking foreign investor rights with good governance. In *Metalclad*, the tribunal demanded states to be totally transparent and create the conditions 'so that investors can proceed with all appropriate expedition in the confident belief that they are acting in accordance with all relevant laws'.[105] Doubts or uncertainties about the state of the law would be the sole responsibility of states. Metalclad acted 'in the full expectation that the permit would be granted', and

97 *Generation Ukraine v Ukraine*, ICSID Case No ARB/00/9, Award (16 September 2003) 20.29.

98 *Saluka v Czech Republic*, PCA–UNCITRAL, Partial Award (17 March 2006) 263.

99 Dolzer and Schreuer (n 6) 101, 112.

100 ibid.

101 Bruce Ackerman, *Private Property and the Constitution* (YUP 1977) 5, 23, 29; Frank Michelman, 'Property as a Constitutional Right' (1981) 38 Washington and Lee Law Review 1097, 1099.

102 Rose (n 10).

103 See US Model Bilateral Investment Treaty 2012 (Annex B); Canadian Model Bilateral Investment Treaty (Annex B.13(1)); Comprehensive and Progressive Agreement for Trans-Pacific Partnership (Annex 9-B); EU–Canada Comprehensive Economic and Trade Agreement (Annex 8-A).

104 Notably, Susan Rose-Ackerman, 'Against Ad Hocery: A Comment on Michelman' (1988) Columbia Law Review 1697; see also Gregory Alexander (n 37) 203–14. Alexander claims that balancing, or proportionality, ultimately depends on the 'core purpose of constitutional protection of property'; ibid 215.

105 *Metalclad v Mexico* (n 20) 76.

denying this permit—together with other related measures—was found to be tantamount to expropriation.[106]

But subsequent tribunals have not followed this sort of reasoning, preferring a more open-ended balancing approach. Arbitrators have noted that investment treaties do not require states to adhere to this high level of transparency,[107] or that the protection of legitimate expectations falls more appropriately under the fair and equitable standard of treatment.[108] Most arbitrators instead prefer a detailed examination of the facts of a case to a complex doctrinal analysis.[109] This does not mean that arbitrators' normative preferences no longer play a role in these decisions. Controlling the narrative is an integral part of the political struggle over international investment law.

In deciding a claim of indirect expropriation, tribunals pay significant attention to the effects of a measure on a foreign investment project. An indirect expropriation requires effects that are 'equivalent to' or 'tantamount to' a direct expropriation. But some arbitrators have gone further and relied solely on the effects of a measure to resolve a claim of expropriation.[110] The *sole effects* doctrine states that a regulation constitutes an indirect expropriation when it radically deprives the foreign investor of the control or enjoyment of the investment. For these tribunals, the regulatory purpose of a measure is not a significant aspect because a radical deprivation of foreign investor rights, in every case, requires compensation.[111] A state's intention is less important or a secondary consideration.[112]

Assessing the significance of the effects of a measure, in any event, is not a trivial question. As explained earlier, arbitrators may look at the effects of the measure on the value of the project or on the bundle of foreign investor's rights. This reasoning may lead to different outcomes. Further, ISDS practice has focused on two other questions, namely the duration of the measure and how serious the effects need to be (ie the threshold). Regarding duration, some

106 ibid 104, 107.

107 *Feldman v Mexico* (n 92) 113, 133.

108 See Fietta (n 38) 385. The investment treaties and chapters in FTAs that have incorporated the Penn Central test, however, include a reference to investment-backed expectations; see Rose (n 10).

109 The preference for this case-by-case approach extends to other standards, such as the fair and equitable standard of treatment. Perrone (n 18) 689.

110 *Metalclad v Mexico* (n 20) 103. Dolzer claims that some awards of the Iran–US Claims Tribunal, particularly *Tippets*, played an important role in the development of the sole effects doctrine. Rudolf Dolzer, 'Indirect Expropriations: New Developments' (2002) 11 New York University Environmental Law Journal 64, 86.

111 *Compañía del Desarrollo de Santa Elena v Costa Rica*, ICSID Case No ARB/96/1, Award (17 February 2000) 72; *Tecmed v Mexico* (n 9) 121; *Azurix v Argentina* (n 26) 309–11; Rosalyn Higgins, 'The Taking of Property by the State: Recent Developments in International Law' (1982) 176 Recueil des Cours 259, 331.

112 *Tecmed v Mexico* (n 9) 116; Dolzer and Schreuer (n 6) 112–15; Reinisch (n 7) 446.

awards highlight that effects have to be 'irreversible and permanent'.[113] Others have observed that they may be only temporary 'in some contexts and circumstances'.[114] In relation to the intensity of the effects, on the other hand, tribunals have agreed that the threshold needs to be high for a public measure to constitute an indirect expropriation. The *National Grid* tribunal explains that the measure should imply a 'neutralization, radical deprivation, irretrievable loss, inability to use, enjoy or dispose of the property'.[115]

This high threshold may correct the imbalance created by the 'sole effects' doctrine. If the doctrine overlooks regulatory purposes, threshold considerations can be somewhat responsive to public needs. A central distinction between regulations and expropriations, as the *SD Myers* tribunal underscored, is that '[e]xpropriations tend to involve the deprivation of ownership rights; regulations a lesser interference'.[116]

However, the sole effects doctrine has been strongly criticized for leaving out not only the states' right to regulate but also public and constitutional law considerations.[117] For arbitrators, this critique poses an interpretative challenge. The tribunals that initiated the sole effects doctrine (e.g. the Iran-US Claims Tribunals) did not reject states' right to regulate. They instead focussed on the effects of the measure to resolve the dispute, interpreting the right to regulate restrictively. Aldrich explains that the Iran-US Claims Tribunals recognized the states' right to regulate but, in practice, only one case was rejected on this ground.[118] The formal recognition of this right, in other words, did not affect the application of the sole effects doctrine. The issue is that the public and constitutional law critique of this doctrine demands more. It asks arbitrators to take seriously both foreign investor rights and legitimate democratic decisions.

The question is of paramount importance. In a claim of indirect expropriation, arbitrators can decide the dispute showing a high degree of deference towards democratic authorities or could instead choose to distrust public initiatives.[119] In the first scenario, they would apply judicial restraint when

[113] *Tecmed* (n 112) 116.

[114] *SD Myers v Canada* (n 12) 283.

[115] *National Grid v Argentina*, UNCITRAL, Award (3 November 2008) 177. Similarly, *Sempra v Argentina*, ICSID Case No ARB/02/16, Award (28 September 2007) 113, 147; *MTD v Chile*, ICSID Case No ARB/01/7, Award (25 May 2004) 63, 133.

[116] *SD Myers v Canada* (n 12) 282.

[117] Notably, Van Harten criticized this approach for overlooking the public law dimension implicated in ISDS, while Schneiderman argued that this reasoning promotes a 'constraining' version of constitutionalism. See Gus Van Harten, *Investment Treaty Arbitration and Public Law* (OUP 2007); Schneiderman (n 4).

[118] George H Aldrich, 'What Constitutes a Compensable Taking of Property? The Decisions of the Iran–United States Claims Tribunal' (1994) 88 American Journal of International Law 585, 605.

[119] See Gus Van Harten, *Sovereign Choices and Sovereign Constraints: Judicial Restraint in Investment Treaty Arbitration* (OUP 2013) 1–9.

revising general and non-discriminatory public measures, while in the second they would review the means and ends of the measure; the intensity of this review could also be more or less deferential.[120]

The first awards dealing with claims of indirect expropriation made a quite clear choice in favour of distrusting democratic authorities, focusing on the effects of a measure and showing limited or no interest in the intention of states. Three unrelated awards rendered in 2000 developed and consolidated this approach. In February, the arbitrators in *Santa Elena* observed that states should pay compensation when they make the rights of foreign investors 'practically useless', irrespective of whether or not the measure is 'beneficial to society as a whole'.[121] A few months later, the *Metalclad* tribunal further observed that 'covert or incidental interference with the use of property' can also amount to an expropriation if it deprives the owner 'of the use or reasonably-to-be-expected economic benefit of property'.[122] In this award, again, the arbitrators did not delve into the environmental implications of the measures or the reasons why the local community resisted the project. Given the implications of this approach, it was unsurprising that Canada suggested the tribunal to follow precisely the opposite interpretation in *Pope and Talbot*. Canada argued that the expropriation clause in NAFTA's Chapter 11 should not apply to non-discriminatory regulations. But these arbitrators rejected this position in June 2000. They observed that such 'a blanket exception for regulatory measures would create a gaping loophole'.[123]

Subsequent tribunals have continued to review regulations. Some of these awards have been more deferential to public authorities, but arbitrators still do not show a degree of judicial restraint comparable to domestic judges in analogous cases.[124] Two influential more deferential awards are *Saluka* and *Methanex*. In *Saluka* (a non-NAFTA dispute), the arbitrators concluded that it is now established in international law that States are not liable to pay compensation to a foreign investor when, in the normal exercise of their regulatory powers, they adopt in a non-discriminatory manner bona fide regulations that are aimed at the general welfare.[125] The *Methanex* tribunal (a NAFTA dispute) reasoned that:

[120] William W Burke-White and Andreas von Staden, 'Private Litigation in a Public Sphere: The Standard of Review in Investor-State Arbitrations' (2010) 35 Yale Journal of International Law 283.

[121] *Compañía del Desarrollo de Santa Elena v Costa Rica*, ICSID Case No ARB/96/1, Award (17 February 2000) 72.

[122] *Metalclad v Mexico* (n 20) 103.

[123] *Pope & Talbot v Canada* (n 12) 99. Similarly, *Tecmed* (n 112) 121.

[124] Van Harten (n 119) 157–64.

[125] *Saluka v Czech Republic* (n 98) 255.

> [a]s a matter of general international law, a non-discriminatory regulation for a public purpose, which is enacted in accordance with due process and, which affects, inter alios, a foreign investor or investment is not deemed expropriatory and compensable unless specific commitments had been given by the regulating government to the then putative foreign investor contemplating investment that the government would refrain from such regulation.[126]

These tribunals explicitly recognize states' right to regulate and subject this right to an arbitral review according to international law and investment treaties. This review contributes to drawing a line between legitimate regulation and indirect expropriation. Arbitrators, in this way, moved the focus from the inside to the outside of property (ie from ownership to the public regulations that shape ownership).[127] But these two sides remain closely intertwined. An expansive interpretation of foreign investor rights affects states' right to regulate and vice-versa. As in the United States, during the *Lochner* era, tribunals can recognize states' right to regulate and still hold a sense of distrust for public power.[128]

As Dolzer and Schreuer predicted, tribunals have not arrived at a precise formula to distinguish legitimate regulation from indirect expropriation. Neither should we expect they do so in the future, as most property scholars surmise, even if aided by the US doctrine of balancing that some new investment treaties have incorporated via annexes.[129] Instead, we will probably continue to see arbitrators relying on different doctrines or formulas to assess the effects of a measure on the investment project and whether the regulation complies with the requirements imposed by international law and investment treaties. Two points should be emphasized here. One is that claims of indirect expropriation rarely succeed because regulations only create lesser interferences. As explained earlier, the investor usually remains under control and enjoys the benefits of the investment. The other is that some tribunals have confirmed the non-expropriatory effects of measures by reviewing the public regulation. The reasoning in some awards, such as *Tecmed*, is prone to this circularity. Arbitrators confirm the non-expropriatory effects by examining

[126] *Methanex v USA* (n 16) pt IV, ch D, 7.
[127] Singer (n 31) 7.
[128] David Schneiderman, 'NAFTA's Takings Rule: American Constitutionalism Comes to Canada' (1996) 46 The University of Toronto Law Journal 499, 508.
[129] See Rose (n 10).

whether the regulation is reasonable and proportionate.[130] The interpretation of these requirements will be discussed later in the chapter on the right to regulate.[131] Here, it is enough to say that it is unlikely that a regulation that passes the *Saluka* or *Methanex* tests creates effects on the foreign investment that meet the high expropriatory threshold.

Yet, it is not impossible. Legitimate regulation may radically deprive a foreign investor of her rights. In *Philip Morris v Uruguay*, the arbitrators highlighted that this dispute was easier to resolve than *Methanex* precisely because Uruguay's measures did not ban 'the production and sale of the subject product'.[132] Tribunals have taken different approaches in this regard. While the *Methanex* tribunal confirmed that the public measure was a legitimate regulation, although it closed down the market for the controversial additive, other awards have reasoned that not compensating a total deprivation would impose an excessive burden on the foreign investor.[133] These arbitrators suggests that there is a sort of limit to any balancing exercise, a position that is akin to Michelman's argument in his famous 1967 article where he claimed that courts should be attentive to 'demoralising costs'.[134] The premise is similar. If the burden goes too far, or the costs are excessive for the individual, then states should pay compensation.

Importantly, two situations should be distinguished here. In cases like *Methanex* and *Philip Morris*, the regulations were aimed to curb a cost or a risk created by the foreign investor and the investment. The state neither contributed nor was in any way responsible for these negative externalities. On the contrary, as the arbitrators highlighted, the foreign investors were aware or should have been aware of these costs and risks.[135] In these circumstances, it was reasonable to expect some reaction from states, and they could legitimately regulate as long as the burden imposed by the regulation was proportional to the risk and imposed according to due process.[136] For these arbitrators, the situation would only have been different if the state had granted a specific commitment that it 'would refrain from such regulation'.[137]

[130] Erlend Leonhardsen, 'Looking for Legitimacy: Exploring Proportionality Analysis in Investment Treaty Arbitration' (2012) 3 Journal of International Dispute Settlement 95, 124.
[131] See Sierra-Camargo and Suárez-Ricaurte in this volume.
[132] *Philip Morris v Uruguay* (n 9) 306 (n 405).
[133] See *Metalclad v Mexico* (n 20).
[134] Frank I Michelman, 'Property, Utility, and Fairness: Comments on the Ethical Foundations of "Just Compensation" Law' (1967) 80 Harvard Law Review 1165, 1237.
[135] *Methanex v USA* (n 16) 9; *Philip Morris v Uruguay* (n 9) 392.
[136] *Methanex v USA* (n 16) 11–18; *Philip Morris v Uruguay* (n 9) 305–307.
[137] *Methanex v USA* (n 16) 7; *Philip Morris v Uruguay* (n 9) 429.

Disputes like *Methanex* or *Philip Morris* are different from cases in which host states passed measures to increase their share of the benefits. These measures—commonly taxes—could be challenged for being punitive or extraordinary. Arbitrators recognize states' right to define their level of taxation but subject to the limitations imposed by international law and investment treaties. For the *Encana* tribunal, '[o]nly if a tax law is extraordinary, punitive in amount or arbitrary in its incidence would issues of indirect expropriation be raised'.[138] The tribunals in *Burlington*, *Perenco*, and *Murphy* similarly reasoned that a 99 per cent windfall tax is not expropriatory.[139] These investors could still control and enjoy the benefits of their investment. In *Sergei Paushok*, the tribunal was also unconvinced that windfall taxes constituted a treaty breach even if 'such legislation went beyond the taxation levels in application at the time in most countries of the world'.[140] These arbitrators noted that investors could 'obtain the appropriate guarantees ... in the form of, for example, stability agreements which limit or prohibit the possibility of tax increases'.[141]

All in all, taking seriously states' right to regulate does not provide 'a bright and easily distinguishable line' between legitimate regulation and indirect expropriation, but does reveal the plurality of purposes in property. States adjust the contours of ownership to facilitate social transformations or to protect common, communal, and private property rights. The problem is that these objectives are regularly in tension. When states regulate, foreign investors often win and sometimes lose.[142] Investment law scholars and arbitrators rarely recognize that states' right to regulate also serves to expand and strengthen foreign investor rights. Taking this dynamic factor into account, however, could sharpen the line between regulation and indirect expropriation. This would require rethinking whether every public measure that affects a foreign investor

138 *EnCana Corporation v Ecuador*, LCIA Case No UN3481 (3 February 2006) 177.

139 *Perenco Ecuador v Ecuador*, ICSID Case No ARB/08/6, Decision on Remaining Issues of Jurisdiction and on Liability (12 September 2014); *Burlington v Ecuador* (n 20); *Murphy Exploration v Ecuador*, PCA Case No 2012-16—formerly AA 434, Award (10 February 2017). The tribunal in *Occidental v Ecuador 2*, however, found that Law 42 was a violation of the fair and equitable treatment. This tribunal reasoned that the measure was 'neither a royalty, a tax, a levy or any other measure of taxation under the Participation Contract. 510. It is, as its title makes explicit, a unilateral decision of the Ecuadorian Congress to allocate to the Ecuadorian State a defined percentage of the revenues earned by contractor companies such as OEPC that hold participation contract'; *Occidental Petroleum v Ecuador* (n 52) 509–10.

140 *Sergei Paushok v Mongolia*, UNCITRAL, Award on Jurisdiction and Liability (28 April 2011) 303.

141 ibid 302.

142 According to UNCTAD, since the early 1990s most national investment policies either liberalize or promote foreign investment. Although the trend is changing, the 2018 data still shows that 66 per cent of the measures favour foreign investment while only 34 per cent of them are restrictive or impose regulations. UNCTAD, *World Investment Report 2019: Special Economic Zones* (United Nations 2019) 84.

should be treated as a potential cause of action or, instead, as a regular contribution to the betterment of the host society from which everybody—including foreign investors—benefits. Individuals, communities, and corporations should contribute to social goals and values according to their capabilities and, largely, these contributions compensate each other in the long-term (ie a shared sacrifice and long-term reciprocity). Only excessive burdens, which narrowly single out certain investors, would then require compensation (ie irreducible individual losses).[143]

7 Conclusion

Claims of direct and indirect expropriation bring about fundamental questions about social organization. This chapter has shown that investment treaties and tribunals approach these questions from the perspective of the foreign investor and investment, downplaying the local and social importance of property arrangements. Two problems emerge from this approach. One refers to the standards of compensation. As opposed to the usual narrative, international practice shows a plurality of methods to calculate and pay compensation. During most of the twentieth century, international law showed some responsiveness to the domestic context and efforts of social transformation. This responsiveness, however, was under severe attack during the post-colonial period and, arguably, international investment treaties gave this thinking a *coup de grâce*. Compensation for cases of direct expropriation is no longer responsive to the local context or attempts to reimagine social organization.

The other issue relates to the notion of indirect or regulatory expropriations. Inevitably, the normative preferences of arbitrators shape ISDS awards. But claims of indirect expropriation are particularly controversial. They are resolved on a case-by-case basis, are intensive in facts, and the applicable law plays a limited role as there is no clear legal doctrine or formula to draw the line between legitimate regulation and indirect expropriation. Irrespective of whether or not domestic legal systems should recognize indirect or regulatory expropriations, the problem is more acute in international arbitration. Arbitrators are far from host countries, but make fundamental decisions about their organization and functioning. This lack of proximity has not

[143] What is an excessive burden, then, would be a matter of controversy. A crucial issue, for instance, is whether adjudicators should look at the specific facts of a dispute (static picture) or at the relative situation of the different actors in society (dynamic picture). See Alexander and Peñalver (n 1) 164, 177, 179.

stopped ISDS tribunals from showing limited deference to democratic non-discriminatory decisions. Starting with three influential awards rendered in 2000 (*Santa Elena*, *Metalclad*, and *Pope & Talbot*), arbitrators have applied no or little judicial restraint. This attitude is difficult to reconcile with democratic principles and is more problematic given the evidence suggesting that arbitrators' incentives may be more aligned with global business and the interests of large law firms.[144]

At a point when the future of international investment law is uncertain, it is worth remembering that the basic standards of this regime—such as expropriation—may respond to ideas or premises that today might seem unjust or require rapid rethinking. Colonialism was unfair and promoted economic divergence between the North and the South, which remains unresolved and threatens world stability. In the coming years, moreover, the unsustainable levels of inequality and environmental degradation threaten humanity and our planet. Few disagree that changes in global economic governance are necessary, but it is unclear what direction these changes will take. The expropriation standard in international investment treaties remains problematic because it might make these necessary changes—in particular those we cannot foresee today—more difficult.

[144] Van Harten (n 117) Chapter 7; Cecilia Olivet and Pia Eberhardt, 'Profiting from Injustice: How Law Firms, Arbitrators and Financiers are Fuelling an Investment Arbitration Boom' (2012) Transnational Institute; Sergio Puig, 'Social Capital in the Arbitration Market' (2014) 25 European Journal of International Law 387.

5

The Minimum Standard of Treatment

Fola Adeleke and Gus Van Harten

1 Introduction

The development of international investment law finds its origins in the protection of the economic interests of states whose nationals owned property in other states.[1] More specifically, the development of today's investment treaty framework has its roots in events that shaped the world economy, including the vast increase in the number of sovereign states as countries gained independence from colonialism.[2] With former colonizing countries interested in protecting their citizens' property abroad, various principles for their protection began to emerge.[3] Owing to the different positions[4] of capital-exporting and host states, however, there has been an uncertain and much-contested development of international investment law.[5] Drawing on decades of debate and interpretation, central principles—such as the 'minimum standard of treatment' (MST)—are under increasing scrutiny for their bias against the position

[1] Jeswald Salacuse, *The Law of Investment Treaties* (OUP 2015) 46.

[2] Mathucumaraswamy Sornarajah, *The International Law on Foreign Investment* (OUP 2010) 174.

[3] Jeswald Salacuse, 'From Developing Countries to Emerging Markets: A Changing Role for Law in the Third World' (1999) 33 International Lawyers 875.

[4] A recurring issue under international investment law relates to the standard of treatment that a host country should accord foreign investors and their property. On the one hand, the equality principle was favoured by investment recipients and was eloquently captured by the government of Mexico when arguing that foreign investors should accept the risks and benefits of investing abroad and should not receive preferential treatment. On the other hand, European countries and the USA argued for an international minimum standard, which can potentially supersede the protections domestic law offers. Richard Lillich (ed), *The International Law of State Responsibility for Injuries to Aliens* (University of Virginia Press 1983).

[5] Prior to the development of the BIT framework which saw the first BIT signed between Germany and Pakistan in 1959, treaties were initially developed to establish mutual economic interests between the sixteenth and the eighteenth centuries. This later evolved to the treaties on friendship, commerce, and navigation in the nineteenth and twentieth centuries and led to various unsuccessful attempts at multilateralization before the historic establishment of the International Centre for Settlement of Investment Disputes (ICSID). For more on this historical development see Sornarajah (n 2); Robert Wilson, *United States Commercial Treaties and International Law* (Hauser Press 1960).

Fola Adeleke and Gus Van Harten, *The Minimum Standard of Treatment* In: *Rethinking Investment Law*. Edited by: David Schneiderman and Gus Van Harten, Oxford University Press. © Fola Adeleke and Gus Van Harten 2023.
DOI: 10.1093/oso/9780192871084.003.0005

of host states and the sovereign right of those states to regulate foreign nationals and their property.[6]

This chapter considers the origins of the MST, its evolving interpretation, and pivotal moments when a notable shift took place in the development of this standard. In analysing the MST, particular attention is paid to its application in the laws and treaties of some African states. The treaties of African states are used for contextual analysis considering the historical reluctance of host states to embrace the MST principle under customary international law, as contrasted by those states' acceptance of an extraordinarily broad form of the MST in bilateral investment treaties (BITs).

2 International Law Background for the MST

Historically, the MST, also known as the international standard for the treatment of aliens (ie foreign nationals), operated as an element of the standard of 'civilization' in European conceptualizations of statehood during the sixteenth to the nineteenth centuries.[7] The MST was envisioned as an obligation of states that established corollary protections for foreign nationals subject to the regulatory authority of the host state within its territory.[8] Recognizing also the right and responsibility of states to protect their own nationals abroad, Root argued on behalf of US capital-exporting interests, in the ongoing imperialist period of the early twentieth century, that a range of measures was available to states to protect their nationals, including military intervention and diplomatic protection.[9] Other defenders of the capital-exporting or imperialist perspective asserted that reprisals by states, with a view to protecting their nationals, was permissible where the foreign national had been denied justice in another

[6] Fola Adeleke, *International Investment Law and Policy in Africa: Exploring a Human Rights Based Approach to Investment Regulation and Dispute Settlement* (Routledge 2018).

[7] At the end of the Second World War, four main sources of foreign investment protection were identifiable. These were: the customary rule on diplomatic protection and minimum standard of treatment of aliens; the treaties of friendship, commerce, and navigation; the prohibition of the use of force to recover contract debts; and the jurisprudence of the various claims commissions and tribunals dealing with injuries to aliens. See Joost Pauwelyn, 'Rational Design or Accidental Evolution? The Emergence of International Investment Law' in Zachary Douglas, Joost Pauwelyn, and Jorge Viñuales, *The Foundations of International Investment Law: Bringing Theory into Practice* (OUP 2014) 22–23.

[8] Hersch Lauterpacht, *Oppenheim's International Law* (OUP 1936) 283; According to Lauterpacht, '[t]here exists in this matter a minimum standard of civilization, and that a State which fails to measure up to that standard incurs international liability'.

[9] Elihu Root, 'The Basis of Protection to Citizens Residing Abroad' (1910) 4 American Journal of International Law 517.

state.[10] From a perspective more sympathetic to host states, the early development of prohibitions on the use of force in international law was itself a response to the assertion by militarily powerful states of the right to use force to protect their nationals. This perspective is indicated by the Drago doctrine and, in turn, by early twentieth century prohibitions on the use of force to support the collection of debts.[11]

While the central idea underpinning MST is the right and responsibility of states to protect foreign nationals, many questions arise over the scope of this principle. On the one hand, capital-exporting states tended to claim an international minimum standard of treatment for foreign nationals and their property, which could be higher than the national standard of treatment provided by a state to its citizens and foreign nationals.[12] On the other hand, other states, typically as an assertion of post-colonial independence, characterized the treatment of foreign nationals as a matter of equality and non-discrimination between the state's citizens and foreign nationals permitted to enter the state.[13] Most notably, the equality principle offers the foundation for the Calvo doctrine, which provides that a state has discharged its obligations under customary international law once equal treatment is afforded to citizens and foreign nationals, irrespective of whether the foreign national is dissatisfied with the treatment given to all.[14] Considering these origins, the doctrine of national treatment for foreign nationals—if it is treated as the sole protection for foreign nationals (once admitted to the host state)—can be understood as a powerful alternative to the MST.

Yet even the early twentieth-century proponents of the MST, such as Root, structured their argument around the principle of non-discrimination and national treatment under domestic law.[15] Only later was the MST expanded

[10] A formulation of this rule was the 1907 Hague Convention Respecting the Employment of Force for the Recovery of Contract Debts. See Martins Paparinskis, 'Investment Arbitration and the Law of Countermeasures' (2008) 78 British Yearbook of International Law 268.

[11] Jochen von Bernstorff, 'The Use of Force in International Law before World War I: On Imperial Ordering and the Ontology of the Nation-State' (2018) 29(1) European Journal of International Law 248.

[12] Root (n 9); This standard has been described by Root as '[t]he condition upon which every country is entitled to measure the justice due from it to an alien by the justice which it accords to its own citizens, is that its system of law and administration shall conform to the general standard. If any country's system of law and administration does not conform to that standard, although the people of that country may be content or compelled to live under it, no other country can be compelled to accept it.'

[13] This is represented through the Calvo doctrine. For an excellent analysis see Oscar Garibaldi, 'Carlos Calvo Redivivus: The Rediscovery of Calvo Doctrines in the Era of Investment Treaties' (2006) 3 Transnational Dispute Management; Salacuse (n 1) 58.

[14] This position is also consistent with Art 9 of the 1933 Convention on the Rights and Duties of States, which provides that 'nationals and foreigners are under the same protection of the law and the national authorities, and foreigners may not claim rights other than or more excessive than those of nationals.'

[15] Root (n 9) 27.

to envision equal protection under a standard of law and order that is acceptable to international law regardless of domestic law.[16] The MST espoused by Root was also limited by a focus on procedural protections related to denial of justice as opposed to substantive protection of property rights. This limitation is evident from state practice, which accepted the decision of the US–Mexico General Claims Commission in *LFH Neer-Pauline Neer* in 1926 as setting out the customary law rule on denial of justice.[17] In the *Neer* tribunal's decision, the MST was effectively equated to denial of justice, applying to the various arms of government and with various qualifiers—such as bad faith or arbitrariness—to limit the scope of the MST.[18] Thus, the MST allowed space for host states to regulate foreign nationals as they would other actors in their economy and society. For a state to advocate on behalf of its nationals and their property interests abroad, it or they had to establish an exceptionally serious failure by the host state in the protection of the foreign nationals' interests.[19] Such legal affirmations of the regulatory authority of states, as part of the MST, have been under steady pressure from those seeking broader private property protections in all countries. This pressure culminated in the vastly more expansive standards of foreign investor protection found in today's investment treaties.[20]

3 Core Components of the Original MST

As mentioned above, Root is credited for elaborating the MST based on the following statement from an article published in the *American Journal of International Law* in 1910:[21]

> There is a standard of justice ... of such general acceptance by all civilized nations as to form part of the international law of the world. The condition upon which any country is entitled to *measure the justice due from it to an alien by*

[16] Martins Paparinskis, *The International Minimum Standard and Fair and Equitable Treatment* (OUP 2013) 41–46.

[17] The government of Argentina in *National Grid v Argentina*, UNCITRAL Case, Award (November 2008); the government of Canada in *Pope & Talbot v Canada*, UNCITRAL Case, Award on Damages (May 2002); and the government of Mexico in *Cargill Inc v Mexico*, ICSID AF Case No ARB/AF/05/2, Award (September 2009) have all referred to the *Neer* case in their pleadings in citing the authority for denial of justice.

[18] *LFH Neer-Pauline Neer (USA) v United Mexican States* (1926) 4 RIAA 60 [4].

[19] In the nineteenth century, the UK, in making the case for expropriation, argued arbitrary deprivation. See Paparinskis (n 16) 55.

[20] Edwin Borchard, 'The "Minimum Standard" of the Treatment of Aliens' (1939) 33 Proceedings of the American Society of International Law 452.

[21] Root (n 9) 521–22 (emphasis added).

> *the justice which it accords to its own citizens* is that its system of law and administration shall conform to this general standard. *If any country's system of law and administration does not conform to that standard*, although the people of that country may be content or compelled to live under it, no other country can be compelled to accept it as furnishing a satisfactory measure of treatment to its citizens.

Embedded within Root's statement are two primary principles, non-discrimination and denial of justice (or due process). Together, these principles form the original core of the MST. Their content and evolution is elaborated below.

3.1 Non-discrimination

Very clearly, international law has recognized the duty of states to treat foreign nationals, once admitted to a country, in a non-discriminatory manner.[22] States that supported the Calvo doctrine, as well as those that supported the MST, have agreed at least on this fundamental principle.[23] Yet the principle is beguiling for its apparent simplicity. Various questions follow from any effort to interpret and apply it to actual cases that engage the relative treatment of citizens and foreign nationals. Moreover, the principle has been given widely varying definitions, with important implications for the regulatory space of host states.[24] Considering that investor–state dispute settlement (ISDS) tribunals have at times taken exceptionally expansive approaches,[25] one may usefully refer back to the *ELSI* decision of a chamber of the International Court of Justice, which identified four components for a measure to be discriminatory.[26] According to this decision, there must be (1) an intentional act of the state that is (2) in favour of a national and (3) against a foreign investor and that is (4) not taken under similar circumstances against another national.[27]

[22] ibid 246.

[23] ibid.

[24] See Schneiderman in this volume.

[25] See eg *Occidental Petroleum v Ecuador*, in which the tribunal found the treatment of a US oil company to have been discriminatory by comparing it to the treatment of Ecuadorian companies in other sectors acknowledged not to have been in like circumstances to the oil sector. In contrast, the *Methanex v USA* tribunal rejected non-discrimination as an element of MST. For the tribunal, this element could not exist if rules in the same treaty otherwise prohibited discrimination in clear terms, as NAFTA did. *Methanex Corporation v USA*, UNCITRAL Case, Final Award (August 2005), 16 ICSID Rep 40 Part IV Ch C [14]–[26].

[26] *Elettronica Sicula SpA (ELSI) (US v Italy)* [1989] ICJ Rep 15.

[27] ibid.

3.2 Denial of Justice (and Due Process)

The *Neer* decision of 1926, as mentioned above, is an authoritative elaboration of the standard of denial of justice as part of the MST.[28] In *Neer*, the tribunal stated that the safeguard against denial of justice applied to acts of executive, legislative, and judicial authorities of the host state; further, the standard was identical in all cases.[29] Yet the tribunal also acknowledged that it was difficult to define the difference between a wrongful act, on the one hand, and, on the other, 'an unsatisfactory use of power included in national sovereignty'.[30] In this respect, the tribunal stated that, for state conduct to violate the MST, the treatment of foreign nationals 'should amount to an outrage, to bad faith, to wilful neglect of duty, or to an insufficiency so far short of international standards that every reasonable and impartial man would readily recognize its insufficiency'.[31] These thresholds served to balance the interests in protecting foreign-owned property against those of all states to regulate their economy and society. Not surprisingly, the balance struck in *Neer* has come under attack by foreign investors, and in some cases by arbitrators, in litigation under investment treaties.

Even so, in a key respect the *Neer* decision itself favoured the perspective of foreign investors. Some states, for example, disagreed historically with the presence of state responsibility for the passage of legislation governing property rights.[32] By embracing a broad formulation that applied the MST to all wrongful acts committed by any arm of the state, the *Neer* decision also expanded the potential liability of states for executive or legislative acts not yet subject to judicial review and thus to confirmation in its own courts. This approach opened the door to litigation strategies by foreign investors that attack a decision of one arm of the governing apparatus that is not yet final—for the state as a whole—because other arms have not yet had the opportunity to apply their intended checks and balances. Reflecting this concern, other constructions of denial of justice limit the concept to state obstruction of a foreign national's fair access to the state's judicial system. In turn, there is an accepted

[28] *Pope & Talbot v Canada*, UNCITRAL Case, Award on Damages (May 2002); *Mondev v USA*, ICSID Case No ARB(AF)/99/2, Award (October 2002); *Tecmed SA v Mexico*, ICSID Case No ARB (AF)/00/2, Award (May 2003).

[29] ibid.

[30] *Neer* (n 18) [4].

[31] ibid.

[32] Egypt for instance acknowledged state responsibility, while South Africa did not. See Paparinskis (n 16) 61.

recognition that denial of justice can arise only from a breach of international obligations on the administration of justice.[33]

Owing to its intimate connection to a state's judicial system, the standard of denial of justice also invokes the customary duty to exhaust local remedies. Alleged misconduct or procedural errors by state officials generally require domestic remedies to be used by a foreign national before a denial of justice can be established under international law.[34] Yet, once again, the meaning of this duty to exhaust has been interpreted in widely varying ways by ISDS tribunals. For example, in *Saipem v Bangladesh*, the tribunal held that the non-exhaustion of local remedies was justified after the foreign investor had pursued years of litigation in domestic courts,[35] whereas the tribunal in *Loewen v USA* dismissed the foreign investor's claim for its failure to appeal a faint-hope procedural issue to the US Supreme Court after the investor had been bankrupted by an enormous damages awarded in lower courts.[36] In contrast to the state-friendly position in *Loewen*, the tribunal in *Siag v Egypt* held the government's non-compliance with a domestic court judgment itself constituted a denial of justice.[37] As in the case of other aspects of the MST, it is difficult to reconcile the wildly varying and expansive approaches of ISDS tribunals with the international law standards that preceded the post-2000 boom in foreign investor claims against states.

The notion of due process has also played a role in elaborating the MST, given the original focus of the MST on procedural elements and administration of justice. Yet, once again, its invocation under investment treaties has been expansive, especially where the due process principle is expanded to include executive or legislative treatment of foreign investors, beyond the usual context of administration of justice in courts and tribunals. In some investment treaties, due process is expressly linked with MST, but in others it has been said by tribunals to be implicit in one or another standard under the treaty.[38] In any event, due process has now been invoked in ISDS to argue against such matters as the state's refusal to produce documents it considers sensitive, the continuation of domestic proceedings against an investor, or alleged partiality or bias on the part of executive officials.[39] Like other aspects of the MST, therefore,

[33] Roberto Ago, 'Third Report on State Responsibility' UN Doc A/CN4/246, para 143.

[34] ibid paras 182–89.

[35] *Saipem SpA v Bangladesh*, ICSID Case No ARB/05/07, Award (30 June 2009) [183].

[36] *Loewen v USA*, ICSID Additional Facility Case No ARB (AF/98/3), Award (June 2003) [217].

[37] *Waguih Elie George Siag and Clorinda Vecchi v Egypt*, ICSID Case No ARB/05/15, Award (June 2009) [454].

[38] For example, the 2004 Canada Model BIT, the 2008 Germany Model BIT, the Canada–USA–Mexico Trade Agreement, and the Investment Agreement for the Community of East African States (COMESA Investment Agreement 2007).

[39] Paparinskis (n 16) 37, 190–91.

due process has given myriad opportunities for ISDS tribunals to expand the scope of conventional protections for foreign investors at the expense of the regulatory role of host states. For instance, in *Waste Management Inc v United Mexican States (Mexico)*, the tribunal expanded the meaning of due process to include 'an outcome which offends judicial propriety—as might be the case with a manifest failure of natural justice in judicial proceedings or a complete lack of transparency and candour in an administrative process'.[40]

4 The MST in Investment Treaties

Given the historical controversy over the scope of the MST, there has unsurprisingly been thin evidence to support arguments for a customary rule establishing an MST that went beyond the principle of post-establishment non-discrimination. Today's investment treaties have filled the gap, from the perspective of capital-exporting interests, by incorporating express and specific language elaborating on a range of components associated with expansive version of an MST, begetting new and wide-ranging standards of foreign investor protection of which 'fair and equitable treatment' is the most infamous.[41] Thus, the treaties have opened a new era of arbitrator power to interpret and apply investor-friendly concepts historically associated with the MST, but long resisted by host states in debates about the content of international law.

In terms of this curious divergence of investment treaties from long-standing debates about customary international law, it is important to keep in mind that the rapid increase in the number of bilateral investment treaties concluded since the late 1980s and early 1990s has not displaced the complex historical position under customary international law. In the absence of a treaty with more specific language addressing the MST, customary international law remains the applicable legal regime. As recognized by Article 38(1)(b) of the International Court of Justice (ICJ) statute, custom is a source of international law and the scope of any investment treaty—typically bilateral—is limited to the treaty parties. Making matters more complex still, some investment treaties provide for the application of an MST as defined and limited by customary international law. For example, the Canada–Peru BIT and the US Model BIT provide that the MST accorded to a foreign investor is that existing under

[40] *Waste Management Inc v United Mexican States (Mexico)*, ICSID Case No ARB(AF)/00/3, Award (30 April 2004) [98].

[41] See Ostřanský in this volume.

customary international law.[42] These approaches to the treaty language draw on the vexed experience of North American governments that faced early expansive interpretations by ISDS tribunals of the MST in the North American Free Trade Agreement (NAFTA) investment chapter. In *Pope & Talbot v Canada*, for instance,[43] an early tribunal held that 'compliance with the fairness elements [of the MST in NAFTA Article 1105] must be ascertained free of any threshold that might be applicable to the evaluation of measures under the minimum standard of international law' and it based this expansive position on the widespread, if vague, references to 'fair and equitable treatment' (FET) in both NAFTA and bilateral investment treaties.[44] Responding to such interpretations in the early 2000s, the NAFTA governments issued a joint statement which clarified that the MST in NAFTA was limited to its meaning in customary international law and argued repeatedly that this customary MST was described by the classic decisions in *Neer* and *ELSI*. Thus, in *Pope & Talbot*, Canada argued that NAFTA Article 1105 contained a customary international law standard which recognized that impugned state conduct must be egregious before state responsibility can arise.[45] According to Thomas, the word 'egregious' was used by Canada as a reference to the types of adjectives used *in Neer* to describe the seriousness of the state action that will attract responsibility.[46] However, the *Pope & Talbot* tribunal rejected Canada's position on the basis that Canada was addressing the 'contents of the requirements of international law, rather than the other factors referred to in Article 1105, namely, "fair and equitable treatment and full protection and security"'.[47] Soon after, in the *Methanex* decision under NAFTA, the United States refused the *Pope & Talbot* tribunal's expansive characterization, arguing that it was 'poorly reasoned and unpersuasive.'[48]

Other investment treaties do not have the same limiting language as NAFTA, allowing for even more widespread expansiveness by arbitrators in relation to the classical MST, usually by relying on standards of FET and, somewhat less prominently, of full protection and security and indirect expropriation.[49] At

[42] Article 5(1) of the Canada–Peru BIT. Annex A to the US 2012 Model BIT further provides that 'customary international law minimum standard of treatment of aliens refers to all customary international law principles that protect the economic rights and interests of aliens'.

[43] *Pope & Talbot Inc v The Government of Canada*, UNCITRAL, Award on the Merits of Phase 2 (10 April 2001).

[44] ibid [111]. The tribunal saw a contrary reading as doing violence to the BIT language [13].

[45] *Pope & Talbot* (n 43) [108].

[46] JC Thomas, 'Reflections on Article 1105 of NAFTA: History, State Practice and the Influence of Commentators' (2002) 17 1 ICSID Review Foreign Investment Law Journal 74.

[47] *Pope & Talbot* (n 43) [109].

[48] Thomas (n 46) 80.

[49] See Adeleke and Van Harten, as well as Ostřanský, in this volume.

a certain point, their investor-friendly approaches have taken tribunals so far beyond the origins of the MST as to introduce whole new debates about foreign investor protection that were clearly never within the parameters set by decisions like *Neer* and *ELSI*. At this stage, one has moved beyond the debate over MST into new treaty-based quandaries about how far the idea of foreign investor protection can be taken to constrain host states' regulatory space, self-determination, and sovereignty. Therefore, for present purposes, the pivotal turning point in ISDS has rather been a great leap beyond the MST into new domains of legal creativity, as opposed to a turning point in the long history of the customary MST itself. The turn has made obsolete the efforts of host states to preserve sovereignty in the face of assertions by Root and other representatives of capital-exporting interests. Put differently, ISDS tribunals have created a range of new legal encroachments on sovereignty within which even the position presented by Root looks restrictive for purposes of foreign investor protection or, more contentiously, foreign investor privilege.

4.1 A Sojourn into the Relationship between the MST and Fair and Equitable Treatment

The FET standard has become a bugbear of its own in the interpretation of investment treaties by ISDS tribunals, as discussed in more depth elsewhere in this book.[50] Yet a few comments here offer context for how FET can be connected to, or approached autonomously from, the historical MST. Paparinskis helpfully frames this MST–FET interaction along a spectrum.[51] At one end, FET is considered identical to the MST, albeit with residual uncertainty over the meaning of the latter in customary international law. This position is reflected most clearly in the treaty practice of the US and Canada.[52] At the other end of the spectrum, FET is viewed as a separate standard with no reference to MST.[53] Many bilateral investment treaties, as interpreted by ISDS tribunals, fall at this end, typically appeasing the arguments of foreign investors and allowing for wide-ranging expansion of the review power of arbitrators, who have found a range of new standards to exist implicitly in the vague FET formulation.

[50] See Ostřanský in this volume.
[51] Paparinskis (n 16) 93.
[52] See eg art 5 of the 2004 Canada Model BIT and Annex A, art 5 of the 2012 US Model BIT.
[53] For treaties open to this interpretation see art 9 of the Netherlands Model BIT 2019; art 2 of the 2008 Germany Model BIT, and art 2 of the 2008 UK Model BIT. See also Rudolf Dolzer and Christoph Schreuer, *Principles of International Investment Law* (OUP 2012) 134.

Between these ends of the spectrum appears to lie the bulk of state practice in ISDS litigation whereby, for either FET or MST, emphasis is put on more long-standing elements such as non-discrimination, denial of justice, and due process.[54]

On balance, based on the combined effects of loosely worded treaties and expansively minded tribunals, international investment law has been taken well beyond the historical versions of the MST into wide grounds for arbitrator review of host states, most commonly with reference to FET as an autonomous standard. In terms of the historical opposition of host states to an expansive MST, it has been suggested that such states would be unlikely, by the treaty language of FET, to have inferred the inclusion of an expansive MST into their treaties without stating so expressly. However such suggestions on behalf of host state interests appear very unlikely to impact the burgeoning realm of ISDS with its novel foreign investor protections and corresponding powers of arbitrators.

4.2 Examples from the African context

As an illustration of how host states appear to have retreated from the historical position regarding an MST, one may look to bilateral investment treaties signed by African states over a ten-year period (2009–2019). At the outset, one should keep in mind that, when concluding BITs, African states have long been, and continue to be, rule-takers and have not themselves led the development of the MST standard. Rather, in BITs, they have accepted and indeed gone well beyond the historical position of host states.

For example, over this ten-year period, nine African states concluded a BIT with Canada, whose approach in the African context reflects that of a traditional capital-exporter, especially in the resource sector.[55] All nine of these BITs have language on the MST that is similar to that in NAFTA (now CUSMA, although the CUSMA importantly removes ISDS from the Canada–US

[54] As a more recent example of text reflecting this position, the 2016 India Model BIT, Article 3.1, states: 'No Party shall subject investments made by investors of the other Party to measures which constitute a violation of customary international law through: (i) Denial of justice in any judicial or administrative proceedings; or (ii) fundamental breach of due process; or (iii) targeted discrimination on manifestly unjustified grounds, such as gender, race or religious belief; or (iv) manifestly abusive treatment, such as coercion, duress and harassment.' Previously, India's 2003 Model BIT could easily be read as establishing FET as a separate standard from the MST.

[55] These African states concluded BITs with Canada in the listed years: Benin (2013), Tanzania (2013), Côte D'Ivoire (2014), Mali (2014), Nigeria (2014), Senegal (2014), Cameroon (2014), Guinea (2015), and Burkina-Faso (2015).

relationship and much reduces its scope in these countries' relationship with Mexico).[56] This MST language reads as follows:

1. Each Contracting Party shall accord to a covered investment treatment in accordance with the customary international law minimum standard of treatment of aliens, including fair and equitable treatment and full protection and security.
2. The concepts of 'fair and equitable treatment' and 'full protection and security' in paragraph 1 do not require treatment in addition to or beyond that which is required by the customary international law minimum standard of treatment of aliens.
3. A breach of another provision of this Agreement, or of a separate international agreement, does not establish that there has been a breach of this Article.

As one can see, this provision, in its first clause, incorporates broad MST language, as well as, in its second and third clauses, the post-2000 limiting language that was adopted by North American governments after their early NAFTA experience with ISDS tribunals. Thus, the provision reflects the MST 'rule' that has been favoured both by Canada and by the US. With the exception of the Canada–Benin BIT, this provision appears precisely in Article 6 of all nine BITs concluded by an African state with Canada. As rule-takers with Canada, therefore, African states have in general accepted the MST, including potentially expansive concepts of FET and full protection and security, limited only by parameters that were designed by the capital-exporting partner.

The same pattern emerges in African states' BITs with Turkey over the same ten-year period. Seven relevant BITs were concluded and each provides as follows on the MST:[57]

> Investments of investors of each Contracting Party shall at all times be accorded treatment in accordance with the international law minimum standard of treatment, including fair and equitable treatment and full protection and security in the territory of the other Contracting Party. Neither Contracting Party shall in any way impair the management, maintenance,

[56] North American Free Trade Agreement 1994; Canada–United States–Mexico Agreement 2019.

[57] These countries are Gabon (2012), Cameroon (2012), Gambia (2013), Rwanda (2016), Ghana (2016), Ivory Coast (2016), and Burundi (2017).

use, operation, enjoyment, extension, sale, liquidation or disposal of such investments by unlawful or discriminatory measures.

In this provision, the MST incorporates concepts of FET and full protection and security in an undefined and potentially expansive manner, without the further limiting language that emerged from North America. Similar MST provisions are found in the handful of BITs between African states and South Korea or Singapore in the same period, although each takes the approach of describing FET and full protection and security by emphasizing principles of denial of justice and due process and by referring to customary international law for the scope of protection.[58] Such provisions also appear in some intra-African BITs in the same period, such as the Nigeria–Morocco BIT and the Egypt–Mauritius BIT.[59] In each of these contexts, African states emerge again as rule-takers, even when the MST language in the treaties contradicts their own long-standing position in opposition to investor-friendly, but still relatively restrictive, versions of the customary MST.

It is unclear whether the shift by African states away from historical objections to an expansive MST has been deliberate, careless, or an outcome of power dynamics in investment treaty negotiations. The most rigorously-researched empirical explanations suggest at least that it was not deliberate.[60] In any event, the commonalities between African BITs, on the one hand, and the typical BIT language of the respective capital-exporting state, on the other hand, indicate that a pivotal moment for African states' approaches to the MST came at the time of their widespread acceptance of today's investment treaties in the 1990s. As a pivot, it reveals the enhanced and persistent influence of capital-exporting interests in shaping international investment law, and the diminished ability of others to resist. ISDS tribunals have since turned

[58] South Korea: Kenya (2014) and Cameroon (2013). The agreements state: 'Each Contracting Party shall accord to investments of an investor of the other Contracting Party treatment in accordance with customary international law, including fair and equitable treatment and full protection and security. For greater certainty, paragraph 2 of this Article prescribes the customary international law minimum standard of treatment of aliens as the minimum standard of treatment to be afforded to investments of an investor of the other Contracting Party.' Singapore: Nigeria (2016) and Burkina-Faso (2014). The agreements state: 'Each Party shall accord to covered investments treatment in accordance with customary international law minimum standard of treatment of aliens, including fair and equitable treatment and full protection and security.'

[59] The Egypt–Mauritius BIT provides that: 'The concepts of "fair and equitable treatment" and "protection and security" do not require treatment in addition to or beyond that which is required by the customary international law minimum standard of treatment of aliens.'

[60] For discussion and empirical analysis see Jonathan Bonnitcha, Lauge Poulsen, and Michael Waibel, *The Political Economy of the investment Treaty Regime* (OUP 2017) 207–20; Lauge Poulsen, *Bounded Rationality and Economic Diplomacy: The Politics of Investment Treaties in Developing Countries* (OUP 2015).

the dial even further from the protection of host states. The experience has gradually led some states, led in Africa by South Africa, not to renew existing BITs which they consider unduly broad. The South African government has acknowledged that its BITs of the 1990s were adopted without close consideration of the potential risks and costs to the state.[61] The country's foreign investment legislation of 2015—which was adopted after a series of European BITs were not renewed—has effectively replaced FET-driven expansiveness with the standard of fair administrative treatment. The latter aims to 'ensure administrative, legislative and judicial processes do not operate in a manner that is arbitrary or that denies administrative and procedural justice to investors in respect of their investments as provided for in the Constitution and applicable legislation'.[62] Most importantly, the South African legislation reaffirms the role of domestic courts, rather than ISDS tribunals, as the general mechanism for protection of foreign investors alongside other property owners.[63]

At the regional level, African states have been more nuanced in their approach to the MST than one finds in African BITs with non-African capital-exporting states. For example, the SADC Model BIT, adopted in 2012, has no stand-alone provision on MST. Its drafters noted in the Model BIT's commentary that a separate standard on protection and security is needed to limit the scope and potential for huge damages awards.[64] The only references to an MST refer to the protection of human rights, environment and labour, not to the investor-friendly standards that are so commonplace in BITs.[65] Further, the SADC Model BIT focuses on principles of fair administrative treatment rather than foreign investor rights, setting a higher threshold to establish a state violation of the treaty.[66] Article 14 of the Common Market for Eastern and Southern Africa States (COMESA) Investment Agreement takes a different but still cautious approach, providing that the FET standard is limited to the customary MST, without adding any components beyond this historical standard. The Supplementary Act on Investment and the Modalities for their Implementation adopted in 2008 by the Economic Community of West African States (ECOWAS) comes closer to a capital-exporting state's model

[61] Poulsen (n 60); South African government report from approximately 2007.
[62] Protection of Investment Act 22 of 2015, s 6(1).
[63] The legislation also recognizes the standard of full protection and security, as governed by the minimum standard of customary international law. Section 9, Protection of Investment Act 22 of 2015.
[64] Article 14 of the SADC Model BIT (2012).
[65] ibid art 15. Only the labour standards have a clear minimum guidance, which is based on ILO Declaration on Fundamental Principles and Rights of Work 1998.
[66] Article 5 of the 2012 SADC Model BIT. Article 5 commentary, 24.

BIT. It recognizes an MST in accordance with customary international law and includes FET as well as reasonable protection and security under domestic law.[67] Overall, then, the African regional approach is more reflective of the historical opposition to an expansive MST than the approach accepted by many African states in BITs.

5 Conclusion

The historical rejection of an expansive MST in customary international law has been widely undermined by today's investment treaties. Various underpinnings of the customary MST are maintained in BITs, but, according to ISDS tribunals, these roots are merely a supplement to a much wider slate of foreign investor protections. Today, this slate of protections even goes beyond the international MST that was envisioned by Root and others speaking for capital-exporting interests in the early twentieth century. For those who accept that FET exists autonomously (in the treaties) from the customary MST, host states have effectively surrendered to a free-ranging arbitrator power to develop new grounds for reviewing nationals laws, policies, regulations, and judicial rulings.

This evolution of the MST into an amorphous FET standard has arisen from an accumulation of steps by treaty negotiators and ISDS tribunals. Together, they have radically expanded foreign investor protection and gravely undermined the position of host states. While deliberate decisions of ISDS tribunals have been central to this turn in international investment law, the way was paved for a collapse of the capital-importing position by an apparent lack of conscious attention and expertise in treaty negotiations. For African states, at least, the negotiations were driven by the templates of capital-exporting interests, leading to default rules that proliferated versions of the MST and FET that were long resisted by host states. In her study of its origins,[68] Miles shows how international investment law was made to favour capital-exporters, using BITs as instruments of Western hegemony. The present review supports her conclusion that power structures originating in colonialism, and accentuated since the 1990s, have informed the MST and

[67] Article 7 of the 2008 ECOWAS Supplementary Act on Investment and the Modalities for their Implementation A/SA.3/12/08.

[68] Kate Miles, *The Origins of International Investment Law: Empire, Environment and the Safeguarding of Capital* (OUP 2013).

FET in today's investment treaties. For African and other states still struggling for prosperity and stability, the embrace of investment treaties and ISDS appears to have been more a tragic legal accident than a conscious pivot. Like other accidents, the damage can be repaired over time, here by governments giving patient and focused attention to the removal of the treaties' anomalous constraints.

6

Denial of Justice and Judicial Measures

Mavluda Sattorova

1 Introduction

Two intractable and problematic issues bedevil the functioning of the investment treaty regime and its investor–state dispute settlement (ISDS) mechanism. These are (1) the lack of consensus about thresholds triggering state responsibility under the treaties, and (2) the multiplicity and interchangeability of investment protection standards. One standard that neatly encapsulates these issues is the protection against judicial misconduct.

The rise in the number of investment arbitrations over the last three decades has reignited long-standing debates over the contours of state responsibility for judicial conduct. Historically, it was undisputed that denial of justice was a principal legal vehicle to address claims for alleged mistreatment of individuals in a host state's courts. However, international lawyers were divided over the definition of a denial of justice. Early on they split between those advocating an all-encompassing definition that would equate denial of justice to the general notion of an international wrong[1] and those favouring a narrower definition that limited denial of justice to a refusal of access to courts.[2] The contemporary view appears to occupy a middle ground: justice can be denied not only by a

[1] Clyde Eagleton, 'Denial of Justice in International Law' (1928) 22 AJIL 538, 539; Charles Hyde, *International Law Chiefly as Interpreted and Applied by the United States* (Little, Brown, & Co, Boston 1922) 491–92; Andronico Adede, 'A Fresh Look at the Meaning of the Denial of Justice under International Law' (1976) 73 Canadian Ybk Intl L 73, 82; Oliver Lissitzyn, 'The Meaning of the Term Denial of Justice in International Law' (1936) 30 AJIL 632, 636–38. See also the opinion of the Commissioner Nielsen in the *Neer* case, suggesting that it was 'useful and proper to apply the term denial of justice in a broader sense than that of a designation solely of a wrongful act on the part of the judicial branch of the government'. See *LFH Neer & Pauline v United Mexican States* (1926) 4 RIAA 60, 64.

[2] G Guerrero, Annex to Questionnaire No 4, Committee of Experts for the Progressive Codification of International Law, Report of the Sub-Committee, League of Nations Pub C 196, M 70, 1927 V, reproduced in A Freeman, *The International Responsibility of States for Denial of Justice* (Longman & Co 1938) 632. The narrow approach to defining denial of justice was espoused by the Spanish government in the *Barcelona Traction Co Case* (1962–69) 4 ICJ Pleadings 463. See also also G Fitzmaurice, 'The Meaning of the Term "Denial of Justice"' (1932) 13 British Ybk Intl L 93, 95 (noting that 'if used in a more restricted sense, the term has a definite value as describing a particular species of international wrong').

Mavluda Sattorova, *Denial of Justice and Judicial Measures* In: *Rethinking Investment Law*. Edited by: David Schneiderman and Gus Van Harten, Oxford University Press. © Mavluda Sattorova 2023. DOI: 10.1093/oso/9780192871084.003.0006

refusal of access to courts but also by a manifestly unjust decision. There is also a considerable degree of consensus that a denial of justice is not limited to judicial behaviour alone; that is, it can also manifest itself in legislative or executive interference with the administration of justice.[3]

Yet the disagreement over the meaning of denial of justice has persisted in the arbitral awards of ISDS tribunals. Tribunals and commentators have diverged over the types of governmental conduct that can trigger a breach. For one school of thought, denial of justice is 'the sole form of international delictual responsibility towards foreign nationals for acts or omissions within an adjudicative procedure for which the State is responsible'.[4] In other words, the legality of judicial conduct can be determined only through the medium of a denial of justice. This approach implies the need (1) for a tribunal to adopt a highly specific (and deferential) standard of review and (2) for an investor to exhaust local remedies.

At the other end of the spectrum are tribunals and commentators who favour a more fluid approach to claims of judicial misconduct. Their approach frames denial of justice as one of many causes of action available to claimant investors seeking redress for alleged mistreatment in host state courts. On this line of reasoning, judicial behaviour can be contested alternatively as a judicial expropriation, a failure to provide effective means of redress, arbitrary treatment, or a breach of the obligation to ensure full protection and security. By 'dressing up' their claims of judicial misconduct in cloaks other than denial of justice, claimants can avoid satisfying prerequisites that would otherwise apply to their claims. Perhaps unsurprisingly, this school of thought also advocates a less deferential standard of review for judicial measures.

The gap between these opposing schools of thought has major implications. Indeed, it reveals a profound disagreement over the thresholds for triggering state responsibility under investment treaties. Sections 2 and 3 below will discuss the most salient investment arbitration cases concerning judicial measures. The aim of the discussion is (1) to highlight key trends in the evolution of the reasoning in arbitral awards, (2) to identify where the law has taken a wrong turn, and (3) to explore what can be done to address the incoherence and form a more solid foundation for the adjudication of claims of alleged judicial misconduct. Section 4 will highlight the emerging efforts to reign in

[3] See generally Jan Paulsson, *Denial of Justice in International Law* (CUP, 2005).

[4] Zachary Douglas, 'International Responsibility for Domestic Adjudication: Denial of Justice Deconstructed' (2014) 63 ICLQ 867, 900.

discordant arbitral interpretations and restate the investment treaty rules and principles governing state responsibility for judicial measures.

2 Beginnings

Investment treaty obligations for the administration of justice are based on the classical customary law of denial of justice and on the international standard of treatment of aliens.[5] As an international delict, denial of justice has long been intertwined with the requirement of the exhaustion of local remedies. There is broad consensus in customary international law that denial of justice becomes internationally wrongful only after the whole system of administration of justice has been put to the test by way of the exhaustion of local remedies.[6] The requirement to exhaust domestic remedies—prior to instigating an international dispute concerning a denial of justice—is frequently regarded not as a procedural precondition but rather as a substantive duty that forms an inalienable part of the state's obligation not to deny justice.[7]

2.1 The Troubled Legacy of *Loewen v United States*

Loewen v United States was the first investment arbitration case to articulate the legal underpinnings of denial of justice as a cause of action in investment arbitration.[8] It is also somewhat infamous. In *Loewen*, the dispute arose from a private lawsuit in a Mississippi court. The lawsuit had been brought by the local owner of a funeral home business, Jeremy O'Keefe, against his Canadian competitor, Loewen. During the trial, O'Keefe's counsel used xenophobic and racist rhetoric in the course of convincing the jury to rule against Loewen. The jury ordered US$500 million in compensation.[9] After the trial, O'Keefe threatened to execute the judgment immediately. Unable to raise the necessary bond to stay execution, Loewen settled by paying O'Keefe US$170 million.

[5] Martins Paparinskis, *The International Minimum Standard and Fair and Equitable Treatment* (OUP, 2013) 182.

[6] ibid.

[7] Roberto Ago, 'Sixth Report on State Responsibility' in Yearbook of the International Law Commission' (1977) II UN Doc A/CN.4/SER.A/1977/Add.1 (Pt 1) 23–24.

[8] *Loewen v United States*, ICSID Case No ARB AF/98/3, Award (26 June 2003) 42 ILM 811.

[9] ibid para 113. The dispute involved three contracts valued at US$980,000 and an exchange of two funeral homes worth approximately US$2.5 million for the Loewen funeral insurance company valued at approximately US$4 million.

Loewen then brought an ISDS claim, arguing that the trial amounted to a denial of justice and other breaches of the North American Free Trade Agreement (NAFTA).[10] The United States objected that, among other things, state responsibility for judicial acts could arise only from a final action by the state's judicial system as a whole. This argument was predicated on the notion that a judicial decision is a single action at the international level and that the state had not spoken until all appeals had been exhausted.[11]

In its award, the tribunal agreed with the claimants that 'there was a gross failure on the part of the trial judge to afford the due process due to Loewen'.[12] Indeed, 'the whole trial and its resultant verdict were clearly improper and discreditable and cannot be squared with minimum standards of international law and fair and equitable treatment'.[13] Even so, since the trial proceedings were only one part of the framework of judicial remedies available to Loewen, the tribunal found no denial of justice.[14] The rule of judicial finality made it necessary to 'afford the State the opportunity of redressing through its legal system the inchoate breach of international law occasioned by the lower court decision'.[15] Although Article 1121 NAFTA waived local remedies as a precondition for an ISDS claim, the tribunal held that the waiver did not apply in cases where an alleged breach of international law arose from judicial acts.[16]

The *Loewen* award supports the view that claims concerning judicial behaviour should be addressed only through the prism of a denial of justice. Denial of justice was the governing standard even if an investor argued that judicial behaviour breached fair and equitable treatment or failed to ensure due process. In turn, it was necessary to establish whether the state failed in its obligation to provide a *system* of justice. The rule of finality of judicial action was seen as an essential element of the sovereign right to administer justice by its own means. By extension, the state could be found to have denied justice only where the claimant exhausted all available local remedies. Thus, the local remedies

[10] ibid.

[11] ibid para 143.

[12] ibid para 87.

[13] ibid para 137.

[14] Some of the available remedies were arguably too burdensome for the investor, in particular the 'supersedeas bond' requirement according to which a stay of execution on assets pending recourse to higher courts was available only subject to the posting of a bond as security for payment of the judgment, in the amount of 125 per cent of the verdict appealed.

[15] ibid para 156.

[16] ibid para 164. It has been observed that, in spite of having distinguished between the rule of local remedies and the rule of judicial finality, the tribunal, at several moments, referred to the exhaustion of local remedies in addressing Loewen's failure to appeal; BK Gathright, 'A Step in the Wrong Direction: The *Loewen* Finality Requirement and the Local Remedies Rule in NAFTA Chapter Eleven' (2005) 54 Emory LJ 1093, 1105.

rule is not just a procedural prerequisite but rather a substantive element of denial of justice. By requiring judicial finality, the tribunal limited the scope for judicial measures to be disputed under investment treaties.

2.2 Judicial Finality as a Precondition for Claims

The *Loewen* tribunal arguably did not err in its application of international law when it found that a waiver of local remedies in Article 1121 NAFTA was inapplicable to claims arising from judicial misconduct. This interpretation is supported by a long-standing doctrine, according to which a denial of justice becomes wrongful only after the whole system of justice has been put to the test.[17] In the words of Roberto Ago, 'an internationally wrongful act as understood in the term "denial of justice" is not considered as complete until the higher courts have successively given their judgment and confirmed the decision of the court of first instance'.[18]

The reinstatement of the local remedies rule in cases concerning judicial measures draws support from a long line of authorities. These include the Second Report on State Responsibility to the International Law Commission, which noted that 'an aberrant decision by an official lower in the hierarchy, which is capable of being reconsidered, does not of itself amount to an unlawful act'.[19] In particular, the principal basis for the local remedies rule lies in the distinctive *nature* of the delict of denial of justice:

> [t]he obligation which the State owes the foreign national in this context (whether under general international law or under the specific provisions of a treaty like NAFTA or a bilateral investment treaty) is to provide a system of justice which affords fair, equitable and non-discriminatory treatment. So long as the system itself provides a sufficient guarantee of such treatment, the State will not be in violation of its international obligations merely because a trial court gives a defective decision which can be corrected on appeal.[20]

[17] See eg Paulsson (n 3) 104.
[18] Ago (n 7) 57; Paparinskis (n 5) 182–83.
[19] ILC, 'Second Report on State Responsibility' (3 May–23 July 1999) UN Doc A/CN.4/498, 34; See also Freeman (n 2) (commenting that the 'responsibility [of a State] is engaged as the result of a definitive judicial decision by a court of last resort which violates an international obligation of the State'); see also Robert Jennings and Arthur Watts (eds), *Oppenheim's International Law* (9th edn, Longmans 1992) 543–44.
[20] Christopher Greenwood, 'State Responsibility for the Decisions of National Courts' in Malgosia Fitzmaurice and Dan Sarooshi (eds), *Issues of State Responsibility before International Judicial Institutions* (Hart Publishing, 2004) 61.

More broadly, the *Loewen* tribunal was justified in insisting on denial of justice as the appropriate framework for claims of judicial misconduct. However, its reasoning was not adequately elaborated or convincingly reasoned. As a result, it had the effect of muddying the waters of subsequent investment treaty jurisprudence. In particular, in the course of drawing on the customary rules for the application of local remedies to denial of justice claims, the tribunal did not articulate why judicial measures—and not other governmental measures—warrant application of the finality rule and exhaustion of local remedies. Arguments offered by commentators also fail to convince. Take, for instance, the argument that the judicial finality rule is based on a distinction between 'obligations of conduct' and 'obligations of result'. According to this reasoning, the distinct nature of a denial of justice stems from the state's obligation to create and maintain a *system* of justice.[21] As explained in an earlier ILC Report, an obligation of result presupposes some form of finality of action:

> When the conduct of the State has created a situation not in conformity with the result required of it by an international obligation, but the obligation allows that this or an equivalent result may nevertheless be achieved by subsequent conduct of the State, there is a breach of the obligation only if the State also fails by its subsequent conduct to achieve the result required of it by that obligation.[22]

Conceptualizing denial of justice in this way—as a breach of an obligation of result—ostensibly reinforces the rule of judicial finality. That is, no breach occurs until the state fails to use all available opportunities to produce the required result.[23] Further, there is a consensus that the state is under a duty to provide a fair and efficient system of justice. Therefore, a wrongful decision by a court of first instance would not violate the obligation since redress remains available in a higher court. The courts as a whole make up the domestic system of justice.

[21] Paulsson (n 3) 7, 27–30.

[22] Article 20 dealt with the obligations of conduct. Under the rubric ;Breach of an international obligation requiring the adoption of a particular course of conduct, it provided that: 'There is a breach by a State of an international obligation requiring it to adopt a particular course of conduct when the conduct of that State is not in conformity with that required of it by that obligation.' See ILC, 'Report on the work of the twenty-ninth session' (9 May–29 July 1977) UN Doc A/32/10, 11-9.

[23] Greenwood (n 20) 67, n 28. For critical comment see EJ Aréchaga, 'International Law in the Past Third of a Century' (1978) 159 Recueil des Cours de l'Académie de Droit International 1. The local remedies rule, argued Arechaga, should be applied 'in all cases where the original violation affecting an alien may be corrected by a higher national authority, having jurisdiction over the original act, this subsequent action securing, for the alien concerned, a recognition of the right he sought to exercise, even if the international obligation is one of conduct and not one of result' (ibid 296).

Unfortunately, this distinction between obligations of conduct and obligations of result does not offer a convincing basis for subjecting denial of justice claims to different prerequisites. As I have written elsewhere,[24] most investment treaty obligations can readily be classified as obligations of both conduct and result.[25] For example, fair and equitable treatment can be conceptualized as an obligation of conduct because it requires the state to refrain from unfair treatment of foreign investors (e.g. not to withdraw a licence without prior notice). At the same time, fair and equitable treatment (FET) can be classified as an obligation of result in that the state must provide a system that *ultimately* delivers fair and equitable outcomes to investors.

In the case of alleged misconduct by administrative organs of the state, one could similarly argue that FET is an obligation of result by which the state must ensure a fair and efficient *system of administration*, as opposed to ensuring fairness at each stage of the administrative process. In fact, arbitral interpretations of FET as an overarching good governance standard appear to be underpinned by such systemic notions. This perspective is discernible in Elihu Root's historic definition of the international minimum standard. According to Root, '[i]f any country's system of law and administration does not conform to that standard, although the people of the country may be content or compelled to live under it, no other country can be compelled to accept it as furnishing a satisfactory measure of treatment to its citizens'.[26] Some recent interpretations of FET likewise emphasize its systemic nature, especially in investor–state disputes relating to the administrative law of host states. Such interpretations are said to provide the state with both a yardstick and an incentive 'to review and modernize their domestic legal systems'.[27]

If FET were viewed as an obligation of result, an administrative body would not violate the treaty for just any wrong at any time. Rather, the claimant would need to show that the system of administration has failed to deliver fair and equitable outcomes. Should there be such a rule of administrative (or legislative) finality?[28] Those favouring more restrictive interpretation of investment

[24] See Mavluda Sattorova, 'Denial of Justice Disguised? Investment, Arbitration and the Protection of Foreign Investors from Judicial Misconduct' (2012) 61 ICLQ 223, 231.

[25] Rapporteur Crawford suggested that the distinction between obligations of conduct and obligations of result should be abandoned. See ILC (n 19) paras 88–92.

[26] Elihu Root, 'The Basis of Protection to Citizens Residing Abroad' (1910) 4 AJIL 517, 521–22.

[27] Rudolf Dolzer, 'The Impact of International Investment Treaties on Domestic Administrative Law' (2005) 37 NYU J Intl L & Policy 972. Also see Ostřanský in this volume.

[28] See Andrea Bjorklund, 'Reconciling State Sovereignty and Investor Protection in Denial of Justice Claims' (2005) 45 Virginia J Intl L 809, 858 (observing that 'when the *Loewen* tribunal opined that only a final act of a judicial system may give rise to a NAFTA claim, the logical extension of that concept to requiring "appeals" within different hierarchical structures may lead to claims by states party to NAFTA that eviscerate any waiver of the local remedies rule'). See also Campbell McLachlan, Laurence Shore,

treaties and the return of local remedies as a means of scaling back investor–state disputes might welcome this approach. However, extending the rule of finality to administrative and legislative measures is counter-productive. A more coherent approach would be for states to reintroduce local remedies for cases concerning judicial measures. This could be done through expressly amending the relevant provisions in the treaties. Otherwise, the blurring of the line between obligations of result and obligations of conduct risks weakening the rule of judicial finality and thus undermining the different treatment of judicial measures.

Another common justification for subjecting denial of justice claims to the local remedies rule is the need to respect sovereignty. If a foreign investor could instigate international arbitral review of a lower court judgment without first exhausting the local avenues of redress, then international law 'would find itself intruding intolerably into internal affairs of the host state'.[29] This argument is discernible in *Loewen*, where the tribunal noted that the main purpose of the finality requirement was to 'afford the State the opportunity of redressing through its legal system the inchoate breach of international law occasioned by the lower court decision'.[30]

Again, however, the argument here does not supply a sufficiently cogent justification for the judicial finality rule. If finality of action were required out of respect for sovereignty, the same deference should presumably be afforded to measures of the sovereign administration and the legislature?[31] As Bjorkland puts it, 'it is difficult to distinguish the desirability of requiring a decision of the highest body within a court system from requiring a final decision from the highest official in an administrative system'.[32] The flaw with the argument

and Matthew Weiniger, *International Investment Arbitration: Substantive Principles* (OUP, 2007) 232 (noting that 'since the State has a single legal personality at international law, there would seem to be no reason in principle to distinguish between decisions of inferior courts, and decisions of administrative officials').

[29] Paulsson (n 3) 108.

[30] *Loewen* (n 8) para 156.

[31] According to the *Loewen* tribunal, '[i]t would be very strange if a State were to be confronted with liability for a breach of international law committed by its magistrate or low-ranking judicial officer when domestic avenues of appeal are not pursued, let alone exhausted. If Article 1121 were to have that effect, it would encourage resort to NAFTA tribunals rather than resort to the appellate courts and review processes of the host State, an outcome which would seem surprising, having regard to the sophisticated legal systems of the NAFTA Parties' (para 162). Commenting on this finding, Wallace correctly observed that such 'sophisticated legal systems' are also available for non-judicial breaches; Don Wallace Jr, 'State Responsibility for Denial of Substantive and Procedural Justice under NAFTA Chapter Eleven' (2000) 23 Hastings Intl & Comp L Rev 393, 399.

[32] Bjorklund (n 28) 858 (observing that 'when the *Loewen* tribunal opined that only a final act of a judicial system may give rise to a NAFTA claim, the logical extension of that concept to requiring "appeals" within different hierarchical structures may lead to claims by states party to NAFTA that eviscerate any waiver of the local remedies rule').

is that it does not explain why actions of lower courts should be subject to the stringent rule of local remedies, whereas claims contesting decisions of administrative bodies should not. While *Loewen* was correct in its insistence on the exhaustion of local remedies, its failure to support this conclusion with a compelling and legally sound justification has subsequently opened the door to arbitral interpretations that further exacerbated the incoherence of investment jurisprudence on claims concerning judicial conduct.

3 The Wrong Turn towards a Multiplicity of Interchangeable Claims

The rule of judicial finality emerged as a pragmatic solution to curb the proliferation of claims against judicial measures. Yet, it has not been supported by persuasive reasoning. This inadequate justification can in part be blamed for a welter of ISDS cases where, to avoid the rule and related barriers to their claims, investors have challenged judicial measures by alleging other, distinct breaches of investment treaties. This over-reaching illustrates another systemic issue underpinning investment law: the sheer multiplicity and interchangeability of treaty protections for investors. This multiplicity is a root cause of the current inconsistency of arbitral approaches to claims against judicial measures.

Unlike customary international law and its delict of denial of justice, there is no single treaty standard tasked with protecting investors from judicial misconduct. Instead, claimants have been able to choose from an array of broad and intersubstitutable standards. Early ISDS practice, as well as the texts of the new generation investment treaties, tend to designate the FET as a key provision encapsulating the state's obligation not to deny justice to foreign investors. However, the reinstatement of the local remedies rule in *Loewen* appears to have led many claimants to alternative causes of action. In some cases, investors have challenged judicial measures under the ubiquitous standard of full protection and security. In others, they have resorted to the notion of judicial expropriation. There is also a string of cases in which judicial measures have been said to breach the state's obligation to provide 'effective means of asserting claims and enforcing rights'.

3.1 Judicial Expropriation

The award in *Saipem v Bangladesh* is a prime example of how the multiplicity and interchangeability of investment treaty protections could be used to distort investment jurisprudence on judicial measures. The award has received much critical attention, including by the present author.[33] The case emerged from an essentially contractual dispute between Saipem and Petrobangla, a Bangladeshi national oil company. To resolve a disagreement over contractual performance, Saipem initiated commercial arbitration proceedings before an ICC panel. Unsatisfied with those proceedings, Petrobangla applied to the Bangladeshi courts to revoke the ICC tribunal's authority and, later, to set aside its award. This judicial saga culminated in a holding of the High Court Division of Bangladesh's Supreme Court that the ICC award was itself illegal. Saipem took the matter to ISDS under the Italy–Bangladesh BIT, alleging that the judicial intervention in the contractual arbitration amounted to an uncompensated expropriation of its investment. In objecting to the ISDS tribunal's jurisdiction, Bangladesh invoked *Loewen*, contending that, where a court decision formed the basis of an investor's claim, the local remedies rule ought to be exhausted, regardless of whether the claim was framed as denial of justice or as expropriation.[34]

The *Saipem* tribunal agreed that denial of justice called for finality of judicial action.[35] However, it distinguished denial of justice from expropriation committed by the judiciary. The latter, in the tribunal's view, did not require exhaustion of local remedies.[36] While ostensibly endorsing *Loewen*, the *Saipem* tribunal signalled that the rule of finality could be circumvented if denial of justice is repackaged as judicial expropriation.

After *Saipem*, the notion of judicial expropriation resurfaced in various cases. *Tatneft v Ukraine* arose from a series of judicial and executive measures which the claimant argued were tantamount to a creeping expropriation. With a nod to *Saipem*, the *Tatneft* tribunal observed that the analysis of judicial expropriation in ISDS awards had been intertwined with that of denial of justice and other standards. The tribunal held that expropriations can originate in judicial acts and, as such, were not excluded under investment law. Citing the complexity of the factual background of the dispute, however, the tribunal did not explain further how denial of justice differed from judicial expropriation.

[33] *Saipem v Bangladesh*, ICSID Case No ARB/05/7, Award (20 June 2009).
[34] ibid para 178.
[35] ibid para 176.
[36] ibid para 181.

Eli Lilly v Canada added another layer of complexity. It acknowledged the possibility of judicial expropriation, but made it as demanding a standard as denial of justice. The tribunal stated that 'it is possible to contemplate circumstances in which a judicial act (or omission) may engage questions of expropriation under NAFTA Article 1110, such as, perhaps, in circumstances in which a judicial decision crystallizes a taking'.[37] However, unlike other arbitral panels, the *Eli Lilly* tribunal reasoned that a judicial expropriation, regardless of whether the judicial conduct is disputed as a denial of justice, must still be sufficiently egregious and shocking.[38] *Eli Lilly* thus echoed the first NAFTA case in which a tribunal considered a claim of judicial expropriation: *Azinian v Mexico*.[39] Frequently cited in subsequent cases, the *Azinian* tribunal accepted that judicial measures were not beyond the reach of investment arbitration tribunals, but held that, to amount to an expropriation, such measures would need to rise to a denial of justice. Without denial of justice, a merely incorrect decision by a local court would not constitute expropriation.[40]

3.2 Effective Means of Redress

Another standard that has been invoked frequently in cases concerning judicial measures is the so called effective means standard. This standard arises from the obligation 'to provide effective means of asserting claims and enforcing rights with respect to investment, investment agreements, and investment authorisations'.[41] The provision is found in a handful of US bilateral investment treaties (BITs) and the Energy Charter Treaty. One of the first cases to analyse its meaning and scope was *Chevron v Ecuador*.[42] At the heart of the dispute were seven cases the investor had brought in the Ecuadorian courts over its contract-based claims against the government. Having failed to obtain redress in these cases, the investor argued that an unreasonable delay in deciding its

[37] *Eli Lilly v Canada*, ICSID Case No UNCT/14/2, Final Award (16 March 2017) para 221.
[38] ibid para 223.
[39] ibid.
[40] *Robert Azinian and Others v United Mexican States*, ICSID Case No ARB AF/97/2, Award (1 November 1999) 98.
[41] See eg art II(7) of the Treaty Between the United States of America and the Republic of Ecuador Concerning the Encouragement and Reciprocal Protection of Investment (adopted 27 August 1993, entered into force 11 May 1997) Treaty Doc No 103-15; also art 10(12) of the Energy Charter Treaty.
[42] *Chevron Corporation and Texaco Petroleum Corporation v Ecuador*, PCA Case No 34877, Partial Award on Merits (30 March 2010) (Ad hoc—UNCITRAL Arbitration Rules).

contractual claims and a wrongful dismissal of some cases contravened, among other things, Ecuador's effective means obligation.[43]

In response, the tribunal observed that the provision overlapped significantly with the customary standard of denial of justice.[44] However, since the US–Ecuador BIT did not expressly elaborate on this relationship to denial of justice, the tribunal assumed that the standard was intended to go beyond a restatement of the customary position and create a *lex specialis*.[45] Thus, the tribunal arrived at the position that the effective means standard was a distinct and 'potentially less demanding' standard than denial of justice.[46]

By characterizing the effective means standard as 'less demanding', it in turn became possible to do away with the limiting factors of judicial finality and exhaustion of local remedies. Chevron argued, and the tribunal accepted, that exhaustion was required for denial of justice claims, but not for other treaty obligations.[47] In particular, a breach of the effective means standard called for a "qualified" application of the local remedies rule. Instead of resorting to all available remedies in the host state law, the investor was required only 'adequately' to use the means available to it.[48]

One may question what makes the effective means standard so distinctive from customary denial of justice as to require a different application of the local remedies rule. Unfortunately, the *Chevron* tribunal did not offer robust reasoning to support its interpretation. This weakness was evident when the tribunal turned to the substantive content of the effective means standard. It held that the standard encompassed a guarantee against indefinite or undue delay.[49] Yet, according to many authorities, so too does the delict of denial of justice. Indeed, when the tribunal evaluated whether the disputed judicial delays justified the finding of a breach, it expressly relied on the customary law on denial of justice.[50] In other words, the effective means standard was based on the same principles as denial of justice. Yet, if establishing a breach of the effective means provision turns on essentially the same principles as denial of justice, there is no basis to treat them as different standards. As in

[43] ibid paras 206–207.
[44] ibid para 242.
[45] ibid.
[46] ibid para 244.
[47] ibid para 321.
[48] ibid para 268.
[49] ibid para 250.
[50] See eg para 250: '*As with denial of justice under customary international law*, some of the factors that may be considered are the complexity of the case, the behaviour of the litigants involved, the significance of the interests at stake in the case, and the behaviour of the courts themselves' (emphasis added).

Saipem, the *Chevron* tribunal did not offer convincing reasons for departing from customary denial of justice. In turn, and again as in *Saipem*, the tribunal opened the door to cherry-picking treaty standards in cases concerning judicial measures.

Despite this basic flaw, *Chevron v Ecuador* has inspired copycat claims and rulings. The distinct and loosened effective means standard has helped to circumvent the well-established substantive and procedural thresholds for denial of justice. An example is *White Industries v India*. In that case, the effective means standard was imported from another BIT of India for application under the India–Australia BIT.[51] The *White Industries* tribunal appeared so impressed by the reasoning in *Chevron* that it offered no interpretation of its own for this interpretive routine, and simply quoted from *Chevron* in characterizing the effective means standard as entailing 'a distinct and potentially less demanding test, in comparison to denial of justice in customary international law'.[52]

Not surprisingly, in endorsing this view of the effective means standard, the *White Industries* tribunal had to confront its potential as a 'whole of the system' standard. This expansive position emerged from India's submission that, when evaluating the administration of justice in Indian courts, the tribunal ought to take into account the country's developing status: '[A] developing country, with a population of over 1.2 billion people and an over-stretched judiciary, must be held to different standards than, for example, Switzerland, the United States or Australia.'[53] The tribunal disagreed, but sheepishly explained itself only in a footnote. According to the tribunal, the host state's population or the current state of its court system(s) had limited relevance. Rather, the effective means standard required the state to ensure that 'the system of laws and institutions work effectively at the time [the investor] seeks to enforce its rights/make its claims'. For India, the uncompromising implication is that courts and institutions must be built and maintained especially for foreign investors. Remarkably, the systemic orientation in *White Industries* implied a state duty to transform local remedies for the benefit of investors in India, while prudent attention to customary law in *Loewen* required investors to exhaust such remedies in the United States.

[51] *White Industries Australia Ltd v India*, Final Award (30 November 2011).
[52] ibid para 11.3.2.
[53] ibid para 5.2.18.

3.3 Arbitrary Treatment

Besides concepts of judicial expropriation and effective means, investors can also use other standards to evade the local remedies requirement and other customary thresholds. For instance, claims under BIT prohibitions on arbitrary and discriminatory measures are also exempt from the local remedies requirement.[54] In *Alghanim v Jordan*, the claimants disputed the state's imposition of a tax on proceeds from the sale of a telecommunications licence.[55] They had previously challenged the tax unsuccessfully in Jordanian courts, including by final appeal to the Court of Cassation. Under the BIT, the claimants argued that the tax measures were an arbitrary, politically motivated decision. Moreover, the Jordanian courts' dismissal of their challenge to them was a denial of justice as well as a breach of a prohibition of arbitrary measures. A majority of the tribunal dismissed the allegation of arbitrary treatment by the courts on the basis that they did not rise to denial of justice. Even so, the investors' efforts demonstrated how the availability of potentially interchangeable treaty standards gives investors an opportunity to choose among causes of action and undermine the customary constraints and thresholds for denial of justice.

4 In Defence of Multiple Causes of Action?

Nearly two decades after *Loewen*, arbitral tribunals continue to disagree over the contours of state responsibility for judicial measures. Yet the proliferation of cases has at least allowed the opposing views to crystallize and, in turn, has illuminated their respective merits and shortcomings. On the one hand, there are the tribunals that have scrutinized judicial measures under the overarching standard of denial of justice. These tribunals have heeded the customary prudence and deference towards domestic courts. They have limited state responsibility to sufficiently serious failings of the entire judicial system. Some proponents of this approach acknowledge that there are alternative rubrics, such as judicial expropriation or the effective means obligation, but they maintain the same exacting criteria as for denial of justice. As summarized in *Philip Morris v Uruguay*, for a denial of justice to be proven there must be

[54] For example, art II(3)(b) of the US–Ecuador BIT provides that '[a] measure may be arbitrary or discriminatory notwithstanding the fact that a party has had or has exercised the opportunity to review such measure in the courts or administrative tribunals of a Party'. Chevron sought to deploy this BIT provision but its argument was not discussed by the tribunal.

[55] *Alghanim v Jordan*, Case No ARB/13/38, Award (14 December 2017).

clear evidence of 'an outrageous failure of the judicial system' or a demonstration of 'systemic injustice' or of a 'clearly improper and discreditable' judicial decision.[56]

On the other hand, there are those who defend investors' ability to choose how best to present their case against domestic courts. They see no reason why denial of justice should be the sole basis of state responsibility for judicial measures. According to Douglas, 'litigants are motivated by pragmatism rather than fidelity to historical usage'.[57] The flexibility to dress a denial of justice claim as the claimant prefers is a by-product of treaty drafting, which has enabled multiple, overlapping and often interchangeable protections. Douglas asks: 'Why plead a denial of justice, with its substantive requirement that the victim must have had recourse to local procedures when a range of other international obligations might be interpreted as also extending to the same acts or omissions relating to the administration of justice in the particular State?'[58]

Krederi v Ukraine[59] neatly captures the disagreement over how to review judicial behaviour in ISDS, while also highlighting the opposing schools of thought. The dispute arose from transactions to purchase land from Kiev City Council. The transactions were invalidated by Ukrainian courts due to deficiencies identified in the City Council's conduct of the sale. Following these court decisions, title to the land was returned to the City Council. However, the investor was not refunded the purchase price. The investor argued that the totality of actions by the courts amounted to a denial of justice in breach of fair and equitable treatment and to a judicial expropriation. The tribunal disagreed. First, it stressed the distinct nature of denial of justice—arising from a sufficiently serious deficiency—and failure to accord due process.[60] After examining each strand of the alleged judicial failures, the tribunal concluded that the disputed conduct of the courts did not meet the required threshold of severity; that is, it fell below 'an outrageous failure of the judicial system'. Since the courts did not administer justice in 'a seriously inadequate way', the tribunal saw no denial of justice.[61]

Responding to the investor's claim of judicial expropriation, the *Krederi* tribunal accepted that it could be a distinct cause of action. The tribunal stressed, however, that judicial expropriation would be an exception rather than the

[56] *Philip Morris v Uruguay*, ICSID Case No ARB/10/7, Award (8 July 2016) 500.
[57] Douglas (n 4) 868.
[58] ibid.
[59] *Krederi Ltd v Ukraine*, ICSID Case No ARB/14/17, Award (2 July 2018).
[60] ibid para 442.
[61] ibid para 631.

norm.[62] Crucially, it would require a serious procedural illegality and a denial of justice. Since the tribunal had otherwise found no denial of justice, it also dismissed the judicial expropriation claim.[63]

Critics of *Krederi* object to this requirement for serious procedural illegality in the case of judicial conduct. The same objection informs those who call for more causes of action than denial of justice alone.[64] In effect, those who support challenges to the domestic courts based on multiple and interchangeable standards are not concerned so much with denial of justice as an overarching rubric as they are with the fact that denial of justice requires claimants to establish a particularly grave violation of international law. This view epitomizes the profound disagreement over the investment arbitration regime and its function: should tribunals intervene only for sufficiently serious misconduct by state organs? Or do the treaties offer safeguards against a relatively lower degree of inappropriateness?

Another general objection is that subjecting judicial measures to a different threshold of illegality leads to incongruous or irrational outcomes. For Gharavi, 'elevating the standard for judicial expropriation to the level of the denial of justice standard' or, alternatively, 'applying to judicial expropriation a threshold that is different from the threshold for expropriation through the executive or legislative branches of the State' creates a risk of 'absurd results'.[65] That is, states could potentially arrange for judicial involvement to shield the state's interference from future claims.[66] Other critics similarly argue that, if denial of justice were to become the sole ground of state responsibility for judicial measures, 'a sprinkling of judicial involvement in a case would inoculate all of the rest of the state action involved'.[67] Further, why impose an additional requirement of grave illegality, or an obligation to exhaust local remedies, if the same is not required for administrative or legislative measures?[68]

[62] ibid para 709.
[63] ibid paras 713–15.
[64] *Infinito Gold v Costa Rica*, ICSID Case No ARB/14/5, Award (3 June 2021) paras 359–67 is among recent cases where tribunals supported the view that denial of justice was not the sole standard and that reviewing judicial measures under other investment treaty standards, such as FET, was subject to different, less stringent requirements than under denial of justice.
[65] Hamid Gharavi, 'Discord over Judicial Expropriation' (2018) 33 ICSID Rev 349, 354.
[66] ibid.
[67] James Egerton-Vernon and Ananda Burra, 'Is Denial of Justice the Only Substantive Standard Theory of Liability for Judicial Measures?' *Transnational Dispute Management* (April 2019) 3.
[68] ibid; see also Martin Jarrett, 'The Only Thing We Have to Fear about Judicial Expropriation Is the Fear of It' http://opiniojuris.org/2020/05/20/the-only-thing-we-have-to-fear-about-judicial-expropriation-is-the-fear-of-it/.

At first blush, both views—that denial of justice is a single and unifying rubric and that there are multiple and interchangeable standards for judicial conduct—appear to share the goal of more coherence and predictability in ISDS. Those opposed to stringent thresholds appear to champion uniform criteria for judicial as well as administrative and legislative decision-makers. The message seems to be that universal standards will bring consistency and prevent absurd outcomes. Yet if one looks closely at cases in which denial of justice was side-stepped in favour of a more flexible alternative standard, it is clear that these cases have not helped consistency and uniformity in arbitral outcomes. Rather, they have created ad hoc diversions from the otherwise applicable protections expressly agreed to by states in the treaties.

Consider, again, the leading authority on judicial expropriation, *Saipem v Bangladesh*. The facts behind the dispute readily supported a finding of denial of justice. Yet the tribunal preferred a tenuously reasoned claim of judicial expropriation to condemn the Bangladeshi courts. The reasons for this choice were practical. Article 9(1) of the Italy–Bangladesh BIT limited the tribunal's jurisdiction to claims of expropriation.[69] Had the tribunal described the judicial conduct as a denial of justice, the dispute would have been outside the states' treaty-based authorization of the arbitration. The label of judicial expropriation conveniently expanded the tribunal's jurisdiction. Ultimately, however, the tribunal sacrificed clarity and stability in the review of judicial conduct for an expansion of its own adjudicative power.

Of course, the *Saipem* tribunal could have done what later panels did. That is, it could have stressed that, regardless of whether a disputed measure is described in terms of denial of justice or judicial expropriation, a high threshold applies, necessitating evidence of an outrageous failure of the national judicial system.[70] Instead, the *Saipem* tribunal manufactured an exception that facilitated the investor's claim to proceed. In turn, it fragmented the standard of denial of justice as compared to other potential measures of judicial misconduct.[71]

These observations lead to a crucial contradiction on the part of those supporting judicial expropriation as a distinct standard. While they question the wisdom of treating judicial measures differently from legislative and

[69] *Saipem* (n 33) para 121.
[70] *Infinito Gold* (n 64).
[71] *Saipem* (n 33) para 183. It could be argued that, by placing emphasis on illegality of the conduct of the Bangladeshi judiciary, the *Saipem* tribunal moved beyond the standard expropriation analysis and effectively used a higher, more stringent standard to establish judicial misconduct. Yet the ultimate effect of the tribunal's reasoning on subsequent jurisprudence has been to encourage the invocation of judicial expropriation in lieu of a denial of justice. This strategy that would enable investors to use causes of action that are less demanding than denial of justice.

administrative ones, they are surprisingly content with different applications of the local remedies rule for different categories of judicial misconduct. In other words, they reject differential rules for expropriatory acts of the state, but are content to create tenuous subcategories of judicial misconduct, each with its own set of substantive and procedural thresholds. Yet, as the cases amply demonstrate, the dismissal of denial of justice as a unifying rubric does not reduce the likelihood of irrational or absurd outcomes in ISDS. Rather, it breeds more inconsistency by enabling claimants to subvert the established conditions for claims, even when expressly agreed by the state parties to investment treaties.

5 A Reconfiguration of Denial of Justice?

Unsurprisingly, states are concerned by the ISDS discord over judicial measures. Even those states that have long worked for strong investor protections have sought to rein in the existing disarray by reasserting control over the interpretation of their treaties and by stating the law of state responsibility for judicial misconduct. States have also increasingly resorted to third party submissions to tribunals, where permitted by the relevant treaty.

One such submission was made in *Gramercy v Peru*.[72] Drawing on Article 10.20.2 of the US–Peru trade agreement, the US filed a submission clarifying that, while judicial measures applying domestic law may give rise to a claim for denial of justice under the FET standard, 'decisions of domestic courts acting in the role of neutral and independent arbiters of the legal rights of litigants do not ... give rise to a claim for expropriation'.[73] Mexico expressed a similar view in its non-disputing party submission in *Eli Lilly v Canada*. Its submission pointed out that, because of the unique role of adjudicative power in the organization of states, denial of justice was the only customary rule for addressing the international legal consequences of judicial misconduct.[74]

The US Submission in *Gramercy* acknowledged that there may be instances in which a host state judiciary is not separate from other organs of the state. In such cases, expropriation may indeed be effectuated through a series of measures culminating in a judicial act or omission. Indeed, '[s]tates might seek to

[72] *Gramercy v Peru*, ICSID Case No UNCT/18/2 (21 June 2019) Submission by the United States of America pursuant to Article 10.20.2 of the United States–Peru Trade Promotion Agreement.
[73] ibid para 28.
[74] *Eli Lilly v Canada* (n 37)Submission of the United Mexican States Pursuant to NAFTA Article 1128 (18 March 2016) 14.

evade international responsibility for wrongful acts by using the courts as the conduit of executive or legislative action'.[75] However, in cases where executive or legislative organs interfered with the judicial process to cause an expropriation, the appropriate avenue to dispute such interference was the expropriation clause.[76] Likewise, the US stressed in *Gramercy* that the obligation to provide effective means of redress is the same as the FET obligation not to deny justice in criminal, civil, or administrative proceedings.[77] The customary standard for denial of justice, already encapsulated by the FET obligation, made it unnecessary to formulate a separate treaty obligation. (Indeed, the United States has removed the effective means provision entirely from its more recent treaties.[78]) The US also stressed the high threshold for judicial measures to rise to a denial of justice, including the importance of demonstrating 'a notoriously unjust' or 'egregious' misconduct or inaction by the host state's judiciary.[79] Quoting *Apotex*, the US also noted the indispensability of the judicial finality rule: '[a] claimant cannot raise a claim that a judicial act constitutes a breach of international law, without first proceeding through the judicial system that it purports to challenge, and thereby allowing the system an opportunity to correct itself.'[80]

These non-disputing party submissions have helped to clarify the fundamental question left open by the tribunal in *Loewen*: why treat judicial measures differently? Proponents of denial of justice as the unifying standard for mistreatment of investors in the courts effectively advocate a vision of investment law as a mechanism to sanction only serious departures from prescribed standards of behaviour. Denial of justice is thus seen as a special delict, due to the uniqueness of adjudication as an exercise of state authority. As Douglas puts it, adjudication is 'something special' as a form of decision-making and it calls for both an 'additional burden for establishing liability' and 'the existence of a separate delict' for judicial acts or omissions.[81] The exceptional nature of adjudication long ago generated a distinctive customary approach.[82] Yet what are these exceptional considerations?

An answer can be gleaned from state submissions and from the jurisprudence of international courts and tribunals. It is that courts ought to be treated

[75] US Submission in *Gramercy v Peru* (n 72) 29.
[76] ibid para 29.
[77] ibid para 36.
[78] ibid.
[79] ibid para 46.
[80] ibid para 47.
[81] Douglas (n 4) 869.
[82] ibid.

differently owing to 'the principle of judicial independence, the particular nature of judicial action, and the unique status of the judiciary in both international and municipal legal systems'.[83] As observed in the United States' submission in *Eli Lilly*, national judicial measures are accorded a greater presumption of regularity and a greater degree of deference because of the special role the judiciary plays in the state machinery.[84] To quote Douglas again, '[a]ll national legal systems rely upon corrective mechanisms to alleviate the risk of substantive error in adjudicative procedures' just as they 'accept by the very architecture of the institutions created for adjudicative procedures that substantive errors do routinely occur at the first level of the institutional hierarchy'.[85] For these reasons, there is a burgeoning consensus among many tribunals that denial of justice should be the sole basis of state responsibility for judicial measures. A decision by a lower court, if capable of being reconsidered, does not of itself amount to an unlawful act and a denial of justice presupposes a serious defect in the adjudicative process. In evaluating the latter, ISDS tribunals are 'not sitting as appeal courts over domestic adjudicators' and are required to apply only a limited review.[86]

6 Conclusion

The doctrine and scholarship show that, by subjecting judicial measures to special rules and high thresholds, there is a growing effort to curb the reach of investment treaties. Some tribunals and states have sought to create at least one category of state measures that are insulated from claims through stringent substantive and procedural conditions. This category of claims has been increasingly subjected to demanding benchmarks of egregiousness, judicial finality, and limited review. The multitude of methods through which states and select tribunals have been seeking to reinstate special rules applicable to judicial measures can be seen as a still somewhat sporadic but increasingly coordinated attempt to isolate at least one area where the investment treaty protections would not reach easily.

There is a growing number of cases in which states are engaging as non-disputing treaty parties to rein in the interpretation of international norms

[83] US Submission in *Gramercy v Peru* (n 72) 46.

[84] Submission of the United States of America pursuant to Article 1128 of the North American Free Trade Agreement in *Eli Lilly v Canada* (n 37) 22.

[85] Douglas (n 4) 895.

[86] *Krederi* (n 59) 449.

applicable to judicial misconduct. While only a few states, notably Canada, Mexico, and the United States, have so far been actively making non-disputing party submissions in cases concerning judicial measures, the emerging trends can be seen as evidence of a growing dissatisfaction with arbitral practice on denial of justice. This dissatisfaction with the status quo is also discernible in recent innovations in investment treaty practice. Fewer of the newly concluded treaties now contain the problematic 'effective means' standard.[87] Recognizing the need to limit tribunal review of judicial decisions, a small but growing number of treaties seek to exclude judicial conduct from the scope of investment arbitration or otherwise delimit tribunals' powers to determine the legality of national judicial measures.[88]

These innovations in arbitral and treaty practice can be seen as a reaction by states to the rampant growth of investment arbitration beyond its original scope. State efforts to reassert control over arbitral practice highlight the growing recognition of the need to rethink the law and practice on denial of justice. They also illustrate some of the strategies that can be used to address inconsistency and overreach in arbitral jurisprudence. At the same time, the vast number of investment treaties are yet to be modernized or otherwise updated. Even if this patchwork of treaties were to be comprehensively overhauled, an overarching issue is the willingness and ability of arbitral tribunals to depart from how states envisage that investment treaties should apply to judicial action. As the last three decades of investment arbitration practice have demonstrated, the wording of investment treaty standards alone—however detailed, nuanced, and comprehensive—may not prevent future tribunals from enforcing their own vision of where the boundaries of state responsibility for judicial conduct should lie. Rethinking investment protection against denial of justice and judicial measures therefore cannot be limited to amending and restricting the scope of standards of treatment but necessitates a broader and systematic re-evaluation of the incentives underpinning arbitral decision-making in investor–state dispute settlement.

[87] The effective means standard is no longer included in the recent generation of US BITs.

[88] See eg art 13.5 of the Belarus–India BIT (2019) whereby investor–state tribunals are precluded from reviewing the merits of a decision made by a judicial authority of the contracting state parties. Another noteworthy example of excluding certain judicial measures from the scope of investment protection and investor–state arbitration is art 8.12 of the Comprehensive Economic and Trade Agreement between Canada and the European Union.

7

Fair and Equitable Treatment

Josef Ostřanský

1 Introduction

Suppose we judge the fair and equitable treatment (FET) standard by the frequency of its invocation in investment treaty claims. In that case, it is no exaggeration to call the FET standard the most important substantive standard in the modern practice of international investment law. This is quite an achievement for a treaty provision that has seldom, if ever, been negotiated.[1] It is, moreover, quite a feat for a legal standard that witnessed almost no judicial and arbitral practice until less than thirty years ago. Of course, legal standards do not exist of their own accord. Whereas we often think of legal developments like we do people—birth, growing pains, maturity, settlement, and eventually retirement—it is more what people do with legal texts that matters. Texts and accumulated professional practice constrain what one can do with any legal concept. Yet, it is just as much about channelling the relevant actors' prevalent discursive frameworks, their social milieus, and the political economy of the field that shape the actual impact a legal standard achieves.

This chapter asks how a legal standard that played, at best, a supporting role for much of its history has become foreign investors' most popular weapon of choice in investment treaty arbitration and, not independently, the legal standard that arbitral tribunals have found most often in the breach.[2] To do so, the chapter will first revisit the debate about the origins of the FET standard. Then, it hones in on recent debates about the key elements of the standard. Here, the chapter discusses how the legal content of the standard has been construed in investor–state dispute settlement (ISDS) practice, with a view to identifying the pivotal moments of its interpretation and application. This

[1] Christoph Scheuer's expert statement in *Wintershall Aktiengesellschaft v Argentine Republic*, ICSID Case No ARB/04/14, Award (8 December 2008) [85].

[2] UNCTAD Investment Dispute Settlement Navigator lists an FET breach alleged in 592 out of 807 concluded cases in the database; breach was found in 167 out of the 592 cases. See https://investmentpolicy.unctad.org/investment-dispute-settlement.

Josef Ostřanský, *Fair and Equitable Treatment* In: *Rethinking Investment Law.* Edited by: David Schneiderman and Gus Van Harten, Oxford University Press. © Josef Ostřanský 2023. DOI: 10.1093/oso/9780192871084.003.0007

discussion focuses on the key elements of legitimate expectations, legal stability, arbitrariness, and transparency. Whereas other elements of FET have been identified in practice, these key ones have proven the most controversial. The chapter ends with an analysis of recent FET trends in both treaty-making and ISDS practice.

2 Another Origin Story? Fair and Equitable Treatment and the International Minimum Standard

Common accounts of the FET standard link it to the so-called minimum standard of treatment (MST).[3] Alongside the protection against uncompensated expropriation, the MST has long been part of the international law on the protection of aliens and on state responsibility.[4] It is considered a valid part of customary international law. The traditional content of the MST dealt with the administration of justice for foreigners, epitomized in the international rule against denial of justice.[5] The link between the MST and FET standard has been supported by occasional references to customary international law in FET provisions in bilateral investment treaties (BITs). Much ink was spilt over this link in the early 2000s international law scholarship and practice. There is little point in rehashing those discussions here.[6] It is acknowledged that the term was employed in mid-twentieth century US practice of concluding treaties on friendship, commerce, and navigation, and that much of its current content has been justified by analysing past practice in the application of the MST.[7] It must also be acknowledged that much of the content of customary

[3] See eg Martins Paparinskis, *The International Minimum Standard and Fair and Equitable Treatment* (OUP 2013); Rudolf Dolzer, Ursula Kriebaum, and Christoph Schreuer, *Principles of International Investment Law* (3rd edn, OUP 2022) 188–205. Also see Adeleke and Van Harten in this volume.

[4] See Perrone in this volume.

[5] Oliver J Lissitzyn, 'The Meaning of the Term Denial of Justice in International Law' (1936) 30 The American Journal of International Law 632; Edwin Borchard, 'The "Minimum Standard" of the Treatment of Aliens' (1939) 33 Proceedings of the American Society of International Law at Its Annual Meeting (1921–1969) 51; Jan Paulsson, *Denial of Justice in International Law* (CUP 2005); Paparinskis (n 3). Also see the discussion of denial of justice by Sattorova in this volume.

[6] Stephen Vasciannie, 'The Fair and Equitable Treatment Standard in International Investment Law and Practice' (2000) 70 British Yearbook of International Law 99; Rudolf Dolzer, 'Fair and Equitable Treatment: A Key Standard in Investment Treaties' (2005) 39 International Lawyer (ABA) 87; Rudolf Dolzer, 'Fair and Equitable Treatment: Today's Contours' (2013) 12 Santa Clara Journal of International Law 7; Christoph Schreurer, 'Fair and Equitable Treatment in Arbitral Practice' (2005) 6 Journal of World Investment & Trade 357; Kenneth J Vandevelde, 'A Unified Theory of Fair and Equitable Treatment' (2010) 43 New York University Journal of International Law and Politics 43; Paparinskis (n 3).

[7] See eg *Oil Platforms (Iran v US)* 1996 ICJ 803, 858 (December 12) (separate opinion of Judge Higgins); *Waste Management Inc (II) v United Mexican States*, ICSID Case No ARB AF/00/3 (30 April 2004); *Glamis Gold Ltd v United States of America*, UNCITRAL, Award (8 June 2009); NAFTA Free

international law on the protection of foreign property had been developed by a handful of mostly metropolitan states.[8] For present purposes, the most important point is that the modern practice of investment treaty arbitration has developed a far-reaching conception of FET that puts a premium on particular values most beneficial to the foreign investor.

Most of the current ISDS practice related to FET, specifically, and the protection of foreign investment, more generally, has a distinctive value framework. The framework projects a knee-jerk suspicion towards state intervention going beyond market inducement and correction of market failures.[9] It gives preference to the wealth maximization over other social and political functions of property.[10] It supports the state's maintenance of generalized competition.[11] It projects an idea of one-directional regulatory stability. For example, it condones or is indifferent towards regulatory changes that create possibilities for investors' capital accumulation ('regulatory givings'). At the same time, it rejects regulatory changes that limit capital accumulation in order to advance other societal goals ('regulatory takings').[12] Concomitant to this view is an understanding of state–investor relations as essentially transactional.[13] Finally, broader legalization and formal adjudication are framed as institutional vehicles for enforcing this economic constitution; specifically, a type

Trade Commission, Notes of Interpretation of Certain Chapter 11 Provisions (31 July 2001) http://www.sice.oas.org/tpd/nafta/commission/ch11understanding_e.asp.

[8] Jeffry A Friedman, 'International Investment and Colonial Control: A New Interpretation' (1994) 48 International Organization 559; James Gathii, 'War's Legacy in International Investment Law' (2009) 11 International Community Law Review 353; Kate Miles, *The Origins of International Investment Law: Empire, Environment and the Safeguarding of Capital* (CUP 2013); Kathryn Greenman, *State Responsibility and Rebels: The History and Legacy of Protecting Investment Against Revolution* (CUP 2021).

[9] Perrone documents how UNCTAD's narratives post-2008 crisis have been more sensitive to public regulation of investment for certain goals, but they still do not abandon the commodity conception of investment, let alone move towards the conception of investment which would reflect local preferences. Nicolás M Perrone, 'UNCTAD's World Investment Reports 1991–2015: 25 Years of Narratives Justifying and Balancing Foreign Investor Rights' (2018) 19 The Journal of World Investment & Trade 7.

[10] Nicolás M Perrone, 'The Emerging Global Right to Investment: Understanding the Reasoning behind Foreign Investor Rights' (2017) 8 Journal of International Dispute Settlement 673.

[11] Ntina Tzouvala, 'The Ordo-Liberal Origins of Modern International Investment Law: Constructing Competition on a Global Scale' in John D Haskell and Akbar Rasulov (eds), *New Voices and New Perspectives in International Economic Law* (Springer International Publishing 2020).

[12] Nicolás M Perrone, *Investment Treaties and the Legal Imagination: How Foreign Investors Play by Their Own Rules* (1st edn, OUP 2021); Akbar Rasulov, 'The Empty Circularity of Regulatory Takings: The Legacy of a Legal-realist Critique for a 21st Century Context' in Hugo Mattei and John Haskell (eds), *Research Handbook on Political Economy and Law* (Edward Elgar Publishing 2017); Josef Ostřanský, 'From a Fortuitous Transplant to a Fundamental Principle of Law? The Doctrine of Legitimate Expectations and the Possibilities of a Different Law' in Ingo Venzke and Kevin John Heller (eds), *Contingency in International Law: On the Possibility of Different Legal Histories* (OUP 2021).

[13] Perrone (n 12).

of adjudication that is transnational in its practice and spirit, abstracted from local contexts, and operated by people with a globalized outlook.

There is much to consider in the previous paragraph, and this chapter will gradually elaborate on the claims made. The immediate point is that—even though there are some constraints in the language of FET treaty provisions and some linkages with past, functionally similar, international law norms accepted by the community of international lawyers—there is little preordained in the way the standard is applied. Today's context matters just as much. I would wager that, regardless of the links with the MST and colonial heritage of international investment law, if investment treaty arbitration were invented today, the subsequent application of FET would be very different from its current application drawing on more than twenty years of arbitration practice since the 1990s. In other words, the link between the MST and FET is not at the heart of today's FET standard. The heart of FET now lies in this more recent arbitration practice. The policy-making trends I discuss towards the end of the chapter, which react to the recent arbitration practice regarding FET, hint at a possibility that what is taken in the social circles of investor–state arbitration as an established practice might be more of a strange and extravagant period of legal developments. No matter how strange and extravagant, it is this period that weighs most heavily on the minds of policy-makers today and that makes it so difficult to change course in the face of great threats to humanity.

3 The Content of FET: Key Elements and Pivotal Moments

As should be clear by now, the FET standard is not treated here as a more or less determinate legal artefact, the content of which can be elaborated by careful legal exegesis. I will highlight the main elements that ISDS practice considers part of the standard. Yet, I am also interested in how some of these elements came into being within specific parameters. In this sense, I will consider the legal texts but also the people and events that produced them.

The typical wording of the FET standard in many 1990s BITs says something along these lines:

> Investments of nationals or companies of each Contracting Party *shall at all times be accorded fair and equitable treatment* and shall enjoy full protection and security in the territory of the other Contracting Party.[14]

[14] Albania–United Kingdom BIT (1995) art 2 (emphasis added).

> Each Contracting Party *shall ensure fair and equitable treatment within its territory of the Investments of the Investors* of the other Contracting Party.[15]
>
> Each Contracting State shall in its territory promote as far as possible investments by nationals or companies of the other Contracting State and admit such investments in accordance with its legislation. *It shall, in any case, accord such investments fair and equitable treatment.*[16]
>
> *Each Contracting Party shall ensure fair and equitable treatment to investments of investors of the other Contracting Party* and shall not impair, by unreasonable or discriminatory measures, the operation, management, maintenance, use, enjoyment or disposal thereof by those investors.[17]

A few points can be highlighted about the above excerpts. First, the text does not give much guidance on the standard's legal content, leaving arbitrators with a great deal of interpretative latitude. Secondly, the standard is often listed in the same provision as other legal standards—eg alongside promotion obligations as in the Bahrain–German BIT, the full protection and security standard like in the Albania–UK BIT, or together with the prohibition of arbitrary and discriminatory measures as in the Argentine–Dutch BIT. ISDS practice has generally considered these other standards as separate but overlapping with FET. Third, more recent treaty practice has sought to provide more precision in the legal content of FET or even to omit the standard altogether. These steps respond to the interpretative leeway left by earlier BITs to arbitral tribunals.[18]

Although the FET's precise contours and normative content are not entirely clear and still debated, it seems that certain statements about its juridical content, derived from arbitral practice, can be accepted with a fair degree of certainty:

- It is an absolute standard, connoting a minimum threshold.
- It is not limited to bad-faith conduct, ie it is an 'objective standard'.[19]

However, these statements do not get us far in ascertaining the legal content of FET, let alone in assessing how it will be applied to the facts of any case. There

[15] Poland–Switzerland BIT (1993) art 4.2 (emphasis added).
[16] Bahrain–Germany (2010) art. 2.1 (emphasis added).
[17] Argentina–Netherlands BIT (2008) art 3.1 (emphasis added).
[18] See section 4.1 Recent Treaty Practice below.
[19] The idea is that the adjudicator assesses the state's conduct based on its factual manifestations without searching for or regard to the intention of the conduct's author.

have been numerous scholarly attempts to define FET by reference to a unifying principle, such as good faith, the rule of law, good governance, or justice.[20] All of these approaches are problematic, and none is entirely coherent.[21] Hence it is better to approach the FET standard as having several elements of investment protection. Even here, however, scholars and practitioners do not agree on what elements are validly included.

Scholarly accounts often reached different conclusions about the content of FET depending on their methodology. For instance, according to Dolzer, Kriebaum, and Schreuer, FET protects stability and legitimate expectations, transparency, compliance with contractual obligations, procedural propriety and due process, good faith, and freedom from coercion and harassment.[22] Bonnitcha's functional division includes legitimate expectations, procedural aspects, the examination of substantive justifications, and discrimination.[23] Paparinskis's traditional doctrinal method leads him to divide the content of FET into administration of justice and protection of property, with the latter further including non-arbitrariness, due process, transparency, non-discrimination, good faith, and respect for legitimate expectations.[24] For their parts, both arbitral practice and treaty-making are inconsistent and thus do not support any stable and clearly ascertainable meaning. For this reason, the rest of this section focuses on the FET elements that have proven most controversial in ISDS practice, scholarship, and policy-making. As mentioned above, these are legitimate expectations, legal stability, arbitrariness, and transparency.

[20] Todd Grierson-Weiler and I Liard, 'Standards of Treatment' in Petr Muchlinski, Federico Ortino, and Christoph Schreuer (eds), *The Oxford Handbook of International Investment Law* (OUP 2008) 272; Dolzer (n 7) 91; Kenneth Vandevelde, 'A Unified Theory of Fair and Equitable Treatment' 43 (2010) NYU Journal of International Law and Politics 43, 49; Stephan W Schill, 'Fair and Equitable Treatment, the Rule of Law, and Comparative Public Law' in Stephan W Schill (ed), *International Investment Law and Comparative Public Law* (OUP 2010) 151; Roland Kläger, *Fair and Equitable Treatment in International Investment Law* (CUP 2013) 153.

[21] Bonnitcha argues that good faith fails to explain the FET as an objective standard not dependent on whether respondent acted in good faith; the rule of law, itself a contestable concept, fails to explain why a reasoned change in policy arrived at through lawful and reasoned procedures can violate the FET; and finally, justice, an inherently contestable concept, fails to explain many aspects of arbitral practice, such as the protection of expectations or why distributive social welfare objectives, a typical objectives of any theory of justice, do not play role in arbitral decision-making. See Jonathan Bonnitcha, *Substantive Protection under Investment Treaties: A Legal and Economic Analysis* (CUP 2014) 164.

[22] Dolzer, Kriebaum, and Schreurer (n 3) 186–295.

[23] Bonnitcha (n 21) 166.

[24] Paparinskis (n 3) 181–259.

3.1 Legitimate Expectations

The concept of legitimate expectations features in all accounts of FET over the last two decades.[25] Despite numerous scholarly accounts justifying the emergence of a legitimate expectations doctrine as a logical application of investment treaties, its emergence appears highly dependent on the recent history. From the ISDS practice on legitimate expectations, it is clear that the doctrine became part of investment law by a rather fortuitous reference to 'expectations' in early investment treaty arbitration cases. These early cases described the investor's expectations, but only in a non-technical sense. They did not elaborate any legal justifications for the relevance of the investor's expectations, apart from a general reference to good faith. Nevertheless, later cases and scholarship elevated this early case law to a status of legal authority that then gave an ex post juridical justification for the doctrine.

The first investment treaty case that referred to investors' expectations was *Metalclad v Mexico*. In this well-known NAFTA arbitration, the investor's purchase of a waste management company and its unclear landfill rights ended in the denial of municipal permits and other approvals, despite alleged (and oral) federal assurances. The tribunal in that case held the state to this exacting standard:

> [A]ll relevant requirements should be capable of being readily known to all affected investors ... there should be no room for doubt or uncertainty ... Once central authorities become aware of any scope of uncertainty in this connection, it is their duty to ensure that the correct position is properly determined ... Metalclad was entitled to rely on the representations of federal officials and to believe that it was entitled to continue its construction of the landfill ... Metalclad was merely acting prudently and in the full expectation that the permit would be granted.[26]

This statement by the tribunal has since been taken to support the sweeping proposition that legitimate expectations exist whenever a state official advises an investor on the content of law, even requiring officials to dispel possible

[25] This section draws on Ostřanský (n 12); Josef Ostřanský, 'An Exercise in Equivocation: A Critique of Legitimate Expectations as a General Principle of Law under the Fair and Equitable Treatment Standard' in Andrea Gattini, Attila Tanzi, and Filippo Fontanelli (eds), *General Principles of Law and International Investment Arbitration* (Brill Nijhoff 2018).

[26] *Metalclad Corporation v The United Mexican States*, ICSID Case No ARB AF/97/1, Award (30 August 2000) [76], [89].

uncertainties. As Campbell has observed, one can hardly think of a commercial or administrative relationship—other than where a body is tasked with providing an official, authoritative interpretation—where one party must act as legal counsel to the other, and in which that other party can rely wholly on the advice.[27] The tribunal seemed to assume that an investor's entitlement to have expectations protected stems from the subjective expectation itself. According to the tribunal, this entitlement was required implicitly by the NAFTA states' obligations of transparency, which were taken, again implicitly, to be part of FET.[28]

The *Metalclad* arbitrators were high calibre. The tribunal's president was Elihu Lauterpacht, a towering figure in international law, and the wing arbitrators, too, were of important stature and reputation. Benjamin Civiletti was a former US Attorney General who appeared before the International Court of Justice in the *Tehran Hostages* case.[29] José Luis Siqueiros, a late professor at Universidad Iberoamericana in Mexico, was a former President of the Inter-American Juridical Committee of the Organization of American States.[30] Lauterpacht, in particular, left an important legacy in the field of international investment law. Among other things, he was a crucial figure in the drafting of important twentieth-century documents aimed at codification of international investment law, such as the Abs-Shawcross Draft on Protection of Foreign Investment and OECD Draft Convention on Investment Abroad.[31] His ideas, informed by the experience of the nationalization of Anglo–Iranian Oil Company in the 1950s, contributed in important ways to creating the modern mechanism of treaty-based investor–state arbitration and to the emergence of umbrella clauses.[32] Serving as a president of the World Bank Administrative

[27] Christian Campbell, 'House of Cards: The Relevance of Legitimate Expectations under Fair and Equitable Treatment Provisions in Investment Treaty Law' (2013) 30 Journal of International Arbitration 361, 366.

[28] Interestingly, the decision was partly annulled on the grounds that the NAFTA Chapter 11 does not include a stand-alone obligation of transparency, which the tribunal read into art 1105 (FET) via reference to art 102(1). *The United Mexican States v Metalclad Corp* [2001] BCSC 664 (Supreme Court of British Columbia, 2 May 2001).

[29] 'Remembering Former U.S. Attorney General Benjamin Civiletti' *Maryland State Bar Association* (21 October 2022) https://www.msba.org/remembering-benjamin-civiletti/; United States Diplomatic and Consular Staff in Tehran *(United States of America v Iran)*, Verbatim Record [1979], Oral Arguments on the Request for the Indication of Provisional Measures, Minutes of the Public Sittings 15.

[30] International Council for Commercial Arbitration, https://www.arbitration-icca.org/jose-luis-siqueiros-1924-2020.

[31] Yuliya Chernykh, 'The Gust of Wind: The Unknown Role of Sir Elihu Lauterpacht in the Drafting of the Abs-Shawcross Draft Convention' in Stefan Schill and others (eds), *International Investment Law and History* (Edward Elgar Publishing 2018) 241; Squire Law Library, 'Eminent Scholars Archive, Sir Elihu Lauterpacht' www.squire.law.cam.ac.uk/eminent-scholars-archive/professor-sir-elihu-lauterpacht.

[32] Chernykh (n 31); Anthony Sinclair, 'The Origins of the Umbrella Clause in the International Law of Investment Protection' (2004) 20 Arbitration International 411.

Tribunal from 1996 to 1998, he decided cases based on a notion of legitimate expectations, although in an entirely different legal and adjudicative context.[33] Importantly, however, besides its passing reference to investors' expectations, the tribunal did not apply anything resembling a doctrine, principle, or rule of legitimate expectations from any existing source of law.

The second case alluding to expectations also dealt with the denial (and, more specifically, revocation) of a landfill operating permit in Mexico.[34] In *Tecmed v Mexico*, the tribunal effectively divined a standard that has since been criticized as an idealized demand for good, not to say near-perfect, governance.[35] Similar to *Metalclad*, the concept of legitimate expectations was not even applied in the case, as the tribunal found an FET violation based on procedural propriety.[36] Even so, a far-reaching conception of legitimate expectations, once again unsupported by any authority beyond the principle of good faith, has been taken from this statement:

> [Good] faith principle established by international law requires the Contracting Parties to provide to international investments treatment that does not affect the basic expectations that were taken into account by the foreign investor to make the investment. The foreign investor expects the host State to act in a consistent manner, free from ambiguity and totally transparently in its relations with the foreign investor, so that it may know beforehand any and all rules and regulations that will govern its investments, as well as

[33] See eg *Joseph Lopez v IBRD*, WBAT Decision No 147 (14 May 1996). The case dealt with the question of whether Lopez's service was properly terminated by the bank for unsatisfactory performance. Lauterpacht and others found that the delay of the bank's review of Lopez's objection 'infringed upon his procedural rights and his legitimate expectation to have a speedy disposition of his complaints (para 54)'. As a side note, one of the vice presidents of the tribunal deciding on the *Lopez* case was the late Francisco Orrego Vicuña, who later became an important arbitrator in many investor–state treaty disputes and one of the early scholars justifying reference to legitimate expectations in arbitral practice; Francisco Orrego Vicuña, 'Regulatory Authority and Legitimate Expectations: Balancing the Rights of the State and the Individual under International Law in a Global Society' (2003) 5 International Law FORUM du droit international 188.

[34] *Técnicas Medioambientales Tecmed SA v The United Mexican States*, ICSID Case No ARB AF/00/2, Award (29 May 2003). Composition of the *Tecmed* tribunal was also interesting. The tribunal was presided by the former Secretary General of the ICC Court of Arbitration, an expert in private international law and commercial arbitration, Argentine professor Horacio Grigera Naón. The other two arbitrators were José Carlos Fernandez Rosa, professor of private international law at Universidad Complutense in Madrid and later a member of l'Institut de droit international, and Carlos Bernal Verea, a private practitioner in Mexico, who later became a professor at ITAM in Mexico City—one of the most elite private educational institutions in Mexico known for its close links with US neoclassical economics and the training of economically minded lawyers.

[35] Zachary Douglas, 'Nothing if Not Critical for Investment Treaty Arbitration: Occidental, Eureko and Methanex' (2006) 22 Arbitration International 27.

[36] ibid 28.

> the goals of the relevant policies and administrative practices or directives, to be able to plan its investment and comply with such regulations.[37]

This sweeping dictum, and that in *Metalclad*, were subsequently adopted by later tribunals and elevated to a status of legal authority for a doctrine of legitimate expectations.[38] Neither of the early tribunals had invoked such a doctrine themselves, but merely used the term expectations in describing the investors' ultimate disappointment.

It was not until *Thunderbird v Mexico* that a 'doctrine' of legitimate expectations was applied in investment treaty arbitration.[39] The *Thunderbird* tribunal, particularly in Wälde's lengthy separate opinion, gave a nod to *Tecmed* and *Metalclad* and then went to great lengths to portray legitimate expectations as a general principle of law. The tribunal's president was Albert Jan van den Berg, a renowned expert on the New York Convention with an extensive practice in commercial and investment arbitration, with Agustín Portal Ariosa, a Mexican private practitioner who had worked for the Mexican government, and the late Thomas Wälde as co-arbitrators. Wälde was a prominent if enigmatic figure in investment treaty arbitration during its initial emergence as a field of practice. He was a former UN Inter-Regional Adviser on Petroleum and Mineral Legislation, a seasoned UN official, and an international law practitioner and academic who had worked with Detlev Vagts, Richard Baxter, and Rosalyn Higgins. He came to prominence in the investment law community upon creating important platforms for exchange of opinions among the constituencies that were interested in investment law and arbitration. Institutionally, he set up the Centre for Energy, Petroleum and Mineral Law and Policy at the University of Dundee. Most importantly, he established the OGEMID, an ongoing and influential listserv which connects actors in the emerging, mostly investor-side, community of practitioners and academics.[40] Similarly, he was an active commentator on investment and oil and gas law in the *Transnational*

[37] *Tecmed v Mexico* (n 34) [154].

[38] See eg *Bayindir Insaat Turizm Ticaret Ve Sanayi AS v Islamic Republic of Pakistan*, ICSID Case No ARB/03/29, Award (27 August 2009) [179]–[80]; *MTD Equity Sdn Bhd and MTD Chile SA v Republic of Chile*, ICSID Case No ARB/01/7, Award (25 May 2004) [114]–[115]; *LG&E Energy Corp, LG&E Capital Corp, and LG&E International Inc v Argentine Republic*, ICSID Case No ARB/02/1, Decision on Liability (3 October 2006) [127]; *Saluka Investments BV v Czech Republic*, UNCITRAL, Partial Award (17 March 2006) [302].

[39] *International Thunderbird Gaming Corporation v The United Mexican States*, UNCITRAL, Award (26 January 2006).

[40] 'About OGEMID' www.transnational-dispute-management.com/ogemid/.

Dispute Management (TDM) online journal.[41] Thus, Wälde had created influential early venues for the exchange of information and perspectives among like-minded actors who were interested in the field.

In his separate opinion in *Thunderbird*, Wälde argued boldly that legitimate expectations are a 'self-standing subcategory and independent basis for a claim'.[42] His comparative review of EU law, national administrative law systems, and WTO jurisprudence led him to postulating the existence and validity of a doctrine of legitimate expectations under investment treaties. While he admitted that the doctrine's exact contours were not yet clear, Wälde claimed that international law had long applied such a doctrine in the manner of that now deployed by modern investment tribunals.[43]

On closer examination, Wälde's references have little in common with the conception of legitimate expectations we know today in ISDS. For instance, his reference to the 1930s era arbitration in *Schufeldt* did not actually address an illegal contract later reneged on; this point had merely been a defence put forward by Guatemala. The *Schufeldt* arbitrator held the disputed contract to be valid and the state's repudiation decree to be an internationally unlawful sovereign interference in a contract.[44] Similarly, *Aminoil* and *Amoco* only referred to legitimate expectations as a descriptive consideration in the calculation of damages in order to help estimate a reasonably foreseeable profit.

However, around the time *Thunderbird* was decided in 2006, investment law scholars—many of them also practitioners in the field—began publishing articles that sought to explain and justify the application of legitimate expectations as a valid doctrine in investment law.[45] Some spoke of the doctrine as a 'logical and practical necessity'.[46] As it happened, by the 2010s legitimate expectations had been established as the single-most important aspect of FET,

[41] For an impressive list of his commentaries and short articles spanning a wide range of topics related to investment law and arbitration published in TDM see www.transnational-dispute-management.com/journal-author-articles.asp?key=6.

[42] *Thunderbird v Mexico* (n 39) Separate Opinion of Thomas Wälde [37].

[43] He referred to *Shufeldt Claim* (Guatemala, USA), [1949] UNRIAA 2 (24 July 1930) 1079; *Kuwait v The American Independent Oil Company (AMINOIL)* (1982) 21 ILM 976 [149]; *Amoco Intl Finance Corp v Iran* (1987) 15 IRAN-US CTR 189.

[44] *Schufeldt Claim* (n 43) 1088. Alternatively, the circumstances of the *Schufeldt* case may be viewed as an example of estoppel precluding Guatemala's defence of illegality; Derek Bowett, 'Estoppel before International Tribunals and Its Relation to Acquiescence' (1957) 33 British Yearbook of International Law 176, 186.

[45] See eg Vicuña (n 33); Elizabeth Snodgrass, 'Protecting Investors' Legitimate Expectations: Recognizing and Delimiting a General Principle' (2006) 21 ICSID Review 1; Michele Potestà, '*Legitimate Expectations* in Investment Treaty Law: Understanding the Roots and the Limits of a Controversial Concept' (2013) 28 ICSID Review 88.

[46] Snodgrass (n 45) 54–56.

one that arguably has swallowed the bulk of substantive international investment law.[47] Yet, most of the legal justifications for the doctrine suffered from deep flaws and inconsistencies and left many unanswered questions.[48] Commentators have pointed to the dubious juridical basis for applying legitimate expectations at all in the investment context.[49] More muted criticism has recognized the inconsistencies of applying such a doctrine under the rubric of FET, while admitting that they have become embedded in arbitral practice.[50]

Therefore, despite its contingent and, one might have thought, fleeting references in early awards, legitimate expectations are now an established and powerful weapon for claimants in investment disputes. Little more than mentioning of the word 'expectations' by a few influential international lawyers, joined eventually by superficial analogies to domestic administrative law, made the concept of legitimate expectations look natural and practically automatic for modern investment law practice. Now, some twenty years later, tribunals still apply an expansive understanding of legitimate expectations in ISDS cases. Moreover, they do so even as policy-makers have been trying hard to eliminate the doctrine from the investment law repertoire in a new generation of investment treaties.[51] As just one illustration, the raft of investment claims against reforms of renewable energy subsidies in Spain, Italy, and the Czech Republic have proven that the doctrine is alive and well. Thus, the emergence of this doctrine, while historically contingent, continues to weigh heavily on the present and foreseeable future of the investment treaty regime.

3.2 Legal Stability and Predictability

Another creative element found in ISDS application of the FET standard is the requirement for a state to maintain stability and predictability in its legal framework. This profound obligation is said to derive from the vague concept of FET as read in the light of aspirational language in treaty preambles.[52] Some

[47] See eg *Electrabel SA v Republic of Hungary*, ICSID Case No ARB/07/19, Decision on Jurisdiction, Applicable Law and Liability (30 November 2012) [7.75]: 'It is widely accepted that the most important function of the fair and equitable treatment standard is the protection of the investor's reasonable and legitimate expectations.'

[48] See Ostřanský (n 25).

[49] See eg Campbell (n 27).

[50] Paparinskis (n 3) 259.

[51] See section 4 below. Recent Treaty-making and Arbitral Practice.

[52] See eg *Toto Costruzioni Generali SpA v Republic of Lebanon*, ICSID Case No ARB/07/12, Award (7 June 2012) [224]; *LG&E v Argentina* (n 38) [125]; *Bayindir Insaat Turizm Ticaret Ve Sanayi AS v Islamic Republic of Pakistan*, ICSID Case No ARB/03/29, Award (27 August 2009) [178], [240]; *Duke Energy Electroquil Partners & Electroquil SA v Republic of Ecuador*, ICSID Case No ARB/04/19, Award (18

tribunals have also connected the requirement of legal stability to the similarly far-reaching doctrine of legitimate expectations.[53]

In ISDS practice, the legal stability requirement can be attributed to the early case of *Occidental (I) v Ecuador*. The tribunal in this case was chaired by Francisco Orrego Vicuña, who presided over many ISDS tribunals in claims against Argentina after its economic crisis of 2001 and was an important figure in the promotion of an expansive version of, among other investor-friendly concepts, the legitimate expectations doctrine.[54] Another such figure, Charles Brower served as a party-appointed arbitrator alongside (for the state) Patrick Barrera Sweeney. In pushing the boundaries of FET, the tribunal expressed its confidence that 'under international law ... there is certainly an obligation not to alter the legal and business environment in which the investment has been made'.[55] Indeed, it was so sure of the existence of such a sweeping duty of states that it saw no need to cite any authority at all in support of the assertion. Yet, the notion of stability of a legal or environment for doing business is better understood as an aspiration that motivated capital-exporting states in their lopsided push for BITs in the era of decolonization. As a doctrine of international law, however, it is very hard to sustain. The general rule under customary international law is that business conditions are fleeting.[56] This general rule clearly could not be displaced by the vague phrasing of FET. Without a more specifically contracted stabilization clause, legal stability is a hard fit within the law of FET.

Many early cases that used FET to construct the 'stability obligation' were based on the US–Argentina BIT of 1991. This treaty mentions, in its preamble, the importance of FET in maintaining stability: 'Agreeing that fair and equitable treatment of investment is desirable in order to maintain a stable framework for investment and maximum effective use of economic resources.'[57] On

August 2008) [339]; *Occidental Exploration and Production Company v Republic of Ecuador (I)*, LCIA Case No UN3467, Award (1 July 2004) [183]–[186]; *Saluka v Czech Republic* (n 38) [302].

[53] Stability was connected with legitimate expectations explicitly in eg *Duke v Ecuador* (n 52) [339]; *Bayindir v Pakistan* (n 52) [240]; *Occidental (I) v Ecuador* (n 52) [183]–[186]; *LG&E v Argentina* (n 52) [137]; *Saluka v Czech Republic* (n 38) [302]; *MTD v Chile* (n 38) [113].

[54] Vicuña (n 33).

[55] *Occidental (I) v Ecuador* (n 52) [191].

[56] *Oscar Chinn*, PCIJ, A/B63, Judgment of 12 December 1934, 88; *George W Cook (USA) v United Mexican States* (1930) vol IV, RIAA 593, 594; *Toto v Lebanon* [242]–[244], *Parkerings-Compagniet AS v Republic of Lithuania*, ICSID Case No ARB/05/8, Award (11 September 2007) [335]–[336]; *El Paso Energy International Company v Argentine Republic*, ICSID Case No ARB/03/15, Award (31 October 2011) [374]–[375], [394].

[57] *CMS Gas Transmission Company v Republic of Argentina*, ICSID Case No ARB/01/8, Award (12 May 2005) [284]; *LG&E v Argentina* (n 38) [124]; *BG Group Plc v Republic of Argentina*, UNCITRAL, Award (24 December 2007) [307].

this basis, can one credibly say that a specific obligation of legal or regulatory stability was meant to be part of the FET treaty obligation itself? The answer is no. Under the Vienna Convention's rules of treaty interpretation, aspirational statements in a preamble may be taken to reflect a policy goal, but they do not set out binding obligations. One may hope that FET will contribute to more stability, but hopes are not the same as obligations. Indeed, the expression of a preambular aspiration itself demonstrates the intention to separate the ideal of legal stability from whatever is considered obligatory under FET.

Very few investment treaties include this preambular reference to legal stability. Apart from US BITs, such references seem to be almost exclusively found in Japanese and Finnish treaty practice.[58] Turkish investment treaties also link FET to the ideal of a stable investment framework, but again only as a preambular aspiration.[59] Some newer treaties mention stability, predictability, and favourable investment conditions in a separate introductory provision on treaty 'objectives'. Apart from these relatively few contexts, the notion of legal stability is found only in treaty exceptions for prudential measures to stabilize a state's financial system, particularly in Canadian and Japanese practice.[60]

Some tribunals have gone so far as to derive an obligation to deliver legal stability from the free-floating principle of good faith, without requiring any specific text to that effect in the treaty.[61] That said, and to be fair, other (more recent) tribunals have qualified the blanket statements on legal stability by noting that the implying of such an obligation from statements about legitimate expectations, and therefore FET 'may not be correct if stated in an overly broad and unqualified formulation'.[62] Alternatively, they have offered the modest qualification that, while stability can inform the interpretation of specific obligations (like FET), it should not be used as an independent legal

[58] Treaties for the Protection and Promotion of Investment between Japan and Oman, Ukraine, Uruguay, Kazakhstan, Myanmar, Mozambique, Iraq; Treaties for the Protection and Promotion of Investment between Finland and Mauritius, Mongolia, Georgia, Jordan, Belarus, Ethiopia, Zambia, Armenia, Ukraine.

[59] Treaties for the Protection and Promotion of Investment between Turkey and Gambia 2013, Pakistan 2012, Cameroon, Bangladesh, Azerbaijan, Tanzania, Senegal, Kuwait, Slovakia, Singapore. The Turkish practice is in this way similar to the Energy Charter Treaty, art 10, which mentions the stability *desideratum* in art 10, as opposed to Turkish treaties where it retains a separate form in the preamble.

[60] Treaties for the Protection and Promotion of Investment between Canada and Mali, Senegal, Burkina Faso, Serbia, Nigeria, Cameroon, Benin; Treaties between Japan and Kazakhstan, Ukraine, Mongolia, Myanmar, Mozambique, Iraq.

[61] See the discussion above on *Tecmed v Mexico* (n 34); *Metalclad v Mexico* (n 26); *Occidental (I) v Ecuador* (n 52).

[62] *EDF (Services) Limited v Romania*, ICSID Case No ARB/05/13, Award (8 October 2009) [217]; *Saluka v Czech Republic* (n 38) [304]; *Mamidoil Jetoil Greek Petroleum Products Societe SA v Republic of Albania*, ICSID Case No ARB/11/24, Award (30 March 2015) [625]–[629].

concept.[63] For example, the tribunal in *Continental* distanced itself relatively clearly from treating legal stability as an autonomous obligation. Its statement captures the limitations of the original leaps of reasoning by earlier tribunals:

> The stability of the legal framework for investments is mentioned in the Preamble of the BIT. It is not a legal obligation in itself for the Contracting Parties, nor can it be properly defined as an object of the Treaty ... Stability of the legal framework is undoubtedly conducive to attracting foreign investments, especially direct investments where business plans can extend over a number of years; and even more so in respect of those where initial investments are substantial and are recouped only over a long period of time. On the other hand, it would be unconscionable for a country to promise not to change its legislation as time and needs change, or even more to tie its hands by such a kind of stipulation in case a crisis of any type or origin arose. Such an implication as to stability in the BIT's Preamble would be contrary to an effective interpretation of the Treaty; reliance on such an implication by a foreign investor would be misplaced and, indeed, unreasonable.[64]

Accepting this position, the concept of legal stability is unhelpful as a source of guidance let alone as an obligation. The above statement also indicates that, if one accepted the concept as somehow binding, it would be near-impossible for states to operationalize. In turn, if one accepts—as most ISDS tribunals now appear to do—that the notion of legal stability does not require states to forego their regulatory powers—then what is point of asserting it? Put differently, if it is accepted that states can still change and amend their laws, how does a requirement of stability help with the analysis and resolution of any particular case?[65] Clearly something more, such as arbitrariness, than merely change would be needed to establish a treaty violation Yet, the treaties already have obligations to check arbitrary abuse of state power. Moreover, if states are not permitted arbitrarily to modify any of their laws and regulations, is that not itself effectively a self-standing obligation of stability?[66] The key problem with

[63] *Philip Morris Brands Sàrl, Philip Morris Products SA and Abal Hermanos SA v Oriental Republic of Uruguay*, ICSID Case No ARB/10/7, Award (8 July 2016) [426]; *Charanne and Construction Investments v Spain*, SCC Case No V 062/2012, Award (21 January 2016) [492], [499]; *EnCana v Ecuador*, LCIA Case No UN3481, Award (3 February 2006) [173] (in the context of indirect expropriation).

[64] *Continental Casualty Company v Argentine Republic*, ICSID Case No ARB/03/9, Award (5 September 2008) [258].

[65] *CMS v Argentina* (n 57) [284]; *LG&E v Argentina* (n 38) [124]; *BG v Argentina* (n 57) [304]–[307]; *Philip Morris v Uruguay* (n 63) [423].

[66] This distinction was well articulated in *TECO Guatemala Holdings LLC v Republic of Guatemala*, ICSID Case No ARB/10/23, Award (19 December 2013) [617]–[619].

the whole line of reasoning on legal stability is that it reverses the customary international law position that regulatory stability is ephemeral, and 'change is the rule', into the position that change is exceptional and 'stability is the rule'.[67] By extension, any exercise of the usual regulatory role of states is viewed with suspicion. In reversing the international legal position on the role of the state, ISDS tribunals have prioritized, at the most fundamental level, the investor's perspective. In doing so, they have lost sight of the role that investment is supposed to play in any economy and society.

Not all tribunals have taken such an erroneous turn in the expansion of FET obligations in investment law. Some have more realistically underscored that regulations cannot be separated from general business conditions, considering that regulations and business conditions are interconnected and co-created by the state.[68] An investor must accept that regulations evolve as a matter of course. Investors have a duty of due diligence to learn and comply with them. It is the state's duty to act consistently, to abide by due process, to avoid substantive arbitrariness, and to honour specific commitments, all with an acceptance of the need for reasonableness or other qualifications. One important contextualizing factor is the conditions of the host state, including its economic and political volatility. Investment treaties should not seek to eliminate political risk for investors by imposing a blanket obligation of legal stability.

3.3 Arbitrariness and Reasonableness

Less controversial elements of FET are concerned mostly with the procedural and formal characteristics of governmental regulatory action (due process, transparency, non-discrimination). More controversial ones, including legitimate expectations, legal stability, and protections against arbitrariness, reach into the substantive characteristics of regulatory action. The latter notion of arbitrariness, in the sense of its prohibition, has been accepted as part and parcel of international law without much objection.[69] Nevertheless, this does not mean that the incorporation of the notion into FET has been straightforward.

[67] The customary international law rule was specified in eg *Oscar Chinn* (n 56) 88; *George W. Cook v Mexico* (n 56) 594.

[68] See eg *Methanex Corp v US*, Final Award on Jurisdiction and Merits (3 August 2005), Part IV, Ch D [9]–[10]; *Sergei Paushok, CJSC Golden East Company and CJSC Vostokneftegaz Company v The Government of Mongolia*, UNCITRAL, Award on Jurisdiction and Liability (28 April 2011) [302]; *Charanne v Spain* (n 63) [507]; *Bayindir* (n 38) [193].

[69] See eg Frederick Alexander Mann, 'British Treaties for the Promotion and Protection of Investments' (1981) 52 British Yearbook of International Law 241, 243.

International legal discussion of arbitrariness generally starts with a reference to the ICJ Chamber's decision in *ELSI*. The relevant parts of this classic statement warrant quotation in full:

> [T]he fact that an act of a public authority may have been unlawful in municipal law does not necessarily mean that that act was unlawful in international law, as a breach of treaty or otherwise. *A finding of the local courts that an act was unlawful may well be relevant to an argument that it was also arbitrary; but by itself, and without more, unlawfulness cannot be said to amount to arbitrariness.* It would be absurd if measures later quashed by higher authority or a superior court could, for that reason, be said to have been arbitrary in the sense of international law. To identify arbitrariness with mere unlawfulness would be to deprive it of any useful meaning in its own right. *Nor does it follow from a finding by a municipal court that an act was unjustified, or unreasonable, or arbitrary, that that act is necessarily to be classed as arbitrary in international law*, though the qualification given to the impugned act by a municipal authority may be a valuable indication ... arbitrariness is not so much something opposed to a rule of law, as *something opposed to the rule of law*. This idea was expressed by the Court in the Asylum case, when it spoke of 'arbitrary action' being 'substituted for the rule of law'. It is a wilful *disregard of due process of law*, an act which *shocks, or at least surprises, a sense of juridical propriety*.[70]

The quote captures a wealth of vital considerations in relation to arbitrariness and its potential relevance to FET. First, domestic legality is a relevant consideration in the review of arbitrariness. Even so, unlawfulness under municipal law is not determinative. Secondly, since mere illegality is not enough ('not so much something opposed to a rule of law'), the conduct must reach a higher threshold of something akin to systemic failure ('something opposed to the rule of law'). Thirdly, procedural review is an important part of review for arbitrariness. Finally, in the *ELSI* conception of arbitrariness, there is an element of shock or surprise. It is particularly this last element that has been criticized as lacking analytical rigour and, instead, presenting a

[70] *Elettronica Sicula SpA (ELSI) (United States of America v Italy)* (Judgment) [1989] ICJ Rep 15 (20 July 1989) [125], [128] (citations omitted, emphasis added).

subjective test.[71] Yet, this aspect still finds some support in investment arbitration case law.[72]

Arbitrariness is closely connected to reasonableness, which may be viewed as its flipside: what is not arbitrary is reasonable. Of course, one may challenge this articulation as too broad. In different legal systems, when conduct or decision is not characterized as arbitrary, it does not necessarily follow that the conduct or decision were reasonable. Depending on the domestic legal system, the notion of arbitrariness may assume wider or narrower parameters. For example, arbitrariness may refer to situations in which a decision-maker considered irrelevant factors or failed to consider relevant ones.[73] Reasonableness may also itself be an exacting standard depending on the domestic law. For example, it may require a measure to be necessary for a particular purpose; in other words, it may require the least restrictive impact on particular rights or interests or, simply that a decision be substantively adequate and correct.

Regarding reasonableness, its core meaning, it has been noted that its assessment cannot be achieved by a merely technical or dogmatic approach since the word encapsulates a profound ambiguity whereby 'what is reasonable depends on its circumstances'.[74] This problematic aspect of what is reasonable may be extended to the whole question of the meaning of FET.[75] Corten has remarked that reasonableness reflects a 'contradiction between the essentially static character of legal texts and the dynamic character of the reality to which they apply'.[76] This underlying tension gives reason to pause in the face of the stringent requirements of legitimate expectations and legal stability, as interpreted by ISDS tribunals, alongside the imprecision of the notion of

71 See eg Kurt J Hamrock, 'The ELSI Case: Toward an International Definition of "Arbitrary" Conduct' (1992) 27 Texas International Law Journal 837, 849; Jacob Stone, 'Arbitrariness, the Fair and Equitable Treatment Standard, and the International Law of Investment' (2012) 25 Leiden Journal of International Law 77, 89. Of note is similarity between this subjective criterion and the presumption criterion in the famous *Wednesbury* rationality test: 'is it a decision which no reasonable decision-maker in its right mind would take?'; *Associated Provincial Picture Houses Ltd v Wednesbury Corporation* [1948] 1 KB 223.

72 See eg *Mamidoil* (n 62) [769]; *Cargill Incorporated v United Mexican States*, ICSID Case No ARB AF/05/2, Award (18 September 2009) [296]; investment cases distance themselves from the *ELSI* dictum not on the basis of this subjective nature, but because they claim that the level of shock or outrage is not required by the FET, thus they reject it based on a degree, not on its nature. See eg *Eureko BV v Republic of Poland*, Partial Award (19 August 2005) [234]; *Pope & Talbot Inc v Government of Canada*, Award on the Merits, Phase 2 (10 April 2001) [118].

73 See eg *Associated Provincial Picture Houses Ltd v Wednesbury Corporation* [1948] 1 KB 223; 5 'Administrative Procedure Act', U.S. Code § 706(2)A – 'Scope of review'.

74 *Continental Shelf (Tunisia/Libyan Arab Jamahiriya)* (Judgment) [1982] ICJ Rep 18, 46 [72].

75 *Saluka* (n 38) [284]; *Sempra Energy International v Argentine Republic*, ICSID Case No ARB/02/16, Award (28 September 2007) [296]; *British Caribbean Bank Limited v The Government of Belize*, PCA Case No 2010-18, Award (19 December 2014) [281].

76 Olivier Corten, 'The Notion of "Reasonable" in International Law: Legal Discourse, Reason and Contradictions' (1999) 48 International & Comparative Law Quarterly 613, 615.

arbitrariness. States are held to strict standards of conduct under investment treaties, while arbitrators have been unable to devise tests that offer anything resembling a bright-line test for the review of regulatory action. As such, the ambiguous breadth of FET makes it one of the most exacting standards in international law.

3.4 Transparency

On many occasions, FET has been interpreted in various ways as including a notion of transparency of the regulatory framework.[77] Essentially, there are three approaches to the requirement of transparency under FET, all derived from the practice of ISDS tribunals. These are: a strict approach to transparency, a moderate approach, and a qualified approach that requires enhanced transparency only in specific factual contexts.

3.4.1 Strict approach: host state handholding

The strict approach to transparency is based on the maxim that a government must bear any risk of ambiguity arising from its actions.[78] This idea is best expressed in Wälde's Separate Opinion in *Thunderbird v Mexico*. The claim in that case arose from the closure of Thunderbird's gaming facilities. According to what the claimant had told Mexican authorities, these facilities had used 'skill machines', as opposed to 'slot machines', the latter turning solely on chance. The distinction between the machines was important because Mexican law prohibited games of chance and betting.[79] Eventually, the investor's operations were declared unlawful on this basis, as the investor's representations to regulatory bodies had been incorrect, and its facilities were closed down. A majority of the tribunal dismissed the ISDS claim, but arbitrator Wälde added a separate opinion.

Wälde's thesis was that investment treaties are more appropriately analysed using comparative public law rather than private contract law. The former,

[77] Most typically *Waste Management II v Mexico* (n 7) [98]; *Spyridon Roussalis v Romania*, ICSID Case No ARB/06/1, Award (7 December 2011) [314]; *Rumeli Telekom AS and Telsim Mobil Telekomunikasyon Hizmetleri AS v Republic of Kazakhstan*, ICSID Case No ARB/05/16, Award (29 July 2008) [605]; *Saluka v Czech Republic* (n 38) [307], [363], [500]; *Bosh International Inc and B&P Ltd Foreign Investments Enterprise v Ukraine*, ICSID Case No ARB/08/11, Award (25 October 2012) [212]; Paparinskis (n 3) 247–50.

[78] *Thunderbird v Mexico* (n 39) Separate Opinion of T Wälde; *Tecmed v Mexico* (n 34) [154]; *Metalclad v Mexico* (n 26), [76]; *Nordzucker v Poland*, UNCITRAL, Second Partial Award (Merits) (23 November 2009) [78]–[85].

[79] *Thunderbird v Mexico* (n 39) 50.

Wälde said, protected the individual from arbitrary, discriminatory, and excessive exercise of public power.[80] On the face of it, this position was unobjectionable since public law analogies are more appropriate to the structural characteristics of investment treaties and arbitration, especially in the context of regulatory disputes. Yet, Wälde went further by stripping the analogy of countervailing public policy rationales that underpin domestic legal systems. He argued that investment treaties are meant to compensate substantively for a presumed structural weakness in domestic law that disadvantages foreign investors as opposed to nationals. According to Wälde, this structural dynamic works even to diminish requirements for investors' due diligence in relation to transparency and regulation.[81]

Wälde's pro-investor inference was excessive. Suppose that domestic law is ambiguous, contradictory, or not readily available. Such limitations should arguably not harm the investor if it made an effort, from the perspective of a reasonable businessperson, to familiarize itself with the legal requirements. Even then, however, this ambiguity should not itself lead to host state liability if the investor's assessment of the law turned out to be incorrect. The mere fact that an investor is in a subordinate administrative position to that of state regulators cannot alleviate its duty of basic due diligence into the legal framework for its business. Taken to its logical end, such an alleviation of investor responsibility would oblige administrative agencies to counsel investors proactively about applicable rules and regulations and any potential changes.[82] Such a conclusion is fanciful in national law contexts. Public authorities are required to be as forthcoming as domestic law requires, not more so because a regulated actor is a foreign investor.

3.4.2 Moderate approach: due diligence and accessibility

The moderate approach to transparency combines the three propositions: that regulations must be readily available, that an investor must conduct due diligence into regulations covering its investment, and that ambiguity, if it reaches extreme levels (such as requiring mutually exclusive courses of conduct) cannot be interpreted to the investor's detriment.[83] Under this approach, the

[80] ibid para 27.
[81] ibid para 33.
[82] The most extreme version of this criterion can be found in the cases of *Metalclad* and *Tecmed*. See eg, *Metalclad v Mexico* (n 26) [76]: 'Once central authorities become aware of any scope of uncertainty in this connection, it is their duty to ensure that the correct position is properly determined.' *Tecmed v Mexico* (n 34) [154].
[83] *Plama Consortium Limited v Republic of Bulgaria*, ICSID Case No ARB/03/24, Award (27 August 2008) [268]–[270]; *Eudoro Armando Olguín v Republic of Paraguay*, ICSID Case No ARB/98/5, Award

state must create conditions by which investors can familiarize themselves with applicable regulations, but the investor must also be diligent in reviewing the regulations properly.[84] Many recent treaties include a transparency clause as a self-standing obligation of the states parties, while specifying that the obligation pertains only to the publishing of laws and regulations.[85]

This approach eliminates the most extreme consequences of the strict approach to transparency. It recognizes that it is unreasonable to expect public administrators to take a proactive stance whenever foreign investors are affected. Such an attitude would be highly unusual if it concerned a national. As the tribunal in *Invesmart v Czech Republic* put it: 'due diligence is a subjective coin of transparency'.[86] Put differently, the international standard, premised on FET, should not require the state to do the work of any economic actor, whether foreign or national. Investment treaties are not a substitute for any investors' lack of diligence. Thus, the strict approach to transparency is tempered.

3.4.3 Qualified approach: negotiations

In some ISDS cases, the tribunal has extended the strict approach to transparency only to particular contexts, such as where there are direct dealings, on a footing of equality, between the administration and the investor. Thus, in contractual negotiations, governments have sometimes been held to standards more stringent than the moderate approach.[87] The tribunals justified this particularized strictness on the basis that the government has specific notice of direct negotiations with the investor. Further, the government holds the

(26 July 2001) [65]–[76]; *Alasdair Ross Anderson and Others v Republic of Costa Rica*, ICSID Case No ARB AF/07/3, Award (19 November 2010) [58]; *Marion Unglaube and Reinhard Unglaube v Republic of Costa Rica*, ICSID Case No ARB/08/1 + ARB/09/20, Award (16 May 2012) [258]; *Joseph Charles Lemire v Ukraine*, ICSID Case No ARB/06/18, Dissenting Opinion of J Voss [15], [158]–[161].

84 *Invesmart v Czech Republic*, UNCITRAL, Award (26 June 2009) [296], [327]. For an older authority on the requirement of transparency see *Case of 'Fair American' (US, Mexico)* (1841) in JB Moore, *History and Digest of the International Arbitrations to which the United States Has Been a Part*, vol 4 (Government Printing Office 1898) 3369.

85 Mostly Canadian treaties; see eg art XVI(2) of the Canada–Latvia BIT, signed 5 May 2009: 'Each Contracting Party shall, to the extent practicable, ensure that its laws, regulations, procedures, and administrative rulings of general application respecting any matter covered by this Agreement are promptly published or otherwise made available in such a manner as to enable interested persons and the other Contracting Party to become acquainted with them.' Further Canada–Romania BIT, 8 May 2009, art XVI(2); art 4 of the Japan–India CEPA, 16 February 2012; Canada–China BIT, 09 Sep 2012, art 17; Canada–Jordan BIT, 26 June 2009, art 19, combining the general obligation with best efforts obligation to allow 'interested persons and the other Party' for an opportunity to comment.

86 *Invesmart v Czech Republic* (n 84) [272].

87 *PSEG v Turkey*, para 186, 246, 250–51; *Nordzucker* (n 78) [83]–[85]; less explicitly also *Electrabel* (n 47) [7.79]; *Ioan Micula, Viorel Micula, SC European Food SA, SC Starmill SRL and SC Multipack SRL v Romania*, ICSID Case No ARB/05/20, Separate Opinion of G Abi-Saab (5 December 2013) [12]–[13]. Abi-Saab, however, frames this issue as a question of consistency and negligence.

relevant information about the applicable framework and policies, insofar as it authors them. Yet, even this requirement must be qualified by the context. For instance, specialized administrative bodies with limited competence should not be expected to represent policies, or be aware of intricacies and technicalities of matters, that fall within the competencies of other administrative bodies. Unfortunately, very few tribunals have endorsed this more realistic approach to the functioning of public administration.[88]

4 Recent Treaty-making and Arbitral Practice

A predominant theme of this chapter has been that FET is the most controversial and far-reaching standard under investment treaties. Without detailed guidance from the treaty text, early ISDS cases led to expansive conceptions of FET that hold governments to exceptionally demanding scrutiny. Tribunals formulated doctrines that are virtually unheard of in national legal systems or that were imported into ISDS without the concomitant public law doctrines that usually limit state liability in domestic law. What do these developments mean for the future of FET and, more broadly, the international regime of investment protection?

With respect to FET, one observes two somewhat opposing tendencies. On the one hand, policy-makers have been attuned to the developments in practice and have tried to curtail arbitrator discretion by crafting more careful and detailed treaty language. On the other hand, the current ISDS caseload is still mostly authorized by old generation treaties, usually dating from the 1990s, and arbitrators have shown little willingness to accept the accumulated critique.

4.1 Recent Treaty Practice

Responding to ISDS practice, states have concluded various treaties in the last decade with a view to qualifying and detailing the content of FET, or excluding it altogether. International organizations have also called for reform of the existing stock of investment treaties to align them with sustainable development

[88] *Invesmart v Czech Republic* (n 84) [243], [250]–[258].

goals and the green economy transition.[89] These efforts are welcome and well-justified.

As an example, the 2016 India Model BIT does not include any reference to FET. Rather, it limits the relevant protections to violations of customary international law, with an exhaustive list of elements:

> No Party shall subject investments made by investors of the other Party to measures which constitute a violation of customary international law through:
> (i) denial of justice in any judicial or administrative proceedings; or
> (ii) fundamental breach of due process; or
> (iii) targeted discrimination on manifestly unjustified grounds, such as gender, race or religious belief; or
> (iv) manifestly abusive treatment, such as coercion, duress and harassment.[90]

Similarly, the Comprehensive and Progressive Agreement for Trans-Pacific Partnership (CPTPP) states that FET does not go beyond customary requirements and specifies that FET 'includes the obligation not to deny justice in criminal, civil or administrative adjudicatory proceedings in accordance with the principle of due process embodied in the principal legal systems of the world' and that, for greater certainty, 'the mere fact that a Party takes or fails to take an action that may be inconsistent with an investor's expectations' or 'the mere fact that a subsidy or grant has not been issued, renewed or maintained, or has been modified or reduced' will not violate the treaty.[91] Finally, some states' investment treaties exclude FET and common protection standards altogether and move in a different direction of investment governance, prioritizing investment promotion and facilitation instead of protection.[92]

[89] See eg UNCTAD, *Investment Policy Framework for Sustainable Development* (UNCTAD 2015) https://unctad.org/system/files/official-document/diaepcb2015d5_en.pdf; UNCTAD, *UNCTAD's Reform Package for the International Investment Regime* (UNCTAD 2018) https://investmentpolicy.unctad.org/uploaded-files/document/UNCTAD_Reform_Package_2018.pdf; UNCTAD, *International Investment Agreements Reform Accelerator* (UNCTAD 2020) https://unctad.org/system/files/official-document/diaepcbinf2020d8_en.pdf; OECD, *The Future of Investment Treaties*, OECD Work Programme https://www.oecd.org/investment/investment-policy/investment-treaties.htm.

[90] 2016 India Model BIT, art 3 https://dea.gov.in/sites/default/files/ModelBIT_Annex_0.pdf.

[91] CPTPP, entry into force 30 December 2018, ch 9, s A, art 9.6. For another example of similarly worder provision see eg art 5 of the Colombia–UAE BIT.

[92] See eg the Brazilian Cooperation and Facilitation of Investment Agreements. For an overview see eg Nitish Monebhurrun, 'Novelty in International Investment Law: The Brazilian Agreement on Cooperation and Facilitation of Investments as a Different International Investment Agreement Model' (2017) 8 Journal of International Dispute Settlement 79; Joaquim P Muniz, Kabir AN Duggal, and Luis

Despite this awareness of the problem of overly broad FET interpretations, recent treaties are a drop in the bucket of existing treaties. They account for less than five per cent of those in force. More importantly, new ISDS cases are brought regularly under the old treaties. Comprehensive reform of the whole regime is needed either to terminate or substantially rewrite existing treaties. The case for such an overhaul is urgent in the face of climate disruption. According to a recent study, the potential liability of states for ISDS claims arising from climate action measures may rise to hundreds of billions of USD.[93] The FET standard, as it has been shaped over the last two decades, is one of the main obstacles to energy transition. Indeed, energy transition cases are the newest laboratory for FET-based claims.

4.2 Recent Arbitral Practice

In the last decade or so, the Czech Republic, Italy, and Spain have faced dozens of ISDS claims spurred by changes to their respective subsidy programmes for renewable energy. The crux of the disputes is as follows.[94] In the early 2000s, under European Union guidance, European states moved to support investments in renewable energy. For the Czech Republic, Italy, and Spain, the chosen policy was feed-in tariffs designed to incentivize investors to invest where markets in the sector had not yet consolidated and returns were uncertain. The feed-in tariffs included state commitments to purchase the energy at a fixed price, guaranteeing a return over a certain period. These parameters were enshrined in general law. Thus, the states shouldered much of the uncertainty in renewable energy, socializing potential risks in a relatively new sector.

This original regulatory framework did not, however, fully account for future changes in solar technology.[95] With the radical decrease in the technology price, combined with their increased efficiency, investments in the sector

AS Peretti, 'The New Brazilian BIT on Cooperation and Facilitation of Investments: A New Approach in Times of Change' (2017) 32 ICSID Review: Foreign Investment Law Journal 404.

[93] Kyla Tienhaara and others, 'Investor-State Disputes Threaten the Global Green Energy Transition' (2022) 376 Science 701.

[94] For details of the Czech and Spanish regulatory frameworks see eg Anna Bilanová and Jaroslav Kudrna, 'Solar Arbitrations against the Czech Republic: Glimpse of Hope for Investor-State Arbitration' (Arbitration Journal) https://journal.arbitration.ru/analytics/solar-arbitrations-against-the-czech-republic-glimpse-of-hope-for-investor-state-arbitration/; Perrone (n 12) 163–70.

[95] The relevant EU law is Directive 2001/77/EC of the European Parliament and of the Council (27 September 2001) on the promotion of electricity produced from renewable energy sources in the internal electricity market.

became a state-financed gold mine. Investors in solar energy reaped windfall profits. It was a 'solar boom' at massive budgetary cost to government and consumers.[96] Electricity prices increased significantly. When the three states changed their programmes to address the problem, a flood of ISDS claims followed.

In these cases, FET featured prominently. The doctrine of legitimate expectations and requirement for legal stability were invoked contentiously, leading to divergent interpretations by tribunals. These ranged from very expansive to more moderate. Some tribunals decided that general laws could engender legitimate expectations of legal stability.[97] Others held that the changes in the regulatory framework had to be reasonable and proportionate so as not to frustrate the economic basis of the investments. Others decided that new legislation had to ensure a reasonable return to investors.[98] Various tribunals ultimately found the state liable for the changes. Overall, this recent history of ISDS litigation has signalled that regulatory experimentation in the energy sector will be simply unsustainable for many states.

5 Old Habits Die Hard

It is well established in the scholarship that international law sources are generally open-ended and of an indeterminate nature.[99] The language of FET is known to suffer particularly from substantial indeterminacy. This limitation is demonstrated by variety of conclusions that have been reached about its

[96] See eg Jaroslav Dorda, 'Czech Republic "Taming" Solar Boom' *PV Tech Blog* (15 September 2010) www.pv-tech.org/guest_bog_iii_czech_republic_taming_solar_boom/; Energiewende Team, 'The Age of Czech Solar Power: After Years of Stagnation, Is a Rebirth Imminent?' *Global Energiewende* (20 March 2019) https://energytransition.org/2019/03/czech-solar-power-after-years-of-stagnation/.

[97] *9REN Holding Sàrl v Kingdom of Spain*, ICSID Case No ARB/15/15; *OperaFund Eco-Invest SICAV PLC and Schwab Holding AG v Kingdom of Spain*, ICSID Case No ARB/15/36; *Greentech Energy Systems A/S and Others v Italian Republic*, SCC Case No V 2015/095.

[98] *Jürgen Wirtgen, Stefan Wirtgen, Gisela Wirtgen and JSW Solar (zwei) GmbH & Co KG v Czech Republic*, PCA Case No 2014-03; *Isolux Netherlands BV v Kingdom of Spain*, SCC Case V2013/153; *Stadtwerke München GmbH, RWE Innogy GmbH, and Others v Kingdom of Spain*, ICSID Case No ARB/15/1.

[99] This is no place to discuss the varieties of the indeterminacy thesis in legal scholarship, such as American legal realism, structural indeterminacy, linguistic indeterminacy, critical legal studies, Marxism, TWAIL etc; see eg Cameron Miles, 'Indeterminacy' in Jean d'Aspremont and Sahib Singh (eds), *Concepts for International Law* (Edward Elgar Publishing 2018) 447; Martti Koskenniemi, *From Apology to Utopia: The Structure of International Legal Argument* (CUP 2005); David Kennedy, 'When Renewal Repeats: Thinking against the Box' (2000) 32 New York Journal of International Law and Politics 335, 404–408; Robert Knox, 'Marxism, International Law, and Political Strategy' (2009) 22 LJIL 413.

content, as interpreted in jurisprudence and scholarship. Against the backdrop of this indeterminacy, the prevailing political economy of the field of investment arbitration creates reputational and economic incentives for the actors who decide, including the international adjudicators. It also frames what is perceived as a preferable and acceptable outcome.[100]

As this volume reveals, many investment law standards, apart from FET, constitute a legal toolkit that is premised on contingent events. However, their actual application in ISDS reflects a specific political economy. On the one hand, if we look at the application of legal concepts expressing the state's regulatory powers, we see that notions ostensibly available to promote public interest and public welfare objectives are in practice disregarded, stripped to the bare bones, or relegated to an exception.[101] On the other hand, doctrines devised to protect investor interests are expanded so as to become almost all-encompassing and indiscriminate,[102] or, at best, used for idiosyncratic balancing against public interests.[103] Fundamentally, a dispute settlement mechanism with party-appointed side persons offers little incentive and limited opportunity for arbitrators to turn from the path beaten in earlier cases.

Analysis of the arbitral practice and scholarship on FET reveals a political economy that prioritizes individual investors and corporate economic actors in critical matters of national economic ordering. This political economy removes the foreign investor from the regulatory context of host states and socializes risks associated with foreign investment.[104] The leading cases on FET favour this approach to investor–state relations. They have generated a jurisprudence that is too path dependent, drawing heavily on earlier cases that took investor-protecting concepts too far. From 2007 on, the application of FET has

[100] That is adjudicators' worldviews about the role of private property and foreign investment in national, regional, and global economy and about the role and functions of the state vis-à-vis the economy and society.

[101] See most recently *Eco Oro Minerals Corp v Republic of Colombia*, ICSID Case No ARB/16/41, Award, Decision on Jurisdiction, Liability and Directions on Quantum (9 September 2021).

[102] *Tecmed v Mexico* (n 34); *Bilcon of Delaware and Others v Government of Canada*, PCA Case No 2009-04; *Masdar Solar & Wind Cooperatief UA v Kingdom of Spain*, ICSID Case No ARB/14/1, Award (25 September 2018).

[103] *Total SA v Argentine Republic*, ICSID Case No ARB/04/01; *Continental v Argentina* (n 64) [255]–[261]; *Tecmed v Mexico* (n 34) [122], [133]; *Azurix Corp v Argentine Republic*, ICSID Case No ARB/01/12, Award (14 July 2006) [311]; *LG&E v Argentina* (n 38) [194]; *Philip Morris v Uruguay* (n 63) [305]–[306].

[104] Quinn Slobodian, *Globalists: The End of Empire and the Birth of Neoliberalism* (HUP 2018) ch 1. See also Perrone (n 12) 163–71.

been more circumscribed,[105] but we still find recent decisions adhering to the far-reaching interpretations.[106]

Although it is much needed, change in the ISDS practice of FET has been minimal and snail-paced. These limitations are rooted in the normative pull of the early cases, even if tempered somewhat by cosmetic accommodations stemming from external and internal critiques. The existing dispute settlement model, combined with its community of practice, offers little hope for change. New treaties react to the early 'excesses', but they are small in number compared to the universe of old treaties still in force. Moreover, even the new treaties that put limits on FET still give license to broad interpretation. This licence is dangerous because adjudicators often channel and accommodate their political economic preferences through the application of malleable concepts, doctrines, and techniques. The FET clauses in new treaties may be more limited, but they still allow arbitrators to employ ambiguous doctrines such as good faith, vested rights, consistency, estoppel, or proportionality, producing effectively equivalent levels of protection for foreign investment. So long as FET and the international minimum standard are decided within the current or a similar ISDS mechanism, and by the current or a similar group of people, little change can be expected.

[105] *Total v Argentina* (n 103); *Toto Costruzioni Generali SpA v Republic of Lebanon*, ICSID Case No ARB/07/12, Award (7 June 2012); *Gold Reserve Inc v Bolivarian Republic of Venezuela*, ICSID Case No ARB AF/09/1, Award (22 September 2014); A similar account with respect to trade law can be found in Rob Howse, 'The World Trade Organization 20 Years On: Global Governance by Judiciary' (2016) 27 European Journal of International Law 9.

[106] See the cases referred to above in section 4.2 Recent Arbitral Practice. See also *Bilcon v Canada* (n 102) [447]; *Masdar v Spain*; *Antaris Solar GmbH and Dr Michael Göde v Czech Republic*, PCA Case No 2014-01, Dissenting Opinion of Gary Born (2 May 2018).

8

Umbrella Clauses

*Ibironke T. Odumosu-Ayanu**

1 Introduction

International investment law scholars commonly make two points about the discipline and its relationship to politics. First, it is acknowledged that political risk has a significant impact on foreign investment.[1] Secondly, it is said that investor–state arbitration was designed in part to depoliticize[2] investment disputes.[3] Yet political risk and the depoliticization of disputes represent only a fraction of the politics of international investment law. The wider politics that critical scholars have identified emerge from a closer study of the complex relationship between foreign investment and communities in host countries.

This chapter addresses the wider politics in the context of umbrella clauses. International investment law claims to foster a separation of markets and politics.[4] Here, markets are synonymous with foreign capital and politics is often connected with state conduct that responds, among other things, to the demands of citizens as people who engage in complex interactions beyond the market. Certainly, states must make political choices in their interactions with foreign investors, often in response to domestic circumstances.[5] While some

* The helpful comments and edits of Gus Van Harten, David Schneiderman, and the editors on earlier drafts of the present chapter are acknowledged.

[1] Jason Webb Yackee, 'Political Risk and International Investment Law' (2014) 24 Duke Journal of Comparative & International Law 477.

[2] Depoliticization is a contested term. As Fawcett and others note, 'there is a consensus among scholars that, while contested, depoliticization can be defined as the set of processes (including varied tactics, strategies, and tools) that remove or displace the potential for choice, collective agency, and deliberation around a particular political issue'. Paul Fawcett and others, 'Anti-Politics, Depoliticization, and Governance' in Paul Fawcett and others (eds), *Anti-Politics, Depoliticization, and Governance* (OUP 2017) 3, 5.

[3] See Ibironke Odumosu, 'The Law and Politics of Engaging Resistance in Investment Dispute Settlement' (2007) 26 Penn State International Law Review 251; But see Jason Yackee, 'Investor-State Dispute Settlement at the Dawn of International Investment Law: France, Mauritania, and the Nationalization of the MIFERMA Iron Ore Operations' (2019) 59 American Journal of Legal History 71.

[4] Nicolas M Perrone and David Schneiderman, 'International Economic Law's Wreckage: Depoliticization, Inequality, Precarity' in Emilios Christodoulidis, Ruth Dukes, and Marco Godoni (eds), *Research Handbook on Critical Legal Theory* (Edward Elgar Publishing 2019) 446.

[5] See Lorenzo Cotula, 'Democracy and International Investment Law' (2017) 30 Leiden Journal of International Law 351.

Ibironke T. Odumosu-Ayanu, *Umbrella Clauses* In: *Rethinking Investment Law*. Edited by: David Schneiderman and Gus Van Harten, Oxford University Press. © Ibironke T. Odumosu-Ayanu 2023.
DOI: 10.1093/oso/9780192871084.003.0008

may, in some cases, use domestic politics as an excuse to avoid responsibility, the focus in this chapter is on the general labelling of state responses to citizens' concerns as 'politics'. Foreign investors or arbitrators often frame state action as 'politically motivated' and, as a result, not 'rational' or 'impartial'.[6] Also investors appear to use 'the term "political" as part of a strategy to discredit the state conduct in question'.[7] Such characterizations fit the frame of a form of depoliticization that views international investment law itself as apolitical even beyond the depoliticization that follows from separation of investment arbitration and state–state dispute settlement. This problematic interpretation of depoliticization is particularly visible in the interaction between contracts and investment treaties, often arising in the context of umbrella clauses.[8]

Umbrella clauses are themselves products of the politics of the era when they were developed for general usage.[9] They garnered attention in the 1950s and 1960s. This was the era of decolonization in which former colonial powers began to lose direct control over the natural resources and concession contracts of former colonies. At this time, natural resource industries in some Third World states were being nationalized in favour of domestic producers. The politics of decolonization was in turn a major subject at the United Nations (UN). The purpose of umbrella clauses seemed clear; they would ensure that concession contracts were not left to the domestic control of the host state alone. Even so, states that signed early bilateral investment treaties (BITs) that included such clauses did not appear to have much appreciation for their original purpose.[10]

Umbrella clauses frequently implicate public interest issues. Investor–state disputes involving umbrella clauses often arise from contracts for the provision of essential services or development of natural resources. Thus, umbrella clauses reveal challenges with reconciling the public interest and depoliticization (in this case, reading depoliticization as a separation of states from citizens' concerns). As James Crawford put it, '[n]o issue in the field of investment arbitration is more fundamental, or more disputed, than the distinction between

[6] Jonathan Bonnitcha and Zoe Phillips Williams, 'State Liability for "Politically" Motivated Conduct in the Investment Treaty Regime' (2019) 32 Leiden Journal of International Law 1. See also David Schneiderman, 'Hayek's Dream: International Investment Law and the Denigration of Politics' (2022) 35 Leiden Journal of International Law 743; Gus Van Harten, *Sovereign Choices and Sovereign Constraints: Judicial Restraint in Investment Treaty Arbitration* (OUP 2013) 72.

[7] Bonnitcha and Phillips Williams (n 6) 5.

[8] Schneiderman (n 6).

[9] See the discussion in section 2 of this chapter.

[10] See Jonathan Bonnitcha, Lauge N Skovgaard Poulsen, and Michael Waibel, *The Political Economy of the Investment Treaty Regime* (OUP 2017) 223–26. See generally Lauge N Skovgaard Poulsen, *Bounded Rationality and Economic Diplomacy: The Politics of Investment Treaties in Developing Countries* (CUP 2015).

treaty and contract'.[11] Embedded in the treaty/contract relationship is the umbrella clause, which has been called 'the most controversial standard of protection in international investment law'.[12] One arbitral tribunal noted that 'there is no *jurisprudence constante* on the effect of umbrella clauses' and 'the subject is one on which legal opinion is divided'.[13] It is often argued that umbrella clauses transform contract claims to treaty claims,[14] or transform violations of contract to violations of treaty obligations[15] although there is disagreement on the issue.[16] The conflicting views have not changed since the decisions in *SGS v Pakistan*[17] and *SGS v Philippines*.[18] This controversy has been said to threaten the 'long-term stability and workability of international investment law'.[19]

It is argued in this chapter that umbrella clauses purport to serve as a mechanism for depoliticization. Here, depoliticization is understood not only to take the form of separating investor–state arbitration from state–state arbitration but also to ensure that international investment law is devoid of any conduct that may be labelled as politics. The latter form of depoliticization that reads international investment law as apolitical is the subject of this chapter's analysis. Umbrella clauses represent part of an effort to 'treatify' contracts. Before umbrella clauses emerged, many concession contracts were already argued to be internationalized instruments where international law was a source of law for the contract and international arbitration was a dispute settlement option. What umbrella clauses added was the treaty element. In general, 'treatification' denotes the role of treaties as the main source of international investment law in contrast to customary international law.[20] Here, the term is used as a

[11] James Crawford, 'Treaty and Contract in Investment Arbitration' (2008) 24 Arbitration International 351.

[12] Raul Pereira de Souza Fleury, 'Umbrella Clauses: A Trend Towards their Elimination' (2015) 31 Arbitration International 679, 680; David Collins, *An Introduction to International Investment Law* (CUP 2017) 145.

[13] *Bureau Veritas, Inspection, Valuation, Assessment and Control, BIVAC BV v Republic of Paraguay*, ICSID Case No ARB/07/09, Decision of the Tribunal on Objections to Jurisdiction (29 May 2009) [141].

[14] Julian Arato, 'The Logic of Contract in the World of Investment Treaties' (2016) 58 William & Mary Law Review 351, 372.

[15] Christoph Schreuer, 'Travelling the BIT Route: Of Waiting Periods, Umbrella Clauses and Forks in the Road (2004) 5 Journal of World Investment & Trade 231, 250.

[16] See the discussion in section 3 of this chapter.

[17] *SGS Société Génerale de Surveillance SA v Islamic Republic of Pakistan*, ICSID Case No ARB/01/13, Decision of the Tribunal on Objections to Jurisdiction (6 August 2003).

[18] *SGS Société Génerale de Surveillance SA v Republic of the Philippines*, ICSID Case No ARB/02/06, Decision of the Tribunal on Objections to Jurisdiction (29 January 2004).

[19] Yuval Shany, 'Contract Claims vs Treaty Claims: Mapping Conflicts between ICSID Decisions on Multisourced Investment Claims' (2005) 99 American Journal of International Law 835.

[20] On treatification see Jeswald W Salacuse, 'The Treatification of International Investment Law' (2007) 13 Law and Business Review of the Americas 155; Patrick Dumberry, 'A Few Observations on the Remaining Fundamental Importance of Customary Rules in the Age of Treatification of International Investment Law' (2016) 34 Association Suisse de l'Arbitrage Bulletin 41.

transposition of state–investor contracts to the realm of treaties. This transposition has at least two implications. First, if one treatifies concessions and other state–investor contracts, one purports to legitimize sometimes problematic domestic arrangements at the treaty level. Secondly, treatification facilitates engagement outside the domestic space. Essentially, contracts that are formed and contract disputes that occur in the domestic space of, mostly, Third World states are taken beyond the reach of affected citizens.

According to Wälde, the 'very *raison d'être* of investment treaties' is to remove investment disputes from the jurisdiction of domestic courts, especially in the Third World.[21] Umbrella clauses fit this articulation. The mechanisms devised to respond to challenging state–investor relationships during decolonization also created imbalances, such as the exclusion of local communities from measures designed to address tensions between investment protection and various manifestations of state power. International law mostly assumes that engaging with a state means engaging with its peoples, even though states sometimes actively alienate their citizens to secure investment projects.[22] Even though international law proceeds on the basis that the state is the representative of its peoples, proponents of the prevailing version of international investment law designed depoliticization to also involve a position that strips the state of its peoples and formally subjects investment-related domestic engagements to international law. Through the instrumentality of mechanisms such as umbrella clauses, investment law itself adopts a politics of privileging foreign investors and insisting on states being neutral actors in investment engagements.

2 Political Origins of Umbrella Clauses

Umbrella clauses are hard to define. They have been subject to varying interpretations, both restrictive and wide, which sometimes depend on the language of the clause before a tribunal. They are also drafted differently. For the United Kingdom (UK)–Pakistan BIT: 'Each Contracting Party shall observe any obligation it may have entered into with regard to investment of nationals or companies of the other Contracting Party.'[23] The United States (US) has adopted

[21] Thomas W Wälde, 'The Umbrella Clause in Investment Arbitration: A Comment on Original Intentions and Recent Cases (2005) 6 Journal of World Investment & Trade 183, 190.

[22] Kate Miles, *The Origins of International Investment Law: Empire, Environment and the Safeguarding of Capital* (CUP 2013) 105.

[23] Agreement between the Government of the United Kingdom of Great Britain and Northern Ireland and the Government of the Islamic Republic of Pakistan (30 November 1994) art 2(2).

a different approach. While it adopted umbrella clauses before 2012, under its 2012 model BIT the US now lists those 'investment agreements' that may be subject to investment arbitration; that is, agreements related to natural resources, supply of services to the public (including services such as power generation and water treatment and distribution), and infrastructure projects.[24] The model BIT permits foreign investors to submit an arbitral claim that a state has breached an investment agreement. While the tendency is to note the absence of a general umbrella clause in the 2012 model BIT, it retains coverage of the areas in which public interest issues are most likely to arise within the purview of BITs.[25] For its part, the European Union's recent practice is illustrated by the 2018 European Union–Singapore Investment Protection Agreement. It includes an umbrella clause as part of a section in the treaty on standards of treatment, stating that where a state party has 'given a specific and clearly spelt out commitment in a contractual written obligation' to a 'covered investor' such 'party shall not frustrate or undermine the said commitment through the exercise of its governmental authority either deliberately or in a way that substantially alters the balance of rights and obligation in the contractual written obligation unless the party provides reasonable compensation to restore the covered investor or investment to a position which it would have been in had the frustration or undermining not occurred'.[26]

Generally, umbrella clauses seek to entrench, within the ambit of the treaty, a range of contractual (and other) undertakings that the state has made under domestic law. Schreuer observes that umbrella clauses place 'contractual commitments under the BIT's protective umbrella' and 'add the compliance with investment contracts, or other undertaking of the host state, to the BIT's substantive standards', such that 'a violation of such a contract becomes a violation of the BIT'.[27] As this section will demonstrate, the historical account supports this expansive interpretation. For their part, narrower interpretations and more restrictive provisions seek to rein in the implications of this expansive view.

International investment law scholars have tended to avoid critical history of the subject. Tracing the origins of international investment law forces

[24] 2012 US Model BIT, arts 1, 24.

[25] These provisions are not merely theoretical as they formed part of the 2008 US–Rwanda BIT that was drafted before the model BIT was published in 2012. *Treaty between the Government of the United States of America and the Government of the Republic of Rwanda Concerning the Encouragement and Reciprocal Protection of Investment* (19 February 2008) entered into force 1 January 2012.

[26] Investment Protection Agreement between the European Union and its Member States and the Republic of Singapore (15 October 2018) art 2.4(6).

[27] Schreuer (n 15) 250. However, he urges caution, noting that it would be problematic if investors use umbrella clauses for 'trivial disputes' in order to convert 'minor' disagreements into international claims. See ibid 255.

questions about colonialism, domination and the development of rules that were principally designed to protect capital in a manner that largely ignores many legitimate interests. As Schneiderman notes, the denial of this history is 'strategic'. It involves 'cabining investment law's past' in order to make 'the present appear free of the dynamics of domination that characterized prior conflicts'.[28] Pointing to the proliferation of BITs between formally sovereign but politically and economically unequal states, some mainstream scholars go so far as to contend that the history of investment law 'bears no relationship to the meaning and content of contemporary commitments made by states acting in their sovereign capacity and in relative positions of equality'.[29] However, critical scholars have increasingly turned to history to help understand the international law project and its hegemonic character. In his account of the 'colonial origins of international law', Anghie specifically references the 'colonial origins of foreign investment law as an academic discipline'.[30] Similarly, according to Miles, the 'translation of European trading and investment principles into universal rules of international law on foreign investment is bound' with the 'history of colonialism, the calculated, often brutal, use of force, and the manipulation of legal doctrines to acquire commercial benefits'.[31] Simply, this history 'drove the construction of international investment law'.[32]

The flawed historical premises of imperialism and domination continue to impact the character of investment law. In the face of conflicting decisions on issues such as the interpretation of umbrella clauses or, even, necessity clauses[33] scholars have turned to historical accounts of standards of treatment and investor–state arbitration.[34] One needs to trace the history only to the twentieth century to discover that arbitral tribunals, even before the treatification of contracts, sought to adopt laws other than those of distrusted host states.[35] In the *Qatar Arbitration*, for example, Lord Asquith stated that the laws of the

[28] David Schneiderman, 'Book Review: Kate Miles, *The Origins of International Investment Law: Empire, Environment, and the Safeguarding of Capital*' (2014) 25 European Journal of International Law 942.

[29] ibid.

[30] Antony Anghie, *Imperialism, Sovereignty and the Making of International Law* (CUP 2004) 224.

[31] Miles (n 22) 31–32.

[32] ibid 32.

[33] See Ibironke T Odumosu-Ayanu, 'International Investment Law and Disasters: Necessity, Peoples and the Burden of (Economic) Emergencies' in David Caron, Michael Kelly, and Anastasia Telesetsky (eds), *The International Law of Disaster Relief* (CUP 2014) 374.

[34] For an account of some of these works see Stephan W Schill, Christian J Tams, and Rainer Hofmann, 'International Investment Law and History: An Introduction' in Stephan W Schill, Christian J Tams, and Rainer Hofmann (eds), *International Investment Law and History* (Edward Elgar Publishing 2018) 3.

[35] On internationalization of contracts see Jean Ho, *State Responsibility for Breaches of Investment Contracts* (CUP 2018) ch5.

host state were insufficiently mature to apply to petroleum disputes, preferring instead the general principles of law recognized by 'civilized nations'.[36]

Umbrella clauses are most specifically traced to the 1950s, but they emerged within a centuries-old political and economic environment of foreign investment. European states developed rules to protect investors' property and, as Miles notes, changes occurred when the rules were applied to non-European peoples, becoming, as Miles says, 'inextricably linked with colonialism, oppressive protection of commercial interests, and military intervention'.[37] At this stage, the 'law moved from a base in reciprocity to one of imposition'.[38] During this era, the laws of the colonial powers were imposed on other territories.[39] Conquest and colonialism were justified partly in the name of trade and investment.[40] Typically, natural resources were at its centre. No wonder natural resource concession contracts were at the centre of investment law in the decolonization era. Many of these contracts were fundamentally unequal, sometimes even granting investors access to the entire territory of the host country.[41] They were a source of immense legal conflict among Third World states, developed states, and foreign investors. Disputes such as *Texaco v Libya* influenced theories about internationalization of contracts and investment disputes.[42] This was the period when some states nationalized the property of foreign investors and it was also a time of significant political engagement at the UN. Conversations about political risk were essential and they encompassed issues such as military coups, expropriation and 'civilian unrest'.[43] Some Third World states began to contest concession contracts and challenged the prevailing international economic system by proposing a 'new international economic order' (NIEO).[44] Instead of realizing many of the

[36] *Petroleum Development (Qatar) Ltd v Ruler of Qatar* (1951) 18 ILR 161. See *Saudi Arabia v Arabian American Oil Company* (1958) 27 ILR 117 for a more nuanced approach to applicable law that involved a combination of international law and Saudi Arabian law.

[37] Kate Miles, 'International Investment Law: Origins, Imperialism and Conceptualizing the Environment' (2010) 21 Colorado Journal of International Environmental Law & Policy 1.

[38] ibid 3.

[39] M Sornarajah, *Resistance and Change in the International Law on Foreign Investment* (CUP 2015) 81–84.

[40] ibid 84.

[41] For an example of a concession agreement that granted such extensive access see Agreement of 11 January 1939 between the Sheikh of Abu Dhabi and Petroleum Development (Trucial Coast) Limited, art 2(a), cited in *Petroleum Development (Trucial Coast) Ltd v Sheikh of Abu Dhabi* (1951) 18 ILR 144, 147.

[42] *Texaco Overseas Petroleum Co & California Asiatic Oil Co v Government of the Libyan Arab Republic* (1979) 53 ILR 389.

[43] Yackee (n 1) 480.

[44] Declaration on the Establishment of a New International Economic Order, GA Res 3201 (S-VI), 6 (Special) UN GAOR, 6th Special Session Supplement No 1, 3, UN Doc A/9559 (1974) (1 May 1974);

proposals of the NIEO, BITs proliferated and further entrenched umbrella clauses.[45]

The most referenced author on the origins of umbrella clauses is perhaps Anthony Sinclair, who has traced modern umbrella clauses[46] to Elihu Lauterpacht and the resolution of the Iran nationalization dispute with the Anglo–Iranian Oil Company in 1953 and 1954.[47] This dispute emerged and evolved in a troubling political context, although this is not apparent from the International Court of Justice's (ICJ) record of the dispute. A robust history, which is beyond the scope of this chapter, reveals tensions that underlie nationalizations. Pahuja and Storr outline how Iran, typically portrayed as the aggressor, had sought to act lawfully while the British, supported by the US, did not.[48] They note that '[s]eparating the law from the world in this particular instance bolsters misconceptions around who adhered to international law and who did not' in the course of the oil nationalization.[49]

In terms of its legal history, the Anglo–Iranian oil dispute originated in 'the grant of the infamous D'Arcy Concession of 1901' by Iran to William Knox D'Arcy.[50] Although Iran was not formally colonized by Britain at the time, it was the victim of British imperialism and a dominant British presence in its economy.[51] Unsurprisingly for its time, the D'Arcy Concession was extensive in its territorial scope, exclusive to the foreign investor, and deeply financially inadequate for the host country. Some commentators regard it as a factor in the constitutional revolution that occurred in Iran in 1905, which the concession survived.[52] The ensuing foreign investor, the Anglo–Persian Oil Company,

Charter of Economic Rights and Duties of States, GA Res 3281 (XXIX) (12 December 1974), UN GAOR, 29th Session, Supp (No 31) 50, UN Doc A/3235.

[45] As Pahuja observes, the efforts to challenge the international system were 'transformed by, and subsumed within, a nascent regulatory framework dealing with foreign investment'. Sundhya Pahuja, *Decolonizing International Law: Development, Economic Growth and the Politics of Universality* (CUP 2011) 96.

[46] See Anthony C Sinclair, 'The Origins of the Umbrella Clause in the International Law of Investment Protection' (2004) 20 Arbitration International 411, 413–414 for an earlier example which differs from modern versions of umbrella clauses since the treaty that included the umbrella protection was drafted after the breach of the concession contract.

[47] Ibid. See also Yuliya Chernykh, 'The Gust of Wind: The Unknown Role of Sir Elihu Lauterpacht in the Drafting of the Abs-Shawcross Draft Convention' in Stephan W Schill, Christian J Tams, and Rainer Hofmann (eds), *International Investment Law and History* (Edward Elgar Publishing 2018).

[48] Sundhya Pahuja and Cait Storr, 'Rethinking Iran and International Law: The *Anglo-Iranian Oil Company Case* Revisited' in James Crawford and others (eds), *The International Legal Order: Current Needs and Possible Responses: Essays in Honour of Djamchid Momtaz* (Brill 2017) 53, 54.

[49] ibid.

[50] ibid.

[51] See N Saifpour Fatemi, 'Tensions in the Middle East' (1952) Annals of the American Academy of Political and Social Science 53 (July 1952).

[52] Pahuja and Storr (n 48).

was closely tied to the British Government from its incorporation. The Anglo–Persian Oil Company's contributions to the interests of the people of Iran were scrutinized and some took the view that the interests of Iran and its people were 'chronically subordinated' to those of the company and the British empire.[53] Eventually, Iran sought to renegotiate the concession and, following negotiations with the company, cancelled it in 1932. A new concession agreement was concluded the next year between Iran and the Anglo–Iranian Oil Company (the company's name was changed). However, disagreements continued in the 1940s over the company's 'continued economic dominance'.[54]

Ultimately, in 1951, Iran nationalized the oil industry,[55] offering to compensate the Anglo–Iranian Oil Company at market rates.[56] The events leading to the nationalization are described by Pahuja and Storr as a 'struggle for independence against vested interests and imperial entitlement'.[57] In the ensuing dispute, the United Kingdom brought a claim to the ICJ, whose well-known decision provides insight into the position of international law at the time. In particular, the ICJ rejected the UK's argument that, while the concession agreement was a contract between Iran and the company, it was also a treaty between Iran and the UK.[58] The ICJ rejected this argument, noting that:

> The Court cannot accept the view that the contract signed between the Iranian Government and the Anglo-Persian Oil Company has a double character. It is nothing more than a concessionary contract between a government and a foreign corporation. The United Kingdom Government is not a party to the contract; there is no privity of contract between the Government of Iran and the Government of the United Kingdom. Under the contract the Iranian Government cannot claim from the United Kingdom Government any rights which it may claim from the Company, nor can it be called upon to perform towards the United Kingdom Government any obligations which it is bound to perform towards the Company. The document bearing the signatures of the representatives of the Iranian Government and the Company has a single purpose: the purpose of regulating the relations between that Government and the Company in regard to the concession. It does not regulate in any way the relations between the two Governments.[59]

[53] ibid.
[54] ibid.
[55] *Anglo–Iranian Oil Co Case (United Kingdom v Iran)*, Preliminary Objection, Judgment (22 July 1952) [1952] ICJ Rep 93, 102.
[56] Pahuja and Storr (n 48).
[57] ibid.
[58] *Anglo–Iranian Oil Co Case* (n 55) 111–12.
[59] ibid 112.

Following this decision, the UK resorted to economic sanctions against Iran. It prevented Iran from accessing Iranian assets in British banks. It withdrew British nationals from Iran's oilfields. It militarily detained a tanker carrying Iranian oil, arguing that the tanker was in unlawful possession of its property. Eventually, in 1953 a coup was launched with US support to oust the Iranian government that implemented the nationalization.[60] Clearly, the events surrounding the nationalization were political at both the domestic and the international level.

It was against this backdrop that umbrella clauses emerged to protect investors of the colonial powers. Given the timing, it is plausible that the ICJ's decision inspired concern about the unenforceability, by the home state, of a concession contract. Essentially, states could not count on characterizing a breach of contract against their companies as a breach of treaty against themselves. In light of this, Lauterpacht presented the idea of an 'umbrella' or 'parallel protection' treaty. His advice in relation to the settlement of the Anglo-Iranian Oil dispute was that a future oil concession 'shall be incorporated or referred to in a treaty between Iran and the United Kingdom in such a way that a breach of the contract or settlement shall be *ipso facto* deemed to be a breach of the treaty'.[61] Thus, Lauterpacht proposed an umbrella treaty for the 'consortium agreement' between Iran and the oil companies.[62]

Lauterpacht's approach served further to internationalize and treatify the concession. Internationalization was not completely new, since the 1933 concession agreement provided that international law would apply to the resolution of disputes,[63] and the United Kingdom argued before the ICJ that Iran had breached international law.[64] The proposed settlement from Lauterpacht, combining contract and an umbrella treaty, would have added the further step of treatifying the contract and dispute settlement. Breach of the contract would breach the treaty.[65] Lauterpacht's advice did not materialize in this instance, but it later resurfaced for a proposed pipeline that would pass through Iraq, Syria, and Turkey.[66] In 1956–57, Lauterpacht again advised that in addition to the contracts, 'parallel protection' treaties should be drafted 'so that a breach of a pipeline contract would also constitute a breach of treaty'.[67] States whose

[60] Pahuja and Storr (n 48).
[61] Elihu Lauterpacht, 'Anglo-Iranian Oil Company Ltd Persian Settlement, Opinion' dated 20 January 1954, 4, cited in Sinclair (n 46) 415.
[62] Sinclair (n 46) 416.
[63] ibid.
[64] *Anglo-Iranian Oil Co Case* (n 55) 95.
[65] Sinclair (n 46) 416.
[66] ibid 418.
[67] ibid.

nationals invested in the pipeline could then refer disputes to the ICJ, without exhausting local remedies or using the contracts' dispute settlement mechanisms.[68] This pipeline project also failed to materialize.

As Sinclair notes, Lauterpacht's advice focused on specific projects and the related contracts.[69] During the late 1950s, in the discussion of draft conventions for the protection of property in foreign countries, the idea expanded into that of a general umbrella clause for all covered investment projects.[70] Like modern investment treaties, these draft conventions focused on investment protection and they reflected the capital exporter/capital importer dichotomy of their time.[71] Abs stated tellingly that it was to be 'perfectly clear to the capital importing countries that they were expected ... to leave alone the duly established rights of foreigners who were working for their benefit'.[72]

By 1959, a Draft Convention on Investments Abroad (the Abs-Shawcross Convention) was published. It included, in article II, an umbrella clause as follows: 'Each Party shall at all times ensure the observance of any undertakings which it may have given in relation to investments made by nationals of any other Party'.[73] One of the animating discussions was the extent to which the draft convention affirmed international law or created new obligations. The draft convention referred to itself, in the preamble, as 'a restatement of principles of conduct relating to foreign investments'. The attached commentary adopted the view that the umbrella clause 'affirms' what it called the 'universally accepted principle *Pacta sunt servanda*'.[74] It stated further that it was unnecessary to distinguish between contract and treaty in this regard.[75] Schwarzenberger took a different view.[76] He argued that the umbrella clause sought to transform obligations to foreign investors into international obligations.[77] He viewed this step as a departure from customary international law and, indeed, as 'a far-reaching departure from the law' which may 'tilt the

[68] ibid.

[69] ibid.

[70] See ibid 418–20 for a discussion of the draft Conventions by Dr Hermann Abs and by Sir Hartley Shawcross (later Lord Shawcross).

[71] AA Fatouros, 'An International Code to Protect Private Investment – Proposals and Perspectives' (1961) 14 Univ of Toronto Law Journal 77; Arthur S Miller, 'Protection of Private Foreign Investment by Multilateral Convention' (1959) 53 American Journal of International Law 371.

[72] Hermann J Abs, *Proposals for Improving the Protection of Private Foreign Investments* (Institut International d'Etudes Bancaires 1958) 24–25, cited in Sinclair (n 46) 418.

[73] 'The Proposed Convention to Protect Private Foreign Investment: A Roundtable: Introduction' (1960) 9 Journal of Public Law 115, 116.

[74] ibid 120.

[75] ibid.

[76] Georg Schwarzenberger, 'The Abs-Shawcross Convention on Investments Abroad: A Critical Commentary' (1960) 9 Journal of Public Law 147.

[77] ibid 155.

balance too far in favour of the investor'.[78] For Schwarzenberger, legal remedies for 'alleged breaches of noninternational obligations' should first be exhausted but the umbrella clause in the Abs-Shawcross Convention had the effect of making it unnecessary for a foreign investor to first have recourse to the law of the host state.[79] Metzger saw article II as converting state–investor contracts into ' "international" agreements between countries, which they are not under international law'.[80] Metzger called the clause 'one-sided'[81] and argued that developed and Third World countries alike would decline to undermine their ability to regulate business in the public interest.[82] Nonetheless, states have accepted umbrella clauses and have also surrendered some regulatory space in modern investment treaties. Larson, perhaps, had the broadest and most critical view of the draft convention. He noted:[83]

> The principal flaw in the Draft Convention is its one-sidedness. In form it is evenhanded. That is, at every point the rights it confers and the duties it exacts apply identically to 'each party' ... In substance, however, the entire concern of the Convention is the protection of the rights of the investor. There are no provisions motivated by concern for the rights of the host country. The Draft Convention shares this flaw with practically all the other draft conventions on the subject.[84]

The Organization for Economic Cooperation and Development developed its Draft Convention on the Protection of Foreign Property in 1962 and 1967. Article 2 provided that: 'Each party shall at all times ensure the observance of undertakings given by it in relation to property of nationals of any other Party.'[85] The attached commentary asserted again that article 2 was an application of the *pacta sunt servanda* principle.[86] Rights granted by virtue of domestic undertakings would amount to international rights under the commentary's interpretation.[87] Like the Abs-Shawcross draft, the OECD draft convention did

[78] ibid.
[79] Schwarzenberger (n 76) 155.
[80] Stanley D. Metzger, 'Multilateral Conventions for the Protection of Private Foreign Investment' (1960) 9 Journal of Public Law 137.
[81] ibid.
[82] ibid 138.
[83] Arthur Larson, 'Recipients' Rights under an International Investment Code' (1960) 9 Journal of Public Law 172.
[84] ibid.
[85] 'Organization for Economic Co-operation and Development: Draft Convention on the Protection of Foreign Property' (1968) 7 ILM 117.
[86] ibid 123.
[87] ibid.

not garner enough support and was not adopted. While the OECD Council adopted the draft convention, it was not opened for states' signature although, as Yannaca-Small notes, it 'represented the collective view and dominant trend of OECD countries on investment issues'.[88] Today, the provisions of both the Abs-Shawcross draft and the OECD draft have been modified and adopted in many investment treaties. In fact, before the first OECD draft of 1962, the first BIT—the Germany–Pakistan BIT—had been signed and it included an umbrella clause.[89]

Essentially, umbrella clauses are a product of the politics of the decolonization era. While presented as affirming customary international law, in fact, they exceeded it. They responded to domestic changes in newly independent countries and other Third World states which sometimes manifested as nationalizations. The push for a new international economic order also informed the legal developments of that time. In this context, umbrella clauses were designed to entrench imperial and neo-colonial control over concession contracts. The political shifts of this era also engendered legal developments. Investment treaties were being signed and some included umbrella clauses, at the same time the Libya nationalization and other cases were being decided and investment arbitration was witnessing a shift towards formal depoliticization. Umbrella clauses were designed as a response to these difficult relationships. It is not surprising that investment tribunals that have been tasked with interpreting umbrella clauses have handed down inconsistent decisions on several aspect of these clauses.

3 Interpretations of Umbrella Clauses

This section analyses the interpretation of umbrella clauses in the present era where BITs have proliferated. It first highlights the conflicting jurisprudence that has emerged. It then demonstrates that umbrella clauses are part of an attempt to discipline contracts and bring them within the investment treaty framework as the main vehicle for organizing international investment law.

88 Catherine Yannaca-Small, 'Fair and Equitable Treatment Standard in International Investment Law', OECD Working Papers on International Investment Law 2004/03, 4.

89 Treaty between the Federal Republic of Germany and Pakistan for the Promotion and Protection of Investments (25 November 1959) art 7: 'Either party shall observe any other obligation it may have entered into with regard to investments by nationals or companies of the other Party.'

Numerous arbitral awards have considered themes emerging from interpretation of umbrella clauses. Not every theme is examined here.[90] Instead, the analysis focuses on three themes. First, the nature of umbrella clauses is discussed; that is, whether they 'elevate' contract breaches and claims to treaty breaches and claims. Second, the discussion turns to tribunals' conflicting assessments of how an exclusive forum selection clause in a contract should impact a tribunal's jurisdiction over, and admissibility of, a claim. Third, the issue of whether umbrella clauses should be limited based on the sovereign or commercial character of the state's conduct is examined. These themes have been central to the interpretation of umbrella clauses. They are also the most relevant to the politics of umbrella clauses. Finally, in addition to elements of the development of umbrella clauses discussed above, these interpretations allow us to consider whether and, if so, when the treaties with umbrella clauses took a wrong turn.

3.1 The Nature of Umbrella Clauses

The first theme is the most contested. It relates to the elevation of an alleged breach of contract claim to the level of a treaty claim under international law. Here, there is often comparison between the early decisions in *SGS v Pakistan* and *SGS v Philippines*. In *SGS v Pakistan*, the tribunal adopted a restrictive reading of umbrella clauses.[91] SGS argued that the umbrella clause in the Switzerland–Pakistan BIT, which stated that '[e]ither Contracting Party shall constantly guarantee the observance of the commitments it has entered into with respect to the investments of the investors of the other Contracting Party',[92] elevated 'all contract claims to the level of claims of a breach of the BIT'.[93] Pakistan countered that the contract with SGS required disputes to be

[90] For example, the section does not discuss the privity-related issue of whether shareholders or subnational entities should be covered by umbrella clauses. See Raul Pereira de Souza Fleury, 'Treaty-Protected Investment Agreements: Of Umbrella Clauses and Privity of Contract' (2016) 23 Willamette Journal of International & Dispute Resolution 319; Shotaro Hamamoto, 'Parties to the "Obligations" in the Obligations Observance ("Umbrella") Clause' (2015) 30 ICSID Review 449. See generally *Supervision Y Control SA v Republic of Costa Rica*, ICSID Case No ARB/12/4, Award (18 January 2017) [287].

[91] *SGS v Pakistan* (n 17) [164]. In *Vivendi v Argentina*, which preceded *SGS v Pakistan*, the tribunal and annulment committee were confronted with questions regarding the relationship between contract and treaty claims. See *Compania de Aguas del Aconquija SA & Compagnie Generale des Eaux v Argentine Republic*, ICSID Case No ARB/97/3, Award (21 November 2000); *Compania de Aguas del Aconquija SA & Vivendi Universal v Argentine Republic*, ICSID Case No ARB/97/3, Decision on Annulment (3 July 2002) [103].

[92] *SGS v Pakistan* (n 17) [53].

[93] ibid [54], [99].

referred to arbitration under the *Arbitration Act* of Pakistan.[94] For Pakistan, accepting SGS' argument would 'negate' forum selection clauses in state–investor contracts.[95] The tribunal noted in its decision on jurisdiction that the same facts may lead to both a domestic and an international claim.[96] The more difficult question was whether the tribunal had jurisdiction to determine claims based solely on a contract which do not implicate a substantive standard in the treaty.[97] The tribunal concluded that it did not.[98] The umbrella clause did not provide that breaches of state–investor contracts 'are automatically "elevated" to the level of breaches of international treaty law'.[99] For the *SGS v Pakistan* tribunal, it is not that states may not agree, in BITs, to elevate all breaches of such contracts to treaty breaches, there was nothing in the Switzerland–Pakistan BIT leading to this conclusion.[100] Some other tribunals have adopted a similarly cautious interpretation of umbrella clauses. In *El Paso v Argentina*, the tribunal stated that 'an umbrella clause cannot transform any contract claim into a treaty claim, as this would necessarily imply that any commitments of the State in respect to investments, even in the most minor ones, would be transformed into treaty claims'.[101] For that tribunal, a broad interpretation would be 'quite destructive of the distinction between national legal orders and the international legal order'.[102]

In spite of the approach that tribunals such as *SGS v Pakistan* adopted, arbitral decisions appear to prefer a wider interpretation of umbrella clauses.[103] The *SGS v Philippines* tribunal adopted a more expansive, if nuanced, interpretation.[104] In this case, SGS formed a contract with the Philippines regarding the provision of import supervision services. SGS alleged breach of the contract and sought arbitration under the Switzerland–Philippines BIT.[105] Article

[94] ibid [1]. See [15] for the arbitration and governing law clause in the contract.

[95] ibid [56].

[96] ibid [147].

[97] ibid [156].

[98] ibid [162].

[99] ibid [166], [168]. See also *Joy Mining Machinery Limited v Arab Republic of Egypt*, ICSID Case No ARB/03/11, Award on Jurisdiction (6 August 2004) [81]; *Pan American Energy LLC and BP Argentina Exploration Company v Argentine Republic*, ICSID Case No ARB/03/13, Decision on Preliminary Objections (27 July 2006) [100], [105], [110].

[100] *SGS v Pakistan* (n 17) [173].

[101] *El Paso Energy International Company v Argentine Republic*, ICSID Case No ARB/03/15, Decision on Jurisdiction (27 April 2006) [82].

[102] ibid.

[103] Katherine Jonckheere, 'Practical Implications from an Expansive Interpretation of Umbrella Clauses in International Investment Law' (2015) 11 South Carolina Journal of International Law & Business 143.

[104] *SGS v Philippines* (n 18). For a clarification of the scope of the *SGS v Philippines* decision see Ho (n 35) 205–209. Other tribunals have also adopted a broad interpretation. See *Eureko BV v Republic of Poland*, Partial Award (19 August 2005) [246]–[260].

[105] *SGS v Philippines* (n 18) [1].

X(2) of the BIT stated: 'Each Contracting Party shall observe any obligation it has assumed with regard to specific investments in its territory by investors of the other Contracting Party.'[106] SGS alleged breaches of the BIT due to unpaid amounts under the contract.[107] The Philippines argued that it was a contract dispute governed by the dispute settlement provision of the contract. This provision required that all contractual disputes should be submitted to the Philippines' courts.[108] Further, for the Philippines, the BIT did not 'automatically elevate all ordinary contractual disputes into potential international law disputes'.[109] In contrast, SGS adopted the view that an umbrella clause elevates 'a breach of contract claim to a treaty claim under international law'.[110] Departing from some of the views of the *SGS v Pakistan* tribunal,[111] and even calling its interpretation of the umbrella clause 'unconvincing'[112] and 'highly restrictive',[113] the *SGS v Philippines* tribunal concluded that the umbrella clause 'makes it a breach of the BIT for the host State to fail to observe ... contractual commitments'.[114] It added, however, that the clause 'does not convert the issue of the *extent* or *content* of such obligations into an issue of international law'.[115] The tribunal in *BIVAC v Paraguay* adopted a similar view, finding that the language and the context of the umbrella clause in question created an international obligation for the states parties to observe their contractual obligations.[116] In *Noble Ventures v Romania* the tribunal adopted similarly expansive views.[117] For the tribunal, the 'Parties had as their aim to equate contractual obligations governed by municipal law to international treaty obligations as established in the BIT'.[118]

One reading of these conflicting decisions would be that they were driven by textual variations. In *SGS v Pakistan* the tribunal noted that a differently drafted treaty might lead to different results.[119] This suggests that states can improve

[106] ibid [34].
[107] ibid [15]–[16].
[108] ibid [17]; see [22] for the dispute settlement clause, which also indicated that the laws of the Philippines will govern disputes.
[109] ibid [56].
[110] ibid [65].
[111] ibid [97].
[112] ibid [125].
[113] ibid [120].
[114] ibid [128].
[115] ibid [128].
[116] *BIVAC v Paraguay* (n 13) [141]. Like *SGS v Philippines* (n 18), *BIVAC v Paraguay* distinguished between jurisdiction and admissibility; see *BIVAC v Paraguay* (n 13) [142], [159]. See also Katia Yannaca-Small, 'BIVAC BV v Paraguay *versus* SGS v Paraguay: An Umbrella Clause Still in Search of One Identity' (2013) 28 ICSID Review 307.
[117] *Noble Ventures Inc v Romania*, ICSID Case No ARB/01/11, Award (12 October 2005) [61].
[118] ibid.
[119] *SGS v Pakistan* (n 17) [173].

the clarity of umbrella clauses by their treaty practice. Another reading is that tribunals have been willing to adopt restrictive or expansive interpretations of umbrella clauses sometimes with little, if any, significant differences in the clauses themselves. This critique is more complex than an explanation based on the text of BITs alone can substantiate. The *El Paso* tribunal, in the course of ultimately seizing jurisdiction, captured a fundamental concern when it noted that, if the interpretation in *SGS v Philippines* were adopted, 'the violation of *any legal obligation* of a State and not only of any contractual obligation with respect to investment, is a violation of the BIT, whatever the source of the obligation and whatever the seriousness of the breach'. This outcome, according to the tribunal, would make it 'sufficient to include a so-called "umbrella clause" and a dispute settlement mechanism, and no other articles setting standards for the protection of foreign investments in a BIT'.[120] This would, essentially, blur the distinction between the national and international legal orders.[121] Clearly, conflicting interpretations of umbrella clauses suggest that the treatification purpose for which these clauses were developed have never been fully embraced.

3.2 Forum Selection Clauses in Contracts

A closely related theme is the applicability of forum selection clauses in contracts. Again, *SGS v Pakistan* and *SGS v Philippines* are the often referenced arbitral decisions on this subject. The *SGS v Pakistan* tribunal's decision that the umbrella clause did not 'elevate' the contract claim to a BIT claim was partly informed by the contract's forum selection clause.[122] As noted above, the contract in *SGS v Philippines* also included an exclusive forum selection clause and a choice of law clause that referred to Philippine courts and law, respectively.[123] Here, the BIT did not override the exclusive forum selection clause in the contract.[124] Although the tribunal took jurisdiction based on the BIT, it concluded that the contract claim was inadmissible.[125] Such was the tribunal's response to concerns about reading umbrella clauses broadly. *SGS v Paraguay* casts doubt on this resolution.[126] It rejected Paraguay's characterization of SGS' claims as

[120] *El Paso v Argentina* (n 101) [76]. See [84] for clarification of the tribunal's position.
[121] ibid [77].
[122] *SGS v Pakistan* (n 17) [165].
[123] See *SGS v Philippines* (n 18) [22] for the dispute settlement clause, which also indicated that the laws of the Philippines will govern disputes.
[124] ibid [139]–[143].
[125] ibid [155].
[126] *SGS Société Génerale de Surveillance SA v Republic of Paraguay*, ICSID Case No ARB/07/29, Decision on Jurisdiction (12 February 2010).

contract claims. It also found that the forum selection clause in the contract could not deprive the tribunal of jurisdiction to hear treaty claims.[127] On this reading, a claimant's characterization of a breach of contract as a treaty claim would essentially invalidate the forum selection clause in the contract.[128] The more recent decision in *Belenergia v Italy* adopted a similar approach by taking the position that the treaty is the source of the umbrella clause and the claim was admissible.[129]

Some have argued that while umbrella clauses are reminiscent of the historical conflicting positions between Third World states and developed countries, to give contracts (that have exclusive forum selection clauses) primacy over investment treaties (that have umbrella clauses) may be as unconscionable for the investor as not giving effect to the umbrella clause.[130] Such a view, among other things, fails to account for the validity of the domestic legal order under which the investor and the state formed the contract.

3.3 Distinctions between Sovereign and Commercial Acts

The distinction between sovereign and commercial acts is the third theme discussed in this section. Like the other themes, there are conflicting views on this distinction. While some view the distinction as necessary, many umbrella clauses are drafted widely enough that they potentially capture both (or all) types of acts and investments. To support the distinction, Wälde emphasizes that '[t]he discussion in the 1950s and 1960s which gave birth to the umbrella clause envisaged not a commercial law breach, but rather governmental action abrogating a long term – mostly concession-like – agreement'.[131] *El Paso v Argentina* and *Pan American v Argentina* regard the distinction as being between the state acting as a sovereign or as a 'merchant'.[132] On this view, foreign

[127] ibid [138]. On the distinction between contract claims and treaty claims and breaches of contract and treaty see Eric Brabandere, *Investment Treaty Arbitration as Public International Law: Procedural Aspects and Implications* (CUP 2014) 32–38.

[128] *SGS v Paraguay* (n 126) [128]–[134]. The Annulment committee that was constituted after the decision on the merits declined to reopen questions of jurisdiction relating to the umbrella clause in the Switzerland–Paraguay BIT and the forum selection clause in the contract. See *SGS Société Génerale de Surveillance SA v Republic of Paraguay* (ICSID Case No ARB/07/29), Decision on Annulment (19 May 2014) [130].

[129] *Belenergia SA v Italian Republic*, ICSID Case No ARB/15/40, Award (6 August 2019) [356].

[130] Jarrod Wong, 'Umbrella Clauses in Bilateral Investment Treaties: Of Breaches of Contract, Treaty Violations, and the Divide between Developing and Developed Countries in Foreign Investment Disputes' (2006) 14 George Mason Law Review 137.

[131] Wälde (n 21) 193.

[132] *El Paso v Argentina* (n 101) [79], [81]; *Pan American v Argentina* (n 99) [108]–[109].

investors need protection from the state when it acts as a sovereign.[133] That is essential given the inequality between the state as sovereign and the foreign investor as a commercial entity. However, 'elevating' contract claims to BIT claims on this view alone ignores, as the *El Paso* tribunal noted, the fact that investment contracts have their own dispute settlement clauses, which are often dismissed in favour of BIT arbitration.[134]

In *Joy Mining v Egypt* the tribunal found that it lacked jurisdiction partly because the relevant contract did not constitute an investment. It also gave effect to the contract's forum selection clause, and concluded that there was no credible allegation that Egypt as a state interfered with the investor's contract rights.[135] Egypt argued that the contract was a standard supply agreement and its terms were 'ordinary commercial terms'.[136] The tribunal emphasized a distinction between 'commercial aspects' of a dispute and those aspects that involve 'state interference' with the contract.[137] For the tribunal, the bank guarantee raised commercial issues and the tribunal could not accept that not releasing it would violate the treaty.[138] Essentially, for some tribunals, the state must act in the exercise of its public powers for the treaty to apply.[139]

Other tribunals adopt a different view. In *Burlington Resources v Ecuador*, the tribunal stated that Ecuador's argument that Burlington's claims did not relate to the exercise of sovereign power was not supported by the treaty text. It expressed that 'umbrella clauses may apply even if no exercise of sovereign power is involved'.[140] In *Duke Energy v Ecuador*, the tribunal noted that it was an 'open question' whether breach of an umbrella clause required 'sovereign interference'. The tribunal concluded that while 'language to that effect appears in some cases … a majority of decisions do not formulate such distinction'.[141]

The sovereign–commercial act distinction has the potential to limit the scope of umbrella clauses, but, like the other themes, the jurisprudence is inconsistent. Excluding commercial acts from the ambit of umbrella clauses preserves some space to resolve public interest issues in other forums. A state's

133 *El Paso v Argentina* (n 132) [80].
134 ibid [77].
135 *Joy Mining v Egypt* (n 99) [82].
136 ibid [32].
137 ibid [72].
138 ibid [78]. The *Salini v Jordan* tribunal adopted the reasoning in *Joy Mining v Egypt* (n 99). See *Salini Costruttori SpA and Italstrade SpA v Hashemite Kingdom of Jordan*, ICSID Case No ARB/02/13, Decision of Jurisdiction (12 November 2004) [155]. See also *El Paso v Argentina* (n 101) [85]–[86].
139 *Siemens AG v Argentine Republic*, ICSID Case No ARB/02/8, Award (17 January 2007) [246]–[253].
140 *Burlington Resources Inc v Republic of Ecuador*, ICSID Case No ARB/08/5, Decision on Jurisdiction (2 June 2010) [190]; see [204] for the position 'outside the umbrella clause context'.
141 *Duke Energy Electroquil Partners & Electroquil SA v Republic of Ecuador*, ICSID Case No ARB/04/19, Award (18 August 2008) [320].

sovereign acts are more likely to engender political or public interest questions, but commercial acts are not always devoid of such matters. Argentina's cases illustrate that the public interest can be implicated regardless of the categorization of a state's acts as sovereign or commercial. In *El Paso v Argentina*, for instance, the tribunal observed that there is no treaty protection for breaches of commercial contracts.[142] That dispute was not spared from broader public interest and politics contexts with the claimant alleging that Argentina's actions were discriminatory and politically motivated.[143] In *Siemens v Argentina*, the claimant also argued that Argentina's decision to terminate the contract was political.[144] Argentina had indeed suffered a massive economic and sociopolitical crisis. The tribunal in *Continental Casualty v Argentina* commented on the dire situation, which involved:

> [T]he near collapse of the domestic economy; the soaring inflation; the leap in unemployment; the social hardships bringing down more than half of the population below the poverty line; the immediate threats to the health of young children, the sick and the most vulnerable members of the population, the widespread unrest and disorders; the real risk of insurrection and extreme political disturbances, the abrupt resignations of successive Presidents and the collapse of the Government, together with a partial breakdown of the political institutions and an extended vacuum of power.[145]

If all contract violations in such situations as Argentina's were transformed into treaty violations, it would remove contract claims from the domestic domain. That domain is the one in which concerns of citizens have greater potential to be better addressed. Hence, it becomes necessary to have mechanisms that encompass all affected parties in these complex disputes. Cases such as *Tecmed v Mexico*[146] and *Clayton v Canada*[147] demonstrate that investment arbitration is not the most apt mechanism for addressing such complex disputes. These cases engage international investment law's treatment of political considerations

[142] *El Paso v Argentina* (n 101) [81].
[143] *El Paso Energy International Company v Argentine Republic*, ICSID Case No ARB/03/15, Award (31 October 2011) [301].
[144] *Siemens v Argentina* (n 139) [159].
[145] *Continental Casualty Company v Argentine Republic*, ICSID Case No ARB/03/09, Award (5 September 2008) [180].
[146] *Tecnias Medioambientales Tecmed SA v The United Mexican States*, ICSID Case No ARB AF/00/2, Award (29 May 2003).
[147] *William Ralph Clayton, William Richard Clayton, Douglas Clayton, Daniel Clayton and Bilcon of Delaware Inc v Government of Canada*, Permanent Court of Arbitration Case No 2009-04, Award on Jurisdiction and Liability (17 March 2015).

arising from local community preferences; and they view politics as the intervention of third parties, often on the side of the state or the emergence of domestic concerns. Hence, it is informative to consider tribunal decisions where investors plead political intervention. In some of these cases, tribunals read politics as inconsistent with states' legal obligations. In others, they did not so readily dismiss political considerations. *Biwater Gauff v Tanzania* is an example of the former. The case arose from a water and sewer management and operation system.[148] The tribunal found that some of the government's actions were 'motivated by political considerations' and were, as such, inconsistent with Tanzania's obligations under the United Kingdom–Tanzania BIT.[149] An example of the latter situation—where politics are not so readily dismissed—is *AES v Hungary*. In that case, the investor alleged that the measure was 'adopted for purely political reasons'.[150] The tribunal responded that 'any reasonably informed business person or investor knows that laws can evolve in accordance with the perceived political or policy dictates of the times'.[151] Further, it noted that 'the fact that an issue becomes a political matter ... does not mean that the existence of rational policy is erased'.[152] Based on this approach, it appears that there is some space for recalibrating investment law to engage public interest questions but the question remains whether such space is sufficient to address the fundamental nature of public interest considerations. In the context of umbrella clauses, tribunals have continued to adopt inconsistent approaches in their decisions, sometimes with a preference for excluding the domestic legal order.

3.4 Umbrella Clauses, Interpretations, and Wrong Turns

One may ask whether the law of umbrella clauses took a wrong turn and, if so, when. Although there were debates earlier about contract and treaty in *Vivendi v Argentina*,[153] the first targeted discussion of umbrella clauses

[148] *Biwater Gauff (Tanzania) Ltd v United Republic of Tanzania*, ICSID Case No ARB/05/22, Award (24 July 2008) [15]–[16].

[149] ibid [500]. See Agreement between the United Kingdom of Great Britain and Northern Ireland and the United Republic of Tanzania for the Promotion and Protection of Investments (7 January 1994); entered into force on 2 August 1996.

[150] *AES Summit Generation Limited and AES-Tisza Eromu Kft v Republic of Hungary*, ICSID Case No ARB/07/22, Award (23 September 2010) [9.1.7]. See also *Impregilo SpA v Argentine Republic*, ICSID Case No ARB/07/17, Award (21 June 2011) [201].

[151] *AES Summit Generation Limited and AES-Tisza Eromu Kft v Republic of Hungary* (n 150) [9.3.34].

[152] ibid [10.3.23]. See also *Electrabel SA v Hungary*, ICSID Case No ARB/07/19, Award (25 November 2015) [8.23].

[153] *Vivendi v Argentina* (n 91).

is credited to *SGS v Pakistan*.[154] It was immediately followed by the largely divergent decision in *SGS v Philippines*.[155] If one puts aside the origins of umbrella clauses, one might conclude that umbrella clauses took a problematic turn at this stage. The present author adopts a different view. It is suggested instead that the conflicting decisions are symptoms of deeper challenges within the law of umbrella clauses rather than the cause. Umbrella clauses did not take a wrong turn after they were developed; their purpose has always been flawed.

First, umbrella clauses were born in the shadow of decolonization and imperialism. They were a response to what the drafters perceived as a specific problem which is no longer representative of most investment disputes and, perhaps, never was. Since this time, there has been a decades-long attempt to 'treatify' every aspect of foreign investment. Yet, domestically, contracts have retained significance, especially in potentially contentious areas such as natural resource development. States and investors did not abandon the contract mechanism even when treaties became the primary focus of international investment law.

Secondly, umbrella clauses have been drafted differently across investment treaties and influenced by a lack of clarity since their inception. As section 2 demonstrated, even the earliest versions of umbrella clauses were subject to conflicting interpretations by commentators. The interpretive challenges that tribunals have witnessed cannot be separated from the origins of umbrella clauses and the politics that inform those origins. The BIT era served mainly to allow actors in investment law to see how the clauses work in practice. Rather than create the problem, the BIT era revealed the tensions in umbrella clauses which existed from inception.

Thirdly, the development of umbrella clauses in the decolonization era swung the pendulum quite far in favour of investment protection. It allowed the focus to shift from the state to the investor, while largely neglecting people within states. Today, both states and activists alike are adopting approaches to international investment law that seek some balance within the system. Given the origins of umbrella clauses and the continuing challenges with their interpretation in the present era, the last section of this chapter calls for reimagining investment law without umbrella clauses.

[154] *SGS v Pakistan* (n 17) [164].
[155] *SGS v Philippines* (n 18).

4 Reimagining Contractual Relationships in Investment Law

There has been significant and justified outcry over the domination that ensued when influence was concentrated in the hands of colonial powers. The ascendance of the postcolonial Third World state was not met with fanfare either, especially because these states sought to depart from the rules that governed the treatment of foreign property. The tide of international investment law shifted in the twentieth century away from states and towards foreign investors. Attention turned to the foreign investor as an ostensibly benevolent provider of capital who must be protected. These shifts demonstrate the primacy of transnational capital.[156] Now, international investment law has become embedded within a neoliberal capitalist system that privileges capital. Neoliberal capitalism informs the choices in international investment law and constrains the alternatives. It makes the reimagination of investment law challenging. Yet, the status quo is not inevitable. It is not part of a natural order from which the law cannot depart. Instead, approaches to reimagining contractual relationships in investment law should be explored, so long as they do not expose foreign investors to arbitrary treatment. That would swing the pendulum away from fairness, which any system needs to thrive. The two approaches discussed in this section aim to achieve (some) balance which has been lacking in international investment law among states, foreign investors, and local communities. They acknowledge the interests of all these actors and do not seek to privilege the legitimate views of one over the other. Of necessity, they eschew the politics labels by which international investment law has itself been politicized.

The first approach is to eliminate umbrella clauses. Elimination would not mean that contracts should not be performed. The principle of *pacta sunt servanda*[157]—'agreements which are legally binding must be performed'[158]—is a basic organizing principle. Wehberg argues that the relationship between states and foreign investors cannot exist without it.[159] He asserts that

[156] See generally Leslie Sklair, *The Transnational Capitalist Class* (Blackwell 2001); BS Chimni, 'Prolegomena to a Class Approach to International Law' (2010) 21 European Journal of International Law 57.

[157] Hans Wehberg, 'Pacta Sunt Servanda' (1959) 53 American Journal of International Law 775; Christina Binder, 'Stability and Change in Times of Fragmentation: The Limits of *Pacta Sunt Servanda* Revisited' (2012) 25 Leiden Journal of International Law 909.

[158] Anthony Aust, 'Pacta Sunt Servanda' in *Oxford Public International Law: Max Planck Encyclopedias of International Law* (OUP 2007) https://opil.ouplaw.com/view/10.1093/law:epil/9780199231690/law-9780199231690-e1449.

[159] Wehberg (n 157) 786.

international law depends on 'the powerful instrument of the contract'.[160] It is essentially a myth, as Yackee notes, to suggest that, before modern investment treaties, states had the freedom to break their contracts with foreign investors with 'impunity'.[161] Indeed, umbrella clauses and the investment treaties that incorporate them, are unnecessary to facilitate sanctity of contract.[162] If investment contracts could not be breached without consequence before these modern treaties, the purpose of umbrella clauses is open to serious doubt.

It is not radical to argue that umbrella clauses should be eliminated as state practice affirms this position. Umbrella clauses are falling out of favour, as they should.[163] Canada has generally not used umbrella clauses in its BIT practice.[164] An umbrella clause was also excluded from the *Canada–European Union Comprehensive Economic and Trade Agreement*.[165] Norway likewise excluded an umbrella clause from its 2015 model BIT, although the 2007 model included one.[166] States such as Argentina, Paraguay, and the Philippines—all of which have faced cases that led to conflicting interpretations of umbrella clauses—have excluded umbrella clauses from the (few) recent BITs they have concluded.[167] It is also instructive to examine the South African Development Community's Model BIT template. The drafters considered and then rejected umbrella clauses. In article 29.9, the scope of arbitration is specifically restricted to alleged breaches of treaty rights or obligations that are subject to arbitration.[168] The commentary to the Model BIT template notes that an umbrella

160 ibid 782.

161 Jason Webb Yackee, 'Pacta Sunt Servanda and State Promises to Foreign Investors before Bilateral Investment Treaties: Myth and Reality' (2009) 32 Fordham International Law Journal 1550.

162 ibid.

163 Sometimes, states limit the application of umbrella clauses by excluding these clauses from the purview of international arbitration. An example is the Colombia–Switzerland BIT that excludes umbrella clauses from the scope of arbitration. Article 11(3) of the Agreement between the Republic of Colombia and the Swiss Confederation on the Promotion and Reciprocal Protection of Investments, signed on 17 May 2006 and entered into force of 6 October 2009. *Glencore v Colombia* concluded that the claims under the umbrella clause in the Colombia–Switzerland BIT could not be submitted to international arbitration. *Glencore International AG and CI Prodeco SA v Republic of* Colombia (ICSID Case No ARB/16/6) Award of 27 August 2019 [1019].

164 Katia Yannaca-Small, 'Interpretation of the Umbrella Clause in Investment Agreements', OECD Working Papers on International Investment 2006/03, 6 https://www.oecd.org/daf/inv/investment-policy/WP-2006_3.pdf.

165 Canada–European Union Comprehensive Economic and Trade Agreement https://www.international.gc.ca/trade-commerce/trade-agreements-accords-commerciaux/agr-acc/ceta-aecg/text-texte/08.aspx?lang=eng. See Nathalie Bernasconi-Osterwalder, 'Commentary to the Draft Investment Chapter of the Canada–EU Comprehensive Economic and Trade Agreement' (May 2013) 4, 20 https://www.iisd.org/system/files/publications/commentary_investment_chapter_CETA.pdf.

166 See de Souza Fleury (n 12) 689.

167 ibid 690.

168 South African Development Community, 'SADC Model Bilateral Investment Treaty Template with Commentary' (July 2012) 59 https://www.iisd.org/itn/wp-content/uploads/2012/10/sadc-model-bit-template-final.pdf.

clause was deliberately excluded.[169] Article 29.9 is also a specific response to conflicting interpretations of forum selection clauses. Despite the direction towards elimination of umbrella clauses many states maintain support for umbrella clauses, signalling that the controversy may not abate any time soon.[170]

While it may provide some added regulatory space, eliminating or limiting umbrella clauses is not enough. This makes a second approach to reimagining contractual relationships necessary. The politics of local community marginalization in this area exceeds specific standards of treatment. This marginalization is at the core of many arguments against international investment law.[171] More robust contracts could provide a mechanism to respond to aspects of the marginalization. Recourse to contracts is apposite here considering the relationship between umbrella clauses and contracts. As noted above, given the prevalence of *pacta sunt servanda*, the major contribution of umbrella clauses appears to be, historically, the location of contracts within the realm of treaty accessible to home states and, in contemporary times, the provision of access to investor–state arbitration through investment treaties. Yet, absence of umbrella clauses does not preclude access to dispute settlement as contract-based disputes can be submitted to international investment arbitration.[172] This is because dispute settlement forums such as the International Center for Settlement of Investment Disputes (ICSID) permit the submission of disputes that arise under multiple instruments including treaties, contract and legislation.[173] Questions, therefore, remain regarding the nature and appropriateness of dispute settlement mechanisms provided in these contracts and the regulatory and policy space that they provide.

Outside umbrella clauses, contracts have not garnered as much attention in international investment law because of the shift to investment treaties and investment treaty arbitration. Yet, contracts continue to wield significant influence in the world of foreign investment. There is now a move to

[169] ibid 60.

[170] See de Souza Fleury (n 12) 691.

[171] See eg Odumosu (n 3); Nicolas M Perrone, 'Taking Local Expectations Seriously: A Fresh Start for Foreign Investment Governance?' in John D Haskell and Akbar Rasulov (eds), *New Voices and Perspectives in International Economic Law*, European Yearbook of International Economic Law (Springer 2020).

[172] See ICSID, 'Spotlight on Contract-based Disputes at ICSID' https://icsid.worldbank.org/en/Pages/resources/Spotlight-on-Contract-based-Disputes-at-ICSID.aspx.

[173] See art 25 of the Convention on the Settlement of Investment Disputes between States and Nationals of other States (18 March 1965) (1965) 5 ILM 532, entered into force on 14 October 1966. See also Aron Broches, 'Bilateral Investment Treaties and Arbitration of Investment Disputes' in Jan C Schultz and Albert Jan van den Berg (eds), *The Art of Arbitration: Essays on International Arbitration: Liber Amicorum Pieter Sanders 1912-1982* (Kluwer Law & Taxation Publishers 1982) 63.

re-recognize the influence of contracts in foreign investment.[174] Yackee has observed that '[i]nvestment contracts are not a relic of past practice; they remain commonplace in the modern era, and indeed, investors often continue to insist on obtaining them'.[175] Where appropriately constructed, contracts have the potential to serve as a tool for recalibrating investment relationships. They can, however, only achieve such shift under a radically different agenda.

A radical turn in contracts is not and, in fact, cannot be limited only to arrangements between states and investors. Some contractual arrangements with local communities have arisen in the extractive industries.[176] They are especially relevant when extractive projects proceed in territories of Indigenous peoples. Existing versions of these agreements, however, mostly remain limited and situated within the prevailing system such that they hardly move the conversation beyond the current model. Yet, they offer glimpses of what is possible in a reformed investment law regime. It is necessary to reimagine contracts not only as a tool of investment protection but also as a mechanism for recognizing the centrality of local communities in investment projects in a manner that extends beyond limited contractual engagement with Indigenous peoples and local communities through benefits contracts. These more robust contractual arrangements could take a number of forms. Specifically, they could be multi-actor contracts which determine the most important questions about projects, and specifically incorporate local communities that may be directly impacted by an investment project.[177] Such community engagement would embrace and centre issues and relationships that are dismissed as political in the current system.

International law is a product of interactions with the people in the colonies.[178] Those interactions were used to push these peoples to the margins and out of the realm of the legal. Interactions with local communities, through

[174] James Gathii and Ibironke T Odumosu-Ayanu, 'The Turn to Contractual Responsibility in the Global Extractive Industry' (2016) 1 Business & Human Rights Journal 69; Jason Webb Yackee, 'Do We Really Need BITs? Toward a Return to Contract in International Investment Law' (2008) 3 Asian Journal of WTO & International Health Law and Policy 121.

[175] Yackee (n 174) 133.

[176] Ibironke T Odumosu-Ayanu and Dwight Newman (eds), *Indigenous-Industry Agreements, Natural Resources and the Law* (Routledge 2021).

[177] See Ibironke T Odumosu-Ayanu, 'Governments, Investors and Local Communities: Analysis of a Multi-Actor Investment Contract Framework' (2014) 15 Melbourne Journal of International Law 473. See also Lorenzo Cotula, 'Reconsidering Sovereignty, Ownership and Consent in Natural Resource Contracts: From Concepts to Practice' (2018) European Yearbook of International Economic Law 143.

[178] See Anghie (n 30).

states or otherwise, are often deemed political, thus allowing international investment law to treat them as being outside its realm. A reimagination of investment law must read these interactions into the main corpus of the law as these interactions are and have always been an important part of the law. One should aim to disrupt the status quo and affirm the interests of all the core actors, without undermining the agency of any of them.

9

The Right to Regulate

Jimena Sierra-Camargo and Federico Suárez-Ricaurte

1 Introduction

Regulatory disputes between foreign investors and host states are a contentious topic in international investment law. These disputes arise especially when states adopt measures in the public interest, acting within their general regulatory orbit, and investors object that their private interests in the form of 'rights' or 'legitimate expectations' have been violated. Investors have then threatened or launched investor–state dispute settlement (ISDS) disputes, seeking exorbitant compensation and incentivizing 'regulatory chill' on the part of the state.[1] In turn, states may inhibit themselves from adopting autonomous decisions in the public interest, for fear of costly arbitral awards.

In this context, a key question is whether the so-called right to regulate (RTR) offers an avenue for states to respond to these challenges. In the literature, there is intense debate over whether the RTR should be recognized and guaranteed in an explicit or implicit way. Depending on the strength of the 'right', it may be useful for states. That said, it could also create a further obstacle to state action and deepen the asymmetric relationships embedded in investment law, between states and investors and between Global North and Global South. In this chapter, we tease out the ambivalence in the RTR. On the one hand, it may imply per se a restriction on the state's regulatory space. On the other, it may be interpreted as a prerogative granted to the state in the form of a legal right and therefore as an instrument to defend the state's regulatory role. In its latter form, the RTR has some promise to balance a system that emerged, originally, to protect and privilege foreign investors in a (post-)colonial context.

By emphasizing the post-colonial origins of ISDS, this chapter inquires into whether recognition of an RTR would make ISDS more balanced. We argue

[1] See Kyla Tienhara, 'Regulatory Chill in a Warming World: The Threat to Climate Policy Posed by Investor-State Dispute Settlement' (2017) 7(2) Transnational Environmental Law 229; Gus Van Harten, *Sovereign Choices and Sovereign Constraints. Judicial Restraint in Investment Treaty Arbitration* (OUP 2013).

Jimena Sierra-Camargo and Federico Suárez-Ricaurte, *The Right to Regulate* In: *Rethinking Investment Law.*
Edited by: David Schneiderman and Gus Van Harten, Oxford University Press.
 DOI: 10.1093/oso/9780192871084.003.0009

that the RTR is, itself, part of the post-colonial problem of investment law that perpetuates North–South asymmetric relationships. In our discussion of the RTR, we focus on its origins, its normative and jurisprudential development, and its scope and limitations. We review several cases, most notably *Eco Oro v Colombia*, to illustrate how even a new generation treaty can be distorted by a tribunal majority to favour multinationals from capital-exporting countries. The overall purpose of our study is to consider the potential of the RTR to make ISDS fairer and more balanced.

2 Post-colonial Origins of the RTR

At its origins, the RTR was strongly associated with the principle of permanent sovereignty over natural resources (PSNR). This principle was developed in a series of United Nations resolutions between 1952 and 1974.[2] Although these resolutions recognized the sovereignty of newly independent and developing countries over their natural resources, they also restricted the policy space for these countries to regulate in the public interest. For example, Resolution 1803 of 1962 gathered various elements of the principle as part of the classic Declaration on PSNR.[3] However, this resolution also established limits to the exercise of the sovereignty of 'developing countries'[4] over natural resources by integrating into the world economy, cooperating with the so-called developed countries, promoting orthodox economic development, and compensating foreign investors even before the decolonization process had been completed. Newly independent states, operating as development agents in a post-colonial context, were not allowed to create or rethink their own autonomous development models. Instead of challenging the hegemonic model, they were expected to acquire capital and equipment from capital-exporting countries, to exploit their own natural resources, and export commodities in accordance with the needs of the international trade. Moreover, they were expected to compensate investors in cases where their 'acquired rights' were impaired.

[2] See United Nations, General Assembly Resolution 523 (12 January 1952); Resolution 626 (21 December 1952); Resolution 1314 (12 December 1958); Resolution 1515 (15 December 1960); Resolution 1803 (14 December 1962); Resolution 2158 (November 1966); Resolution 3281 (12 December 1974).

[3] See 'A Genealogy on the Principle on Permanent Sovereignty of Natural Resources' in Jimena Sierra, 'Desarrollo y Gobernanza Global: una revisión histórica de la construcción del nuevo paradigma extractivista en el sur global' *Construyendo el futuro: Conversaciones jurídicas sobre la globalización* (Atelier Libros Jurídicos 2017) 205–36.

[4] See Donatella Alessandrini, *Developing Countries and the Multilateral Trade Regime: The Failure and Promise of the WTO's Development Mission* (Hart Publishing 2010) 4–21, 217–18.

Even in this era, disputes over the amount of compensation due in the event of expropriation or nationalization continued to dominate discussions at the United Nations.[5] Investment law purports to settle the dispute over compensation for expropriation by incorporating standards of customary international law in whose formation most decolonized states did not participate.[6] Once those states were able to contribute to the making of international law at the UN, the discussion culminated in 1974 in the Charter of Economic Rights and Duties of States (Resolution 3281).[7] Unlike Resolution 1803 of 1962, the Charter did not rely on international law but rather on domestic law to determine the amount of compensation due to foreign investors in the case of expropriation or nationalization.

Although the Charter of 1974 received majority support in the UN General Assembly, it was effectively disregarded by international lawyers in subsequent resource disputes. Instead, the Charter's provisions were interpreted as non-binding on capital-exporting countries.[8] To counteract provisions that preferred domestic over international law, bankers, business leaders, lawyers, and arbitrators of developed countries promoted the idea of a new transnational law[9] and, with it, arbitration in ISDS.[10] It is evident that the origins of investment law and its dispute settlement are tightly connected to the history of ongoing foreign control over the natural resources of most countries in the decolonization period.

[5] See General Assembly Resolution 1803 (XVII) of 14 December 1962: 'Permanent sovereignty over natural resources', para 4: 'Nationalization, expropriation or requisitioning shall be based on grounds or reasons of public utility, security or the national interest which are recognized as overriding purely individual or private interests, both domestic and foreign. In such cases the owner shall be paid appropriate compensation, in accordance with the rules in force in the State taking such measures in the exercise of its sovereignty and in accordance with international law. In any case where the question of compensation gives rise to a controversy, the national jurisdiction of the State taking such measures shall be exhausted. However, upon agreement by sovereign States and other parties concerned, settlement of the dispute should be made through arbitration or international adjudication.'

[6] See Antony Anghie, *Imperialism, Sovereignty and the Making of International Law* (CUP 2004) 211–23.

[7] See General Assembly Resolution 3821 (XXIX) of 12 December 1974, 'Charter of Economic Rights and Duties of States'.

[8] *Texaco Overseas Petroleum Co & California Asiatic Oil Co v Government of the Libyan Arab Republic*, 53 ILR 389, Preliminary Award (27 November 1975); Award on the Merits (19 January 1977). See also Anghie (n 6) 221–23.

[9] Peer Zumbansen, 'Transnational Law' *Elgar Encyclopaedia of Comparative Law* (Jan Smits ed, Edward Elgar Publishing 2006); Nicolas Perrone, *Investment Treaties and the Legal Imagination: How Foreign Investors Play by Their Own Rules* (OUP 2021)10; Farshad Ghodoosi, *International Dispute Resolution and the Public Policy Exception* (Routledge 2017). According to Ghodoosi, transnational law has caused a 'weak and elusive public policy doctrine which is losing its status as the only internal and jurisprudential control mechanism in arbitration'.

[10] Perrone (n 10).

3 What Is Meant by an RTR?

The first investment treaties were designed as legal devices to protect European investors from actions abroad that an investor's home state deemed expropriatory. If we understand the RTR as 'the policy space available in investment agreements for countries to regulate in the public interest',[11] then it is apparent that investment treaties are intended to restrict a state's RTR—they were meant to inhibit 'regulatory experimentation harmful to foreign investors' rights'.[12] To maintain the legitimacy of this new system, however, it was necessary to stipulate that there was some policy and regulatory space remaining for states. To that end, the RTR has now been incorporated into many bilateral investment treaties and cognate legal orders.[13]

In modern investment law, RTR terminology emerged as an affirmation that 'regulatory freedom is well-anchored in the realm of at least three other international systems', referring to the World Trade Organization, the European Union, and international human rights law.[14] Some can, therefore, claim that the RTR is not particularly novel. Express reference to the RTR emerged in model BITs only in 2004, however, and have been included in investment treaties since then.[15] Titi claims that such treaties create an 'expectation' that the RTR will continue to proliferate 'as a result of a concerted and very conscious effort to reserve a modicum of policy space'.[16] What prompted the shift? It appears that these express references to the RTR were a response by states to investment arbitration outcomes, reflecting a preoccupation with the need to safeguard a modicum of host state policy space.[17] According to Haljan, integrating the interest of the host state with foreign investor interest through the right to regulate clause embedded in the new generation of BITs or FTAs is unachievable. Whereas foreign investment seeks the repatriation of capital

[11] Fabio Morosini, 'Rethinking the right to regulate in investment agreements: reflections from the South African and Brazilian experiences' in Alvaro Santos, Chantal Thomas, and David Trubek (eds), *World Trade and Investment Law Reimagined: A Progressive Agenda for an Inclusive Globalization* (Anthem Press 2019) 162.

[12] ibid.

[13] For an overview of the perspectives adopted by different stakeholders on the desired balance between the right to regulate and investment protection see David Gaukrodger, 'The Balance Between Investor Protection and the Right to Regulate in Investment Treaties: A Scoping Paper' (2017) OECD Working Papers on International Investment 2017/02.

[14] Aikaterini Titi, *The Right to Regulate in International Investment Law* (Hart Publishing 2013) 66. Titi identifies 'WTO law, EU law and the human rights protection system under the umbrella of the Council of Europe'.

[15] ibid 66. Some examples where new formulations of treaty standards were rethought are Canada's 2004 Model BIT, the United States' 2004 Model BIT, and Norway's 2007 Draft Model BIT, and CETA.

[16] ibid.

[17] ibid 58.

and profits, host states pursue the development and welfare of the host society. Hence, there is no 'common starting point for any balancing of values'.[18]

The RTR can be understood as either an explicit or an implicit legal right of states to exercise their sovereign autonomy and regulatory power in the public interest. As an implicit right, the RTR refers to what, historically, has been considered an intrinsic characteristic of states as subjects of international law, a feature connected with the principle of state sovereignty.[19] According to Korzun, an implicit RTR refers to a state's ability to 'adopt, maintain, and enforce the measures necessary for the advancement of its public policy goals' by means of 'its legislative, administrative, and judicial bodies'.[20] By contrast, an explicit RTR refers only to a limited 'right' that can be invoked in exceptional cases by the state to defend itself from an investor's claim. Drawing on investment treaties and ISDS awards, Titi casts the RTR in these narrow terms. That is, the RTR is available as a defence in legal proceedings and requires a specific legal basis—it is embodied in treaty provisions and is subject to interpretation by investment arbitrators.

Giannakopoulos argues that the right to regulate is a 'manifestation of the State's jurisdictional powers'.[21] The right to regulate under international law should be conceptualized under the 'Hohfeldian framework of the law'.[22] In Hohfeld's perspective, 'a power is a special case of a liberty denoting one's legal ability to alter the existing legal condition of others by creating rights, imposing duties, or conferring liberties or powers'.[23] That attribution directly expresses the notion of jurisdiction in its numerous forms, which is strictly connected to the sovereignty principle.[24] Some authors question whether there is an implicit right to regulate at all. They cite cases in which arbitrators have discussed regulatory freedom, traditionally understood as a core state attribute in international law, in the absence of any legal provision on the RTR the relevant treaty. These authors argue, for example, that when tribunals 'have on occasion

[18] David Haljan, 'A Public Law View of the New Generation of FTAs' (2019) 66 Netherlands International Law Review 237, 264–65.

[19] James Crawford, 'Sovereignty as a Legal Value' in James Crawford and Marti Koskenniemi, *The Cambridge Companion to International Law* (CUP 2012) 117–33.

[20] Vera Korzun, 'The Right to Regulate in Investor-State Arbitration: Slicing and Dicing Regulatory Carve-Outs' (2017) 50 Vanderbilt Journal of Transnational Law 355, 373.

[21] Charalampos Giannakopoulos, 'The Right to Regulate in International Investment Law and the Law of State Responsibility: a Hohfeldian Approach' in Photini Pazartzis and Panos Merkouris (eds), *Permutations of Responsibility in International Law* (Brill Nijhoff 2019) 156.

[22] ibid.

[23] ibid.

[24] ibid. In Giannakopoulos's view, three concrete examples reflect the right to regulate as a legal power: in treaty preambles, in clauses protecting investors from expropriation, and in fair and equitable treatment, particularly in the notion of investor's legitimate expectations.

factored in host state legitimate interests in the absence of a concrete right to regulate', these are entirely dependent on 'arbitral discretion'.[25] Moreover, it is said that states must point to express evidence of an RTR and that 'it seems preferable that, insofar as a state wishes to reserve its right to regulate, it does so explicitly by means of concrete provisions in IIAs'.[26] Thus, the RTR is cast in a limited light only when a treaty generates a clearly-stipulated source. Otherwise, it is assumed not to exist, a point that is not supported in either the literature or the jurisprudence.

How does the RTR relates to the state's duty to compensate investors? Somewhat controversially, the RTR conveys the notion that host states need not compensate investors in circumstances that might otherwise amount to violations of a treaty.[27] This aspect of the RTR revives some of the most contentious debates of the 1960s. As mentioned, those debates focused heavily on whether international or domestic law should prevail in relation to the principle of PSNR and, in particular, whether states must compensate foreign investors in all circumstances. As the RTR is meant to expand the space for states to regulate in the public interest,[28] this issue, it is said, will have been resolved in favour of non-compensation.

4 The RTR in Investment Treaties

The RTR makes an appearance in different features of investment law. For example, explicit references to the RTR can be found in preambles to many new treaties. Alternatively, they are included in specific clauses or standards of treatment, such as those on indirect expropriation or fair and equitable treatment (FET). Direct references to an explicit RTR can also be found in exceptions, exclusions, and other treaty safeguard provisions. However, it is important to emphasize that the RTR has been discussed in arbitral awards, beyond explicit treaty provisions, especially in the context of exceptions and in discussions of

[25] Titi (n 14) 296.

[26] ibid 294.

[27] Lone Wandahl Mouyal, *International Investment Law and the Right to Regulate: A Human Rights Perspective* (Routledge 2016) 65. Given that international law is fragmented and, in international investment law, compensation standards cast the balance favouring investor's protection, reducing the domain of regulation of host states even in human rights law, Wandahl proposes a theory of gravitational pull enhancing legal coherence between both regimes to address 'catastrophic economic consequences'. According to that theory, 'BITs should be interpreted in a harmonizing manner with human rights obligations'. Also, 'the interpretation must take into account the particular context of the case as well as inherent limitations to treaty standards such as avoiding catastrophic economic consequences for the host state and its population'.

[28] These two concepts are used interchangeably in the new wave of IIAs. See Titi (n 14) 373–74.

customary international law. We turn now to a discussion of the various manifestations of the RTR that are either explicit within treaty text or implicit within existing standards of protection.

4.1 Preambles

The incorporation of the RTR in recent treaty preambles has been explained as an attempt to limit tribunals and narrow their margin of interpretation. In positive terms, inclusion of the RTR in preambles denotes the intention of states to clarify the scope of their regulatory space, in a general way, to complement the treaty's substantive standards and exception clauses.[29] Although the binding nature of a preamble is, at best, debatable, preambles offer arbitrators guidelines for treaty interpretation, specifically in relation to limits on the regulatory capacity of states.[30]

Some examples of preambular language are provided by the CPTPP[31] and the CETA.[32] According to the CPTPP preamble:

> The Parties to this Agreement: ... REAFFIRM the importance of promoting corporate social responsibility, cultural identity and diversity, environmental protection and conservation, gender equality, indigenous rights, labour rights, inclusive trade, sustainable development and traditional knowledge, as well as the importance of preserving their right to regulate in the public interest.[33]

[29] Elsa Sardinha, 'The Right to Regulate Towards a (Not Entirely) New Regulatory Paradigm under Recent FTA Investment Chapters' in Mesut Akbaba and Giancarlo Capurro (eds), Investment Challenges in Investment Arbitration (Routledge 2018) 81.

[30] For instance, the 2015 Free Trade Agreement Australia–China.

[31] The Comprehensive and Progressive Agreement for Trans-Pacific Partnership (CPTPP) is a free trade agreement between Australia, Brunei, Canada, Chile, Japan, Malaysia, Mexico, New Zealand, Peru, Singapore, and Vietnam. The CPTPP incorporates, by reference, the provisions from the Trans-Pacific Partnership (TPP), with the exception of some provisions to be suspended upon entry into force. The United States was a state party of the TPP when it was signed on 4 February 2016. After the elected US President Donald Trump withdrew the US signature from TPP in January 2017, the agreement could not be ratified as required and did not enter into force. The remaining countries negotiated a new trade agreement, the Comprehensive and Progressive Agreement for Trans-Pacific Partnership (CPTPP) which incorporates most of the provisions of the TPP and which entered into force on 30 December 2018.

[32] The Canada–European Union Comprehensive Economic and Trade Agreement (CETA) is a bilateral agreement between Canada and the EU that covers several sectors and aspects of Canada–EU trade in order to eliminate or reduce barriers.

[33] The Comprehensive and Progressive Agreement for Trans-Pacific Partnership (CPTPP). Preamble (emphasis added).

Providing more detail, but also somewhat repetitively, the CETA preamble provides:

> The parties resolve to: ... RECOGNISING that the provisions of this Agreement preserve the right of the Parties to regulate within their territories and the Parties' flexibility to achieve legitimate policy objectives, such as public health, safety, environment, public morals and the promotion and protection of cultural diversity; ...
>
> AFFIRMING their commitments as parties to the UNESCO Convention on the Protection and Promotion of the Diversity of Cultural Expressions, done at Paris on 20 October 2005, and recognising that states have the right to preserve, develop and implement their cultural policies, to support their cultural industries for the purpose of strengthening the diversity of cultural expressions, and to preserve their cultural identity, including through the use of regulatory measures and financial support;
>
> RECOGNISING that the provisions of this Agreement protect investments and investors with respect to their investments, and are intended to stimulate mutually-beneficial business activity, without undermining the right of the Parties to regulate in the public interest within their territories.[34]

Importantly, both treaties reaffirm an already existing RTR rather than purporting to recognize a new one.[35]

4.2 Provisions on Indirect Expropriation

Some treaties refer to the RTR in substantive clauses or in treaty annexes, such as those on indirect expropriation. In this respect, it has been argued that these provisions 'promote and protect ... states' regulatory autonomy far more than earlier treaties'.[36] Unlike in older treaties, they supposedly provide more specific guidance to tribunals in determining whether the substantive provision on indirect expropriation should be applied or not. It is important to recall here that indirect expropriation is a frequently invoked clause by investors in

[34] The Canada–European Union Comprehensive Economic and Trade Agreement (CETA). Preamble (emphasis added). The European Union–Singapore Free Trade Agreement takes a similar approach to the CETA, stating in its preamble: 'The parties ... REAFFIRMING each *Party's right to adopt and enforce measures necessary to pursue legitimate policy objectives* such as social, environmental, security, public health and safety, promotion and protection of cultural diversity' (emphasis added).

[35] Sardinha (n 29) 81.

[36] ibid 87.

disputes against host states. Treaties like the CPTPP and CETA[37] frame indirect expropriation by drawing a clear distinction between non-compensable acts adopted by the state in the pursuit of legitimate public welfare purposes and acts not in the public interest that require the payment of compensation. Sardinha confidently asserts that, under these treaties, 'it will be a rare case in which a bona fide regulation could constitute an indirect expropriation', thus creating 'a sort of presumption against the finding of an indirect expropriation in cases in which regulatory power is exercised'.[38] Others claim that the new treaty provisions on indirect expropriation 'provide little or no guidance to arbitral tribunals in distinguishing such actions from regulatory measures not subject to compensation'.[39] As a backdrop to these differing forecasts about the utility of an explicit RTR, ISDS tribunals have in some cases relieved states from the duty to compensate investors where regulation has a legitimate public purpose,[40] while in others, they have held the state to a much harsher standard.[41] In any event, an explicit RTR on indirect expropriation is, at present, far from a reliable safeguard of state policy space with respect to natural resources or other essential subject matters of regulation.

4.3 Provisions on Fair and Equitable Treatment

In contrast to indirect expropriation, FET standards rarely make explicit reference to the RTR. Lacking much precision, FET has been interpreted to require a measure of equity by the host state vis-à-vis the investor. According to Titi, the FET standard 'by its very nature requires a balancing of interests' and 'an interpretation that completely ignores the legitimate interests of a host state will hardly appear to be fair and equitable'.[42] In this context, the RTR is usually discussed by tribunals in relation to other standards linked to the broad notion of

[37] See CPTPP, art 9.8 and Annex 9-B; CETA, art 8.12 and Annex 8-A.

[38] Sardinha (n 29) 98.

[39] Korzun (n 20) 375.

[40] See *Methanex Corporation v United States of America*, UNCITRAL, Final Award (3 August 2005). The right to regulate has been protected and ensured under Energy Charter Treaty because arbitral decisions have considered that indirect expropriation just can be declared when there is a lost 'all significant economic value'. Likewise, concerning FET, ECT arbitral decisions have asserted that the obligation to provide protection and security does not protect against state regulation, which may negatively affect the claimant's investment when the state acts accordingly to a reasonable public policy goal; Graham Coop and Isabella Seif, 'Part II Investor-State Arbitration in the Energy Sector, 10 ECT and States Right to Regulate' in Maxi Scherer (ed), *International Arbitration in the Energy Sector* (OUP 2018).

[41] See *Santa Elena SA v Republic of Costa Rica*, ICSID Case No ARB/96/1; *Metalclad Corporation v The United Mexican States*, ICSID Case No ARB AF/97/1; *Azurix Corporation v Argentine Republic*, ICSID Case No ARB/01/12.

[42] Titi (n 14) 276.

FET, such as the international minimum standard, protections against denial of justice, and full protection and security.

Generally, these types of standards are not subject to any exceptions because they are understood to be irreducible minimums from which no derogations are permitted. The wide margin of interpretation and ambiguity of FET allows it to be used to tilt the balance in favour of investors. In turn, it poses a potential threat to the RTR, allowing 'legitimate expectations' of investors to displace other regulatory purposes such as responsiveness to new knowledge, democratic decision-making, and changing conditions. As illustrated in the various ISDS cases discussed in Section 5, tribunals have often invoked FET and proportionality to reduce the scope of state regulatory authority and to favour of investors.[43] Moreover, Ortino argues 'the role of regulatory stability within the FET standard remains at best ambiguous and which thus fails to assuage the fears that the FET standard may indeed function as imposing an obligation of regulatory stability in the strict sense'.[44] With respect to FET, the prospects for the RTR to restore policy space appear dependent on its implicit, not explicit, recognition in international law generally.

4.4 Exceptions, Exclusions and Non-precluded Measures

The RTR can also be found in treaty provisions laying out exceptions, exclusions, and other safeguard provisions. The longstanding purpose of such treaty provisions is to assert that states are allowed to 'act inconsistently with obligations set out in other provisions ... provided that all of the conditions set out ... are satisfied'.[45] Some exceptions also emerge from WTO law converging with investment law treaties, in references to GATT's article XX.[46] Drawing on

[43] Daria Davitti, 'Proportionality and Human Rights Protection in International Investment Arbitration: What's Left Hanging in the Balance?' (2020) 89 Nordic Journal of International Law 343. In a similar perspective, Davitti argues that a 'balancing between investors' rights and human rights is 'neither possible nor desirable'. Henckels argues, following the approach taken by the European Court of Justice and the European Court of Human Rights, that arbitral tribunals when applying proportionality principle should be 'deferential in their assessment of matters that are more appropriately the province of national decision-makers'; Carolina Henckels, 'Indirect Expropriation and the Right to Regulate: Revisiting Proportionality Analysis and the Standard of Review in Investor-State Arbitration.' (2012) 15(1) Journal of International Economic Law 223, 255.

[44] Federico Ortino, 'The Obligation of Regulatory Stability in the Fair and Equitable Treatment Standard: How Far Have We Come?' (2018) 21 Journal of International Economic Law 845, 848.

[45] Korzun (n 20) 391.

[46] Armand de Mestral and Lukas Vanhonnaeker, 'How Best to Ensure Respect for the Right to Regulate in the Face of Foreign Investment Commitments: A Reformed ISA Process or a Return to the WTO' (2017) 1 https://papers.ssrn.com/sol3/papers.cfm?abstract_id=3089060 (accessed 23 August 2022).

this background, newer investment treaties rely on these tools to circumscribe investor protections and impede successful investor claims.[47] Similarly, some treaties mention the RTR as a safeguard for specific objectives such as the protection of public health and the environment.

These types of provisions can be found in annexes, declarations, reservations, etc. For instance, Article 13bis of the FTA EU–Vietnam[48] states:

> The Parties reaffirm the right to regulate within their territories to achieve legitimate policy objectives, such as the protection of public health, safety, environment or public morals, social or consumer protection or promotion and protection of cultural diversity.

Likewise, the US Model BIT[49] expressly mentions the RTR in relation to environmental protection. Such treaty provisions are not uniform and will depend heavily on the understanding of each arbitral tribunal. They also usually require that the state demonstrate that its regulatory measure was necessary to achieve, or otherwise tied to, a specific policy objective.[50]

5 RTR in Investment Treaty Arbitration

5.1 Tribunals that Accepted RTR

Outside of the express language of the treaties, tribunals have, in rare cases, drawn on international law to recognize an implicit RTR of the state. The *Philip Morris* claims against Uruguay and Australia, respectively, are an illustration. In 2010, the tobacco multinational challenged Uruguay's public health measures seeking to restrict the marketing of tobacco products. The first measure was a Single Presentation Requirement, which required that cigarette brands only be sold with a unique presentation. The second required that health

[47] The Treaty Between the Republic of Belarus and The Republic of India on Investments.
[48] The EU–Vietnam Trade and Investment Agreements.
[49] The 2012 U.S Model Bilateral Investment Treaty.
[50] Robert Brew, 'Exception Clauses in International Investment Agreements as a Tool for Appropriately Balancing the Right to Regulate with Investment Protection.' (2019) 25 Canterbury Law Review 205, Brew proposes a model exception clause that balances the state's right to regulate with investors' expectations, limiting the discretion of arbitral tribunals to pass over states' public policy priorities. The model exception clause is the following: 'Provided that such measures are not ultimately intended as a restriction on international investment, nothing in this Agreement shall be construed to prevent a Party from adopting or enforcing measures necessary to achieve a legitimate objective, including, but not limited to: (a) The protection of public morals; ... public order; 215 (c) ... the environment';

warnings on cigarette packages cover 80% of packages sold. Philip Morris challenged these measures under Uruguay's BIT with Switzerland, arguing violations of a 'use and enjoyment of investment' clause, FET, and expropriation. A majority of the tribunal rejected the latter claim, upholding Uruguay`s right to implement measures for the protection of public health in the legitimate use of its police powers.[51] As was discussed in section two of this chapter, implicit RTR is the 'ability to adopt, maintain, and enforce the measures necessary for the advancement of its public policy goals' by means of its public branches of power.[52] Hence, when states have invoked a police powers doctrine in their defence, they are indeed appealing to an implicit RTR.

In Philip Morris' claim against Australia under a BIT with Hong Kong, the tribunal declined to accept jurisdiction in the dispute. Australia had forbidden all tobacco products and packaging sold in Australia that displayed trademarks, symbols, graphics, or images. Philip Morris argued that the regulation was 'expropriatory' because it impeded the use of intellectual property rights on tobacco products.[53] The Tribunal, instead, concluded that the claimant had abused its rights by carrying out a corporate restructuring, by acquiring Australian subsidiaries, for the purpose of securing BIT protection.[54] There was no decision on the merits in *Philip Morris v Australia*, nor a reaffirmation of the state right to regulate. These two cases, however, prompted the inclusion of an explicit, if narrow, tobacco carve-out in CPTPP, which states that a state party may deny the benefits of the investment and ISDS chapter for claims initiated against tobacco measures.[55]

[51] *Philip Morris Brands Sàrl, Philip Morris Products SA and Abal Hermanos SA v República Oriental Del Uruguay*, ICSID Case No ARB/10/7 [408]–[410], [418]–[420]; Prabhash Ranjan, 'Police Powers, Indirect Expropriation in International Investment Law, and Article 31(3)(c) of the VCLT: A Critique of Philip Morris v. Uruguay' (2019) 9 Asian Journal of International Law 98; Rudolf Dolzer and Christoph Schreuer, *Principles of International Investment Law* (2nd edn, OUP 2012) 120. Doctrinally, Dolzer and Schreuer define the police power doctrine as general regulation adopted from bona fide motivation, either in taxation or in other areas that are not discriminatory, nor conceived to harm alien property, or substantially to diminish its selling price.

[52] Korzun (n 20) 373.

[53] Andrina Sukma Dwi, 'Towards a Future Investment Treaty: Lessons from Indirect Expropriation Cases due to Measures to Protect the Environmental and Public Health' (2017) 28(2) European Business Law 245.

[54] Prabhash Ranjan and Pushkar Anand, 'How 'Healthy' are the Investment Treaties of South Asian Countries: An Empirical Study of Public Health Provisions in South Asian Countries' BITs and FTA Investment Chapters' (2018) 33(2) ICSID Review: Foreign Investment Law Journal 406.

[55] Article 29.5: 'A Party may elect to deny the benefits of Section B of Chapter 9 (Investment) with respect to claims challenging a tobacco control measure of the Party. Such a claim shall not be submitted to arbitration under Section B of Chapter 9 (Investment) if a Party has made such an election. If a Party has not elected to deny benefits with respect to such claims by the time of the submission of such a claim to arbitration under Section B of Chapter 9 (Investment), a Party may elect to deny benefits during the proceedings. For greater certainty, if a Party elects to deny benefits with respect to such claims, any such claim shall be dismissed.'

Another illustration of an implicit RTR, albeit in a case against the US, is the *Methanex* award of 2005. The case was prompted by a ban imposed by the state of California on the use and sale of MTBE, a gasoline additive used to manufacture Methanol. A core issue in the case was the extent to which a host state, based on the RTR, can introduce a measure that 'enables or restricts competition from firms operating in similar sectors'.[56] Methanex argued that it was in like circumstances with US-based ethanol producers 'because they both produce oxygenates used in manufacturing reformulated gasoline and because they compete for customers in the oxygenate market' and whose products were not banned.[57] The investor claimed that California banned MTBE and methanol to give ethanol a monopoly in the market based on 'spurious environmental concerns'.[58]

In the course of rejecting this claim on jurisdictional and national treatment grounds, the tribunal permitted the US to introduce its ban on methanol and hand to ethanol producers a monopoly. Rather than accept the investors argument about the legal meaning of 'like circumstances' that drew on WTO law, the tribunal interpreted the comparator group narrowly, upholding the right of the home state to alter its regulatory environment so as to favour ethanol producers.[59] This award is an example of an implicit RTR that generates an unprecedented discretion afforded to California under investment law.

5.2 Tribunals that Rejected RTR

Unfortunately, for states seeking to regulate in the public interest, there are many more cases that reject an implicit RTR than accept it. Illustrations abound. For example, in *Tecmed v Mexico*, the tribunal assumed the power to assess the proportionality of state measures as part of the FET standard. In doing so, it restricted any implicit RTR well beyond what the treaty explicitly provided. The tribunal concluded that Mexico had violated both FET and indirect expropriation by declining to renew the investor's license to operate a landfill for hazardous industrial waste. Mexico had argued that its decision amounted to legitimate regulatory action consistent with the state's discretionary authority

[56] See David Schneiderman's chapter on National Treatment (ch 2) in this book.
[57] ibid Part IV, Chapter B, art 1102 Nafta, para 6.
[58] ibid para 7.
[59] For a further discussion on the scope of WTO standards and its comparison with international investment law see Elizabeth Trujillo, 'Balancing Sustainability, the Right to Regulate, and the Need for Investor Protection: Lessons from the Trade Regime' (2018) 59 Boston College Law Review 2735.

under its police power 'in the highly regulated and extremely sensitive framework of environmental protection and public health'.[60] Incorporating a proportionality analysis, borrowed from European human rights law, the tribunal reviewed and then rejected the Mexican authorities' environmental and health rationales for denying the investor's permit.[61] This conclusion was in stark contrast to the *Methanex* decision discussed above.

One of the first cases to interpret a version of an express RTR, *Bear Creek v Peru*, illustrates how these clauses might be function in the future.[62] A Canadian company, Bear Creek, had been allocated the rights to exploit the Santa Ana silver mine. The project triggered social and political unrest, indicating a gross absence of social license. The government subsequently prohibited mining in nearby areas and suspended further applications to develop mining in the region. Faced with Bear Creek's ISDS claim, Peru argued that these measures emanated from its police powers, which conferred a margin of discretion to the state to check social protest that threatened both the state's internal security and border security with Bolivia.[63] The tribunal rejected the state's reliance on the RTR clause. Citing *Tecmed*, it found the measures disproportionate and discriminatory against the investor and an indirect expropriation of the investment.[64] Like *Tecmed*, the *Bear Creek* ruling demonstrates how arbitrators have shrunk RTR so as to favour claimants. In both cases, there was manifest dissatisfaction with the investor's behaviour and documented violations of either domestic environmental or human rights law. Yet each of the tribunals dismissed these elements in the course of expanding their powers of review,[65] questioning sovereign decisions, and awarding substantial compensation against the state, all at the expense of the discretion of regulatory authorities.

6 A Turning Point in RTR: *Eco Oro v Colombia*

More recently, in *Eco Oro v Colombia*,[66] the tribunal condemned Colombia after it chose to protect a special ecosystem vital to mitigation of climate

[60] *Tecnicas Medioambientales Tecmed SA v United Mexican States*, ICSID Case No ARB AF/00/2, Award (29 May 2003) [97], [201]; *Tecnicas Medioambientales Tecmed SA v United Mexican States*, ICSID Case No ARB AF/00/2 (18 October 2018).
[61] ibid [116], [122].
[62] *Bear Creek Mining Corporation v Republic of Peru*, ICSID Case No ARB/14/2, Award (30 November 2017).
[63] ibid 469.
[64] ibid [347]–[348], [473]–[478].
[65] See Van Harten (n 1) 92.
[66] *Eco Oro Minerals Corp v Republic of Colombia*, ICSID Case No. ARB/16/41, Award (9 September 2022).

disruption. This *páramo* ecosystem is located in Santurbán. It provides water to a large region of the country and plays a significant role in maintaining biodiversity. It has a unique capacity to retain, restore, and distribute water across extended areas.[67]

In 2007, Eco Oro signed a concession agreement[68] with Colombian authorities that allowed the company to carry out mining 'exploration' in a territory overlapping the Santurbán *páramo* ecosystem. As the company was aware, it required a further 'environmental license' before it could start mining. Subsequently, in 2010, a new Colombian law[69] prohibited mining in specially protected environmental areas such as *páramo* ecosystems. The law was framed as part of a lengthy process to strengthen environmental protections, in pursuance of obligations made at the Rio de Janeiro Conference or 'Earth Summit' of 1992.[70] In 2017, the Colombian Constitutional Court issued a judgment[71] recognizing the participatory rights of communities affected by proposed projects in the Santurbán *páramo*. This judgment was premised on an earlier decision by the Court in 2016, which concluded that, by virtue of various articles of the Colombian Constitution,[72] 'the protection of the environment prevails over the economic rights acquired by individuals through environmental licenses and concession contracts'. In circumstances where 'it is proven that the activity produces damage' or where 'there is merit to apply the precautionary principle to avoid damage to non-renewable natural resources and human health', economic interests will yield to environmental measures.[73] Echoing the underlying premises of the RTR, the Court stated:

> The mere existence of a concession contract does not prevent the State from limiting, conditioning or prohibiting the activity that is the object of the concession, when this is intended to protect a legal right of greater constitutional importance.[74]

[67] See Lorenzo Cotula, 'Investment Disputes from Below: Whose Rights Matter? Mining, Environment and Livelihoods in Colombia' International Institute for Environment and Development (23 July 2020).

[68] See Concession Agreement between Eco Oro Minerals and the Colombian Institute of Geology and Mining, INGEOMINAS, Concession 3452 (8 February 2007).

[69] Congress of the Republic of Colombia. Law 1382 of 2010. 'by which Law 685 of 2001 Code of Mines is modified.'

[70] United Nations Conference on Environment and Development. Rio de Janeiro, Brazil (3–14 June 2022).

[71] Colombian Constitutional Court, Ruling T-361 of 2017, Reporting Judge: Alberto Rojas Ríos.

[72] Political Constitution of the Republic of Colombia.

[73] Colombian Constitutional Court, Ruling C-035 of 2016, Reporting Judge: Gloria Stella Ortiz Delgado, para 128.

[74] ibid para 126.

According priority to the concessionary contracts over greater constitutional values, which would be the opposite view, subordinates the activity of the legislator and the government to a particular interest. This interpretation would chill the regulatory capacity of the legislator to respond to legitimate social demands and alter the constitutional principle of general interest prevalence.[75]

Faced with these protections for the environment and local communities, and with its still-pending approval to exploit any proposed mine, Eco Oro opted to sue Colombia using the dispute mechanism in the Colombia–Canada FTA.[76] The tribunal acknowledged that Colombian authorities had acted in good faith in protecting the public interest and the environment.[77] On this basis, a majority dismissed the state's responsibility in relation to Eco Oro's claim of indirect expropriation. Yet, the tribunal continued, with a differently constituted majority of arbitrators, to condemn Colombia premised on a controversial argument about the minimum standard of treatment available to investors under treaty.[78] Despite the provision expressly tying the standard to its meaning in customary international law,[79] the majority, as have other tribunals, adopted a liberal interpretation which defined the treaty's minimum standard as incorporating an investor's legitimate expectations, an entitlement to a stable and transparent investment environment, and good faith on the part of the state.[80] As recognized by the dissenting arbitrator, the interpretation was so broad that it may amount to a rewriting of the treaty itself, undercutting 'the plain meaning of the [treaty] and well-established principles of customary law' with respect to the minimum standard.[81]

Ironically, while one majority of the tribunal found, in the course of rejecting its indirect expropriation claim, that the investor's legitimate expectations had been respected, a different majority reached the opposite conclusion as the basis for finding a violation of the minimum standard. This contradiction undermines the effectiveness of any exercise of the RTR by the state. That is, it incentivizes the state to refrain from protecting the environment for fear of future demands for compensation. The punitive sanctioning of the state based on the minimum standard rendered the RTR inoperative for defending a public interest such as the environment. It bodes poorly, in particular, for two ISDS

[75] ibid.

[76] See Partial Dissent of Professor Philippe Sands in *Eco Oro Minerals* (n 66) [37].

[77] ibid [601].

[78] See Muthucumaraswamy Sornarjah's chapter on the *Eco Oro* decision in this book.

[79] Free Trade Agreement between Canada and the Republic of Colombia signed on 21 November 2008 and which entered into force on 15 August 2011, art 805.

[80] *Eco Oro Minerals* (n 66) [762].

[81] See Partial Dissent of Professor Philippe Sands in *Eco Oro Minerals* (n 66) [36].

proceedings that are still pending also prompted by mining operations being suspended in the Santurbán *páramo*.[82]

Worse, the *Eco Oro* ruling ignored the explicit RTR clause contained in the Canada-Colombia FTA concerning environmental protection.[83] As part of similar 'new generation' treaties, the Canada-Colombia agreement included express provisions aimed at protecting higher interests like the environment. Strikingly, the tribunal simply applied the same interpretive approach as under older investment treaties. *Eco Oro* thus demonstrates a failure of treaty mechanisms that supposedly aim to correct imbalances in the system. Here, a majority of the arbitrators ignored the effort to do so via treaty language. Investment law was applied, once again, to sideline essential interests including, in this instance, local, national, and global interests in counteracting climate disruption, and protecting vital water sources for Colombians.

One must take heed of cases like *Eco Oro*. Yet, in the end, the tribunal took liberties with the treaty, sufficient to find a violation that justified compensation being provided to the investor. Furthermore, the award denotes, as Haljan argues, that ISDS under FTAs 'seems to present an instance (of a sort) of international law judicial review', with domestic institutions 'being held to account under international law'.[84] The majority's reasoning protecting concessionary contract resembles arguments that elevate foreign investment interests above domestic ones by relying on principles associated with 'civilized justice'.[85]

Eco Oro may be a turning point, as is suggested in Professor Sornarajah's concluding chapter to this volume. Despite the relevant treaty's express provisions safeguarding the RTR, and despite acknowledging that Colombian authorities acted in good faith to protect an important ecosystem, a majority of the tribunal overrode an explicit RTR on its way to ruling against Colombia. This is despite the fact that the parties placed their faith in a more balanced international investment instrument that would lead to more equitable outcomes. The treaty included various modifications, including a new environmental chapter and declarations of a 'right to regulate' both as an explicit RTR provision and as a restriction on the scope of other investment protection standards. However, what the arbitral majority did in the Eco Oro decision was to put into

[82] These were initiated under the FTA with Canada after the Colombian Constitutional Court issued judgments forbidding mining. See *Galway Gold Inc v Republic of Colombia*, ICSID Case No ARB/18/13; *Red Eagle Exploration Limited v Republic of Colombia*, ICSID Case No ARB/18/12.

[83] *Bear Creek Mining* (n 62): 'Preamble ... Undertake each of the preceding in a manner that is consistent with environmental protection and conservation; Enhance and enforce environmental laws and regulations, and to strengthen cooperation on environmental matters.'

[84] ibid [243].

[85] Andrea Leiter, 'Protecting Concessionary Rights: General Principles and the Making of International Investment Law' (2022) 35(1) Leiden Journal of International Law 55, 69.

question those new attempts at improving ISDS legitimacy. Instead, *Eco Oro* reaffirms key critiques and the risks that states continue to face when bound by investment law's standards of treatment. Geopolitical and post-colonial biases embedded in investment law remain, while arbitrators render new explicit RTR malleable enough to overlook attempts at moderating the system. We can safely predict that this situation will remain unchanged so long as Global South states are marginalized and remain in weak negotiating positions.

7 Conclusion

Regulatory disputes, and therefore the RTR, should be at the heart of any rethinking of investment law to make it fairer and more balanced. This task can only be undertaken if one keeps in mind the post-colonial origins of ISDS and the RTR. Investment law was conceived to protect the private interests of foreign investors. At the time, such investors controlled natural resources in the territories of former colonies. If the orientation of investment law were to protect them from expropriation by newly independent and developing states, these origins help to underscore the limitations embedded in the system and how futile may be the efforts to reform it.

Considering only its express recognition in recent investment treaties, the RTR may be insufficient to preserve regulatory space and rebalance the inequities of ISDS.[86] It is apparent that the RTR requires a legal basis, whether implicit or explicit, to legitimately serve as a defence of state policy space. As the RTR is invoked on a case-by-case basis, conflicting interpretations by disparate tribunals can result. There is also no consensus on whether the RTR exempts states from the duty to compensate foreign investors when asserting sovereignty over natural resources.

It is doubtful that, by recognizing the RTR, substantial reform of ISDS can be achieved. On the contrary, the concept of the RTR, whether explicit or implicit, does not alter the inherent power imbalances of investment law. Even when the RTR is recognized, it is tribunals that will define and apply it, guided by the rationality of investor protection and privilege and not the logic of public law which otherwise guides the state. In their hands, the RTR appears more likely to re-legitimize than to rebalance a system of law that continues to favour capital-exporting states and powerful home-state economic actors.

[86] See Van Harten (n 1).

For the RTR to be more effective in rebalancing the interests of investors and those of host states, we would expect to see it incorporated into all investment treaties presently in force, not only the new wave of them. It would likewise need to be clearly defined to include all legitimate public policy objectives and without the need to compensate for alterations to the legal environment. These minimal steps would be needed to clarify the investment protection obligations of states and to inform investors of those obligations as a matter of public law at the domestic and international level. The criteria for interpretation of the RTR must likewise be systematized and binding for arbitrators. Without such constraints on arbitral discretion, states are denied a reasonable degree of legal certainty and legal security in the exercise of their regulatory authority.

In this context, it is worth examining the experience of countries that have maintained a different relationship with ISDS, such as Brazil and South Africa.[87] These countries offer insights into the importance of strengthening the state's regulatory space. They point to other avenues for attracting foreign investors without harming other vital interests. The alternatives include proposals to detach the state states from investment treaties and replace ISDS with adjudication by domestic courts,[88] or with state-to-state dispute settlement.[89] They direct us toward new thinking about investor protections and investment law's priority of protecting foreign investors above all else.

[87] Morosini (n 11) 165. For a further discussion on new trends in the African context see Emmanuel T Laryea and Oladapo O Fabusuyi, 'Africanisation of International Investment Law for Sustainable Development: Challenges' (2021) 20(1) Journal of International Trade Law and Policy 42. For a critical view on Africa's BIT and Right to Regulate see Talkmore Chidede, 'The Right to Regulate in Africa's International Investment Law Regime' (2018) 20 Oregon Review of International Law 437, 467.

[88] See the proposal by the German Judges Association under the context of the TTIP negotiations. Mark Juergen, 'German Association of Judges on the TTIP Proposal of the European Commission' *Global Arbitration News* (21 March 2016).

[89] *Galway Gold Inc* (n 82); *Red Eagle Exploration* (n 82).

10

The Determination of Quantum and Claim Inflation

Juan Carlos Boué

> [N]ous n'avons point de lois, mais nous avons cinq ou six mille volumes sur les lois. Nous nous conduisons d'ordinaire par des coutumes; car on sait qu'une coutume, ayant été établie au hasard, est toujours ce qu'il y a de plus sage ... [C]'est une fortune assurée pour les praticiens, une ressource pour tous les plaideurs de mauvaise foi, et un agrément infini pour les juges, qui peuvent, en sûreté de conscience, décider les causes sans les entendre.
>
> [W]e have no laws, but we have five or six thousand volumes on the laws. We are governed in general by customs; for it is known that a custom, having been established by chance, is the wisest principle that can be imagined ... This yields an assured fortune to practitioners. It is a resource for all pleaders in bad faith, and a pastime of infinite amusement for the judges, who can, with safe consciences, decide causes without understanding them.
>
> Voltaire, *André Destouches à Siam*

1 Introduction

Quantification of damages is not, strictly speaking, a standard of treatment in investment law, but it is nonetheless a key feature of the investor–state dispute settlement (ISDS) regime. Indeed, it is often the feature of greatest practical relevance to the parties in any ISDS case. Nevertheless, in the literature on compensation in ISDS, 'quantification of the quantum'[1] (ie how investments are valued) has unfortunately attracted far less attention than, for example, the

[1] Thomas Stauffer, 'Valuation of Assets in International Takings' (1996) 17 Energy Law Journal 459, 460.

Juan Carlos Boué, *The Determination of Quantum and Claim Inflation* In: *Rethinking Investment Law.*
Edited by: David Schneiderman and Gus Van Harten, Oxford University Press.
DOI: 10.1093/oso/9780192871084.003.0010

topic of standards of compensation. As this chapter will endeavour to show, of all the wrong turns that international investment law has taken, none is pregnant with more grave or more explosive implications than that for the issue of quantum.

This wrong turn began to manifest itself in international arbitration during the 1980s,[2] long before the explosive growth of ISDS. It is telling that the World Bank Guidelines on the Treatment of Foreign Direct Investment warned as early as 1992 that 'particular caution should be observed in applying [DCF], as experience shows that investors tend to greatly exaggerate their claims of compensation for lost future profits'.[3] The diagnosis proved accurate, as financial crises in Argentina and Southeast Asia gave rise to the first major wave of ISDS cases a decade or so later. In those early cases, states tended to focus on issues of jurisdiction and law, rather than quantum, and this approach made it easier for claimants to advance inflated claims and secure unwarranted compensation. Even as ISDS was just becoming—to paraphrase George Kahale—the 'Wild, Wild West of international law', quantum had already been revealed as the regime's No Name City (the place where, as the song has it, every vice is 'worser').[4]

2 Quantum as a Facet of the Legitimacy Crisis

Intuitively, it is easy to see why the 'anything goes' ethos of ISDS should manifest itself, with least restraint, in connection with quantum. After all, as a prominent practitioner puts it, 'International arbitrations—it's all about the money'.[5] This truism has an unsurprising corollary; namely, that 'claimants seek to extract the highest amount of damages possible'.[6] Further, and crucially, ISDS allows claimants to pursue maximal damages untrammeled by procedural and evidentiary rules that, in domestic courts, serve to keep the baser instincts of litigants and their counsel in check. As a practical matter, the potential for abuse, inherent in any system that lacks guardrails and is shrouded in confidentiality, is magnified where lawyers 'tend to be less comfortable dealing with

[2] ibid 480–85.

[3] World Bank, 'Legal Framework for the Treatment of Foreign Investment. Volume II: Report to the Development Committee and Guidelines on the Treatment of Foreign Direct Investment' (World Bank 1992) 26.

[4] George Kahale III, 'ISDS: The Wild, Wild West of International Law and Arbitration' (2018) 44(1) Brooklyn Journal of International Law 1.

[5] Lacey Young, 'The Claim/award Mismatch: GAR Live Energy Considers the Reasons' *Global Arbitration Review* (21 June 2017).

[6] ibid.

quantum than they are with jurisdiction and the merits' and arbitrators 'tend to be less comfortable with quantum, as they often have little or no training in that area'.[7] Thus, ISDS quantum has increasingly become a hunting ground for 'a whole new profession of highly skilled experts' who inflate claims 'with extraordinarily complex and lengthy economic and financial reports that most lawyers and arbitrators have difficulty understanding and evaluating in the relatively short time allotted'.[8]

3 Quantum and Anchoring Heuristics

Key concepts in ISDS, such as fair and equitable treatment (FET), are amorphous. Also, ISDS lacks the checks and balances around which credible legal systems are structured. This combination of features makes it more tempting and easier for lawyers to exploit a potent innate cognitive trait called 'anchoring' by the experimental psychologists who first identified it.[9] In simple terms, anchoring refers to a process of decision-making under conditions of uncertainty by which a numerical result is arrived at by making a series of adjustments to an initial value (the 'anchor'). It has been experimentally demonstrated that anchoring heuristics assert themselves no less powerfully in situations where the anchor value is irrelevant to the matter or even absurd on its face.[10]

The profusion of grossly inflated claims in international arbitration can be explained as a form of moral hazard facilitated by anchoring. Claims can be framed with the knowledge that exaggeration may be rewarded by generous increases to the ordered compensation. The epitome of this dynamic can be found in the spectacle of the arbitrations that pitted former Yukos shareholders against Russia, under the aegis of the Energy Charter Treaty.[11] Those proceedings culminated in a colossal award of US$50 billion, twenty times more than any previous arbitral award against a state. Yet the sum was seen in many

[7] George Kahale III, 'Rethinking ISDS' (2018) 5 *TDM* 15, 19.
[8] Kahale (n 4).
[9] Amos Tversky and Daniel Kahneman, 'Judgment under Uncertainty: Heuristics and Biases' (1974) 185(4157) Science 1124.
[10] Chris Guthrie, Jeffrey J Rachlinski, and Andrew J Wistrich, 'Inside the Judicial Mind' (2000) 86 *Cornell L. Rev.* 777, 788–89. For example, people provided higher estimates of the average annual temperature when first asked to determine whether it was higher or lower than 558 degrees, and mock jurors awarded substantially more in damages when the claim was put at US$1 billion than when the claim was a plausible, much smaller, amount.
[11] The cases are *Hulley Enterprises v Russia*, PCA Case No AA 226, Final Award (2005); *Yukos Universal v Russian Federation*, PCA Case No AA 227 (2005); *Veteran Petroleum v Russia*, PCA Case No AA 228 (2005).

quarters as reasonable.[12] Not only was it less than half of the claimed compensation of US$114 billion; but the tribunal also applied a 25 per cent discount to the amount due to contributory fault by claimants.[13] According to the tribunal, the claimants had abused the fiscal arrangements of the Russian low-tax region as well as the Cyprus–Russia tax treaty, and this reduction supposedly reflected a 'fair and reasonable' apportionment of responsibility between the claimants and Russia.[14]

Ordinary court proceedings are not immune to the effects of anchoring heuristics.[15] However, common rules and principles of judicial systems, especially the rules of evidence, combined with the availability of appellate mechanisms (not to mention the fact that the amount of time that may be devoted to complex issues is not limited by travel schedules), serves to expand the risk of negative outcomes for litigants who play fast and loose with figures and data in order to dress up indefensible claims.[16]

4 The Lopsidedness of Anchoring

Given the lack of safeguards to neutralize maximalist positions in ISDS, and the economic incentives to adopt them, it would seem logical to expect claimant investors and respondent states alike to engage in the kinds of antics described above. Yet that is not the case. The explanation lies in the asymmetrical nature of the incentives that ISDS creates.

To an extent, this asymmetry reflects the *raison d'être* of ISDS, which is, after all, *investment* protection. Also, many members of the club of arbitrators that has been at the forefront of ISDS expansion see investment arbitration as merely a variant of commercial arbitration. The latter exists, according to Lord Mustill, 'for one purpose only: to serve the commercial man'.[17] Or, as a

[12] Jennifer Rankin, 'Russia Ordered to Pay $50bn in Damages to Yukos Shareholders' *The Guardian* (28 July 2014).

[13] *Hulley Enterprises v Russia* (n 11) [1825]. The tribunal valued the damages suffered by claimants at US$66.7 billion.

[14] ibid [1637]. In contrast, as noted in Gus Van Harten, *Sold Down the Yangtze: Canada's Lopsided Investment Deal with China* (Lorimer 2015) 124; the European Court of Human Rights also decided a similar complaint brought by former Yukos shareholders against Russia, and ordered that US$2.5 billion in compensation (a figure which nonetheless still represented a record amount for that court).

[15] Christopher R Drahozal, 'Behavioral Analysis of Private Judging' (2004) 67 Law & Contemporary Problems 105.

[16] See eg the short shrift given by the High Court in London to ExxonMobil's attempt to obtain a worldwide asset freeze in connection with an ICC arbitration against the Venezuelan state oil company: *Mobil Cerro Negro Ltd v Petróleos de Venezuela SA* [2008] EWHC 532 (Comm).

[17] Michael Mustill, 'The New Lex Mercatoria: The First Twenty-five Years' (1988) 4(2) Arbitration International 86.

prominent and controversial arbitrator put it (in an article published when the wave of ISDS claims was just beginning to break),

> [i]nternational business ... requires practical and commercially sensible solutions to the myriad practical and economically significant disputes that it spawns. Such solutions are likely more easily found within the realm of commercial practice rather than legislative pronouncement. The application of custom-based solutions, which are by their very nature 'transnational', serves to avoid much of the unpredictability of domestic substantive legal rules.[18]

Such an approach to adjudication, explicitly unmoored from formal legal principle, certainly tends to suit the 'commercial man' who resorts to ISDS. By the same measure, however, it disserves the interests of sovereigns, not least because it often translates into investors and states being held to different standards of conduct. This lopsidedness extends to the reception given by arbitrators to submissions on damages.

Consider a case which, for a while, held the record for the largest ICSID award (at US$1.77 billion plus interest): *Occidental Petroleum v Ecuador*.[19] At issue was the termination by the Ecuadorean government of an exploration and production contract with Occidental. The latter had transferred an economic interest to a third party in a manner alleged to have violated both the contract itself and Ecuadorean law. The tribunal in that case decided unanimously that this transfer had breached contractual terms and municipal law. Yet, by a majority, it held that, in standing on its rights to terminate the contract for this breach, Ecuador had acted disproportionately and therefore violated the US–Ecuador bilateral investment treaty (BIT). The company's breach, 'while imprudent and ill advised, *did not amount to bad faith*' since, in breaching the contract and municipal law, Occidental executives had acted as 'business people, seasoned oilmen, for whom *legal niceties* [*sic*] were not as important as the business realities of the deal'.[20] Having thus driven a coach and horses through the governing law of the agreement, while also standing on its head the fundamental principle of strict liability for contractual breach, the majority awarded a huge sum of damages. Only at that stage did it make a cursory nod toward Ecuador's damages submissions by finding that Occidental's 'damages

[18] L Yves Fortier, 'New Trends in Governing Law: The New, New Lex Mercatoria, or, Back to the Future' (2001) 16(1) ICSID Review 18.

[19] *Occidental Petroleum v Ecuador*, ICSID Case No ARB/06/11, Final Award (5 October 2012). The tribunal was presided over by Maître Fortier.

[20] ibid [384] (emphasis added).

should be reduced by a factor of 25 per cent [a figure plucked out of thin air] because ... their own wrongful act ... [had] contributed in a material way to the damages'.[21] Remarkably, *Occidental* is often hailed in investor-friendly quarters as demonstrating '[a] very rigorous approach to damages with the tribunal carefully guiding the process'. However, even its admirers are forced to concede that the 'discount factor of 25 percent for-contributory fault by the claimant ... [is] maybe one little blemish on it, because they [the arbitrators] didn't really explain how they got to 25 percent'.[22] From the perspective of states, the *Occidental* decision rather shows that ISDS is so fundamentally flawed that governments may find they cannot even afford to win—let alone lose—the issues in dispute.

Another element serves to heighten the asymmetry between the incentives of claimants and those of respondents in ISDS proceedings in their damages submissions. The design of the system means that, by definition, states are always in the dock as respondents.[23] Counterclaims are very rare, and they seldom succeed even if admitted or considered.[24] The most extreme position that a state can take on quantum is to say the value of the investments affected by state action (whether expropiatory or otherwise) is zero. Yet such undervaluation by a state must overcome a strong reality check in the form of the book value (or net book value) of the investments.[25]

The measure of book value is necessarily at the centre of any damages calculation based on actual losses (*damnum emergens*), due to its retrospective purpose. Apart from this, it is undeniably appealing, even if economically unsound, to calculate damages based at least on the restitution of the capital—amortized, generally—that the investor put into the enterprise.[26] Thus, book value may by default crystallize as a *floor* for compensation, even when neither

[21] ibid [825]. An adjustment on similar grounds was made to the amount awarded in the *Yukos Universal v Russian Federation* (n 11) cases; Maître Fortier was also a member of the tribunal which heard those cases.

[22] Daniel Flores and others, 'Damages Issues in Upstream Oil and Gas Disputes' (2018) 5(1) The Journal of Damages in International Arbitration 61, 82–83. These remarks are by George D Ruttinger.

[23] Gus Van Harten, 'Private Authority and Transnational Governance: The Contours of the International System of Investor Protection' (2005) 12 Review of International Political Economy 600.

[24] Ana Vohryzek-Griest, 'State Counterclaims in Investor-State Disputes: A History of 30 Years of Failure' (2009) 15 International Law, Revista Colombiana de Derecho Internacional 83.

[25] World Bank (n 3) 27; Book value 'means the difference between the enterprise's assets and liabilities as recorded on its financial statements or the amount at which the taken tangible assets appear on the balance sheet of the enterprise, representing their cost after deducting accumulated depreciation in accordance with generally accepted accounting principles'.

[26] Book value is irrelevant if a project will not earn a return. The project will be worth zero, regardless of book value.

party argued as much.[27] The question of the *ceiling* of quantum in ISDS is, however, altogether different.

The standard of compensation under investment treaties is a prospective (forward-looking) measure, akin to an estimation of lost profits (*lucrum cessans*); namely, the measure of fair market value (FMV). FMV is a numerical expression of what a willing and informed buyer would pay, today, for the future profit streams a project would generate over its lifetime. It is generally accepted that the best way of determining FMV is through the discounted cash flow (DCF) methodology.[28] In any DCF calculation, historical data is used to establish baselines for investment costs, the reliability of equipment, maintenance schedules, stock turnover ratios, and many other things. However, the key value drivers in a DCF calculation are the *assumptions*, the *price projections* and the *discount rate* embedded in the financial model that seeks to consider all the variables that could affect an enterprise's future cash flows. If the assumptions and projections are sufficiently far-fetched, the sky becomes the limit for damages claims.

In ISDS, misapplication of the DCF methodology has clearly led to claim inflation. The phenomenon can actually be traced to some of the last arbitrations arising from the nationalization of oil concessions in the Middle East and to some of the arbitrations at the US–Iran Claims Tribunal.[29] In 1992, the committee entrusted with developing the World Bank's Guidelines on the Treatment of Foreign Direct Investment probably had such cases in mind when it issued its previously mentioned call for caution in applying DCF due to the tendency of investors to exaggerate claims of lost profits.[30] This admonition was echoed in 1996 by Thomas Stauffer, who pointed out that the DCF method had been 'tainted by misapplication' and 'used to justify valuations [in arbitration processes] which reach beyond the "fanciful" to "wonderland proportions"'.[31] Ironically, the valuation exercises that outraged Stauffer in the mid-1990s look like paragons of restraint when compared to the surreal valuations now habitual in ISDS.[32]

[27] As was the case, for example, in *Caratube International Oil Company v Kazakhstan*, ICSID Case No ARB/13/13, Award (27 September 2017) [1164]–[1166].

[28] William C Lieblich, 'Determinations by International Tribunals of the Economic Value of Expropriated Enterprises' (1990) 7 Journal of International Arbitration 37.

[29] The most notable cases being *The American Independent Oil Company (Aminoil) v Government of the State of Kuwait*, Ad hoc Arbitration, Final Award (24 March 1982); *Amoco International Finance Corp v Iran*, 15 Iran–US CI Trib Rep (1987); *Amoco Iran Oil Company v Islamic Republic of Iran and the National Iranian Oil Co*, I Iran–US CI Trib Rep 493 (1982); *Phillips Petroleum Co Iran v Iran*, 1 Iran–US C1 Trib Rep 487 (1982); *Arco Iran v Iran*, 25 Iran–US CI Trib Rep 339 (1990).

[30] World Bank (n 3) 26.

[31] Stauffer (n 1) 479.

[32] *Aminoil* (n 29). For example, at US$2.5 billion (in 1979 money), equivalent to around US$6 billion in 2008 terms, the *Aminoil* claim looks quaint when compared to the US$30 billion ICSID claim that

5 How Accurate and Objective Is DCF Valuation Anyway?

Before analysing how the DCF method is misapplied to inflate claims, it is worth examining a preliminary point; namely, the degree of precision and objectivity of DCF valuation itself.

Lawyers acting as counsel for ISDS claimants are wont to deride the quantum submissions of states by saying their sole aim is to 'deliberately drag down damages'. This objective is pursued, not only through arguments that try to 'soften up the arbitrators and pull on their heartstrings', but also by 'frequently argu[ing] that the claimant is seeking damages on a "speculative" basis'.[33] The latter course of action, in particular, is decried as epitomizing bad faith, given that DCF

> [i]s widely supported by the professional literature, and its workings are well understood. Indeed, most investors rely on a DCF analysis to determine whether or not to undertake a particular project ... [T]he DCF approach is widely accepted by international agencies, such as the World Bank, as a valid method to estimate damages and fair market valuations in international disputes.[34]

It is indeed indisputable that DCF is used commonly in matters beyond legal proceedings. The DCF methodology is the central plank of the multi-trillion dollar market for corporate control, for example,[35] and is applied every day in innumerable transactions concerning corporate mergers and acquisitions, purchases and sales of shares and other securities, and so on. All of these transactions are forward looking. Therefore, all are predicated on forecasts and 'guesstimates' about the likely behaviour and evolution of many variables. If participants in the market for corporate control regularly take such uncertainties in stride, why should ISDS tribunals harbour misgivings about DCF? All they need is to apply the tried and tested DCF methodology for valuing enterprises in the circumstances of profit interruption by state action. After all, market transactions for corporate control would appear to demonstrate that,

ConocoPhillips raised against Venezuela in 2008. The *Aminoil* claim was the largest in the history of international arbitration until the dawning of the mega-case era from 2005 onwards.

[33] Young (n 5) citing a legal practitioner who usually represents claimants in ISDS proceedings.

[34] Manuel Abdala, 'Key Damage Compensation Issues in Oil and Gas International Arbitration Cases' (2009) 24(3) American University International Law Review 539, 548–49.

[35] Peter L Bernstein, *Capital Ideas: The Improbable Origins of Modern Wall Street* (The Free Press 1992) 154–55.

despite the complexities of forecasting future cash flow, a DCF valuation is akin to an *haute cuisine* recipe. That is, it is a dauntingly complicated exercise best left to capable hands, but almost certain to generate an outcome at the highest standards of discernment, provided the procedures are scrupulously followed and the appropriate techniques are applied.

In response to such assertions, it must be made clear, first, that tribunals should remain wary of DCF valuations and mindful of why, until recently, ordinary courts were unenthusiastic about DCF.[36] Secondly, it is unfortunately the case that DCF techniques will not produce the 'right' result in ISDS proceedings as they might in the market for corporate control. The simple reason is that arbitration valuations always lack a key attribute of valuations arising from actual transactions in the latter market.

What is this missing attribute? One should begin by observing that, when market transactions for corporate control are analysed in hindsight, it is clear that DCF valuations seldom produce the 'right' outcome (in the sense of delivering future results in accordance with expectations):

> [t]he evidence is ... overwhelming that, on average, acquisitions do not create much if any value for the acquiring company's shareholders ... McKinsey research found that one-third created value, one-third did not, and for the final third, the empirical results were inconclusive.[37]

From the perspective of economics, this mediocre success rate is not a problem. That is because 'valuation is all about assessing risk and reward, and finding a price that reasonably balances these two that is ultimately reflected *in the meeting of minds between buyer and seller in the marketplace*'.[38] The existence of market transactions, in other words, demonstrates that the valuations underpinning them faced and overcame the sternest litmus test: getting an informed and un-coerced actor to pay money (or the equivalent) for the valued assets and rights. Thus, even though there is 'virtually no direct evidence as to the determination of a DCF value in cases of real market transactions', it is still

[36] According to *US v 47 14 Acres of Land* 673 F 2d 722 726 (8th Cir 1982): 'Great care must be taken. or such valuations can reach wonderland proportions. It is necessary to take into consideration manifold and varied factors like future supply and demand, economic conditions, estimates of mineral recoverability, the value of currency, changes in the marketplace. and technological advances. Many of the factors are impossible to predict with reasonable accuracy.'

[37] Tim Koller, Marc Goedhart, and David Wessels, *Valuation, Measuring and Managing the Value of Companies* (John Wiley 2010) 449.

[38] Bob George, Bill Cline, and Rawdon Seager, 'Valuation of Upstream Oil and Gas Assets' (2019) 12(2) The Journal of World Energy Law & Business 121 (emphasis added).

valid to 'infer that the market value is the DCF value'.[39] Moreover, one can legitimately conclude that the definitive transaction price in the market 'was most probably determined as the result of discounted cash flow valuations undertaken both by buyer and seller'.[40] This conclusion would be 'true for acquisitions and mergers ... true for project investments, and ... generally true in the case of the stock market valuation of listed companies'.[41] It would emphatically not be true, however, for the valuations 'claimed, or reported, in opinions or arbitration awards'.[42]

As Stauffer explained several decades ago, valuations undertaken in arbitration proceedings

> [f]ail the market test because those reported values reflect only the claims of the parties as to what someone purportedly would have paid. Those figures are not based on a sum actually paid in the marketplace; a willing buyer did not pay such sum to a willing and informed seller. Since there was no transaction, there was no market value proven.[43]

In a situation of actual bargaining, an inflated valuation that wildly overestimates revenues, ignores or understates costs, assumes the rosiest price scenarios, and so forth has little chance of leading to any meeting of minds between seller and buyer. The latter will simply reject the former's offer. In arbitration proceedings, in contrast, no such buyer actually needs to come forward; so for an unrealistic valuation for the claimant investor to win over a tribunal, all that is required is for the majority of that tribunal to lend a sympathetic ear to the claimant's submissions, however dubious these might be.

6 Anchoring in Practice

When Stauffer drew attention to the systematic inflation of claims for anchoring purposes in arbitration proceedings, he felicitously called it the 'Cinderella effect'.[44] The driving force behind this effect is described as follows in a leading practical treatise on enterprise valuation:

39 Stauffer (n 1) 472.
40 ibid.
41 ibid.
42 ibid 459.
43 ibid 472.
44 ibid 480.

> [v]aluation can be highly sensitive to small changes in assumptions about the future ... [For] a typical company with a forward looking price-to-earnings ratio of 15 to 16 ... [i]ncreasing the cost of capital ... by half a percentage point will decrease the value by approximately 10 percent. Changing the growth rate for the next 15 years by one percentage point annually will change the value by about 6 percent.[45]

If small changes produce such impacts, significant changes translate into far bigger ones. And if the latter are applied across the board, to all manner of variables, it becomes possible to conjure a silk purse out of even the vilest sow's ear. Basically, 'every cash flow analysis comprises cash-in items ... and cash out items' and the net cash flow 'represents the residue once the cash-out items have been subtracted from the cash-in items'.[46] In valuations undertaken for arbitrations, claimants will seek to maximize the former by assuming that every revenue generating variable that is capable of improvement will indeed get better. Likewise, they will minimize the latter by assuming that none of the myriad things that could go wrong with a project ever will. The net result of such micro-level assumptions is a great distortion of the whole picture.

The core of valuations done for arbitrations is usually the output and operations forecasts from long-term business plans. These are generally prepared before any dispute might have arisen and, indeed, before the projects got underway. Since no economic actor goes into a venture for disappointing returns, the long-term business plans are usually optimistic. Optimistic assumptions make it unnecessary for the investor to dwell at length on a range of issues that might arise in the actual operations, each of which can sway the DCF calculation by millions of dollars.[47]

To be clear, the above is not meant to question the usefulness or soundness of such business plans in general. They are snapshots which, at the time of their preparation, seek to give a picture of the likely path of a project based on the best available information. Even so, and despite what is asserted in ISDS

[45] Koller and others (n 37) 310.

[46] Nick Antill and Robert Arnott, *Valuing Oil and Gas Companies: A Guide to the Assessment and Evaluation of Assets, Performance and Prospects* (Elsevier 2000) 131.

[47] Such questions include, but are not limited to, whether the availability (on stream) factor of critical pieces of kit has been as expected, whether planned maintenance schedules correspond to the actual wear and tear of equipment and facilities, whether changes in the price of steel and other raw materials, and/or local or generalized shortages of skilled manpower, could have had an adverse cost impact, at the level of both capital expenditure and operational expenditure, and many, many more. The tendency to plan according to best-case scenarios is facetiously called the 'EGAP principle', for Everything Goes According to Plan. See Bent Flyvbjerg, 'Top Ten Behavioral Biases in Project Management: An Overview' (2021) 52(6) Project Management Journal 531, 538.

proceedings, these plans are not assessments of the future that carry a high probability of truth. As Kahale observes, '[n]o one has that kind of crystal ball. The only thing that is virtually certain is that ... assumptions [in the plans] will turn out to be wrong.'[48]

Unfortunately, many ISDS tribunals have been willing to believe that crystal balls are commonplace in the investor community.[49] Moreover, they have been ready to accept that, where a project's performance has fallen short, blame lies with host governments and their alleged interference.[50]

Claimants are keen to assert near infallibility of their output and cost forecasts in business plans. Yet they are also adamant that tribunals should not pay heed to a crucial cash-in element in the same plans; namely, the expected price realization scenario (and its corollaries, expected revenues and returns). The incongruity on the part of claimants is rooted in the fact that, more often than not, state action to rebalance the government's take in natural resource projects tends to occur after sharp price increases in the relevant market (which give rise to windfall profits).[51] In such circumstances, a project may fully recover its costs, in a fraction of the time foreseen in the business plan, and then generate returns far in excess of the most optimistic estimates from the time when the project was originally undertaken.[52]

From the economic perspective, once an investor has realized a market return on the capital invested, a later restructuring of the fiscal arrangements for the project does not harm any vested property interest of the investor. When the restructuring takes the form of a levy on windfall profits (ie profits that

[48] George Kahale III, 'Keynote Address', 8th Annual Juris Investment Treaty Arbitration Conference, Prague, Czech Republic (28 March 2014) 4; Bent Flyvbjerg, 'Make Megaprojects More Modular' (2021) 99(6) Harvard Business Review 50, 51; a foremost authority in project management notes that 'people can forecast certain events—such as GDP growth, macroeconomic policies, business cycles, technological advances, and geopolitical conflicts—with some accuracy over periods of up to one year. After that, however, accuracy declines rapidly, and beyond a time horizon of three to five years, it disappears into the mists of randomness.'

[49] Illustrative examples are *Crystallex v Venezuela*, ICSID Case No ARB(AF)/11/2; *Gold Reserve v Venezuela*, ICSID Case No ARB(AF)/09/1.

[50] See eg *ConocoPhillips Petrozuata BV and Others v Venezuela*, ICSID Case No ARB/07/30, Award (8 March 2019) [364], where the tribunal accepted output figures presented by claimant on the grounds that there was 'no evidence and no convincing argument that would prevent it from retaining these figures ... if ... the operation having the Claimants as partners had remained in place' (para 400), despite the fact that, in internal project meetings before nationalization, officers of claimant had recognized that, for the last eight years of the term of the project, such output figures could not be attained.

[51] Paul Stevens and others, *Conflict and Coexistence in the Extractive Industries* (Chatham House 2013).

[52] In the case of the project at issue in *Venezuela Holdings BV and Others v Venezuela*, ICSID Case No ARB/07/27, the base case cash flow forecast assumed that the nominal price of the crude from this project would increase from US$10.76 per barrel in 2001 to US$15.97 per barrel in 2017 (Cerro Negro Finance Ltd, *Bond Offering Memorandum Dated June 11, 1998*: C-40), and by inflation thereafter. By 2007, on the eve of the nationalization of the project, this crude was fetching an average of US$53.04 per barrel in the market (ie 320 per cent more).

have arisen exogenously, without action on the part of an investor), then this is axiomatically true, which is why, in general, 'taxation ... for windfall profits due to price hikes cannot amount to a taking'.[53]

Windfall taxes may amount to a taking in circumstances where an investment is covered by a tax stabilization or freezing provision. For this reason, arguments aimed at uncovering stabilization language in contractual clauses often take up much of the written and oral submissions in arbitration proceedings.[54] While such arguments often fail,[55] their primary aim is not necessarily to win on an abstruse point of law but rather to give legal cover for inflated damages claims, according to the anchoring playbook.

Besides seeking to exclude a project's originally expected revenues from the assessment of damages from governmental action, claimants exaggerate future flows of funds in another way. They do so by manipulating the price vectors that are fed into DCF calculations. This manipulation tends to be context-driven and can take many forms. For instance, claimants may derive future price projections from a narrow set of bullish price forecasts. Or, they may derive them from a broad set of forecasts, but rely on statistical methods that confer more weight to outliers. They may also derive future revenue scenarios in a way that assumes that the project's output will be sold at a certain benchmark price, without adjusting for quality or locational differences. These strategies are not mutually exclusive or exhaustive. Claims are inflated based on a variety of them.[56]

7 The Discount Rate

Valuations are highly sensitive to any changes in assumptions about the future. No individual variable has a greater practical incidence on the outcome of a DCF calculation, however, than the discount rate. This is the rate used to translate future net cash flows into present values. Unsurprisingly, the damages submissions of ISDS claimants are predicated on low discount rates (preferably

[53] Muthucumaraswamy Sornarajah, *The International Law on Foreign Investment* (CUP 2010) 405.

[54] See eg *ConocoPhillips Gulf of Paria BV v CVP and PDVSA*, ICC Case No 22527/ASAM, for an unsuccessful attempt to transform a boilerplate operational force majeure provision into a clause sheltering a contractual party from the effects of a nationalization measure which was not 'of general applicability' *Investment Arbitrator Reporter* (5 August 2019).

[55] However, some succeed thanks to gross arbitral contortionism, a good example of which is discussed in the coruscating dissent of Hans Smit in *Bridas SAPIC and Others v Government of Turkmenistan and Others*, ICC Case No 9058/FMS/KGA, First Partial Award (25 June 1999) [9]–[10].

[56] Both *Venezuela Holdings BV and Others v Venezuela* (n 52) and *ConocoPhillips Petrozuata BV and Others v Venezuela* (n 50) offer good examples of this kitchen sink approach to claim inflation.

with the integers in single digits). These result in higher present value figures and therefore bigger claims. Yet, the lowballing of discount rates makes a mockery of the fundamental rationale behind a DCF calculation. That rationale is to account for all of the risks assumed by an investor in connection with a specific investment in a specific place. To illustrate, there exists a

> [m]ajor distinction between valuing companies in developed markets and in emerging markets ... Not only do you need to account for risks related to the company's strategy, market position, and industry dynamics, as you would in a developed market, but you also have to deal with the risks caused by greater volatility in the local capital markets and macroeconomic and political environments.[57]

This distinction is obviously made by investors themselves when deciding whether or not to undertake a project or acquisition. It finds concrete expression in higher 'hurdle rates'—meaning the minimum rate of return expected by the investor—for projects to go ahead in riskier places.[58]

These observations lead to the conclusion that, for an investor, the expected value of the same project in different countries will not be the same. Further, if that is the case *ex ante*, then it must be true *ex post* too. Consider the following thought experiment. A large salt dome (the Duck Soup structure) straddles the border between Sylvania and Freedonia. The flanks of the structure harbour identical oil pools, within the countries' respective territories. The fiscal terms in both countries are likewise identical (but the government of Freedonia is of a Marxist persuasion). Development of the two fields entails the same capital investment and variable costs. Each will generate identical cash flows. However, an investor will apply a higher hurdle rate to the Freedonian project, owing to the orientation of its government, which leads to the project having a lower than expected net present value than that in Sylvania. As it happens, both projects are undertaken and come on-stream on the same day. Down the line, the Sylvanian project is sold to a willing buyer for a sum that reflects the buyer's DCF calculation. The next day, Freedonia nationalizes the project in its territory. Would the amount of compensation that Freedonia has to pay equal that which was paid for the Sylvanian project, minus the cash flow from the day before the nationalization? No. Neither would it be that value minus

[57] Koller and others (n 37) 721.

[58] James M Poterba and Lawrence H Summers, 'A CEO Survey of U.S. Companies' Time Horizons and Hurdle Rates' (1995) 37(1) Sloan Management Review 43.

some 'Freedonian haircut' (implying that the Sylvanian price is somehow the 'true' value, subject to some penalty).[59] The correct compensation figure would emerge from a DCF calculation identical to the one undertaken by the buyer of the Sylvanian project, with its starting point shifted one day later and with the future cash flows translated into present value terms by means of a discount rate that reflected the higher likelihood of nationalization in Freedonia compared to Sylvania.

The amount of compensation thus calculated would imply that, when the Sylvanian project was sold, the Freedonian project would have fetched a lower price in the market, even though the projects were identical in every respect except their location. This result may appear counter-intuitive. As the *Himpurna* tribunal reasoned on the issue of discount rate, however, it merely reflects 'the fundamental issue of country risk, obvious to the least sophisticated businessman'.[60]

Thus, when a tribunal is asked to determine the value of an investment, it must first ascertain the profits that the investment is expected to generate over its lifetime. Then it must translate these future money flows into present value terms by means of a discount rate. That rate should be equivalent to the hurdle rate that a rational knowledgeable investor would demand for undertaking an investment with the same characteristics and cash flow profile as the investment at issue, in that industry, in that country, and at that moment in time. Unfortunately, tribunals are too often receptive to submissions from claimants that deny this elementary postulate, leading to discount rate decisions that beggar belief. An example is the recent award of US$6.6 billion against Nigeria in which the tribunal applied a 2.65 per cent discount rate to a gas project that had never got off the ground.[61] Another example is the award that applied a 10.446 per cent discount rate in Turkmenistan less than five years after the collapse of the Soviet Union when the twelve-month LIBOR rate at the time was around 5.78 per cent.[62]

[59] As correctly noted by Flores (n 22) 93.

[60] *Himpurna California Energy v PT (Persero) Perusahaan Listrik Negara*, UNCITRAL, Final Award (4 May 1999) in (2000) 25 Yearbook Commercial Arbitration 13 [348]–[378], [598]. In this case, claimants had argued for a discount rate of 8.5 per cent, but the tribunal applied a discount rate of 19 per cent, and justified its decision by pointing to the 'fact . . . that it is riskier to enter into a 30-year venture in [a country like] Indonesia than in more mature economies. And it is no answer to say that the contract has allocated 99% of the risk to the Indonesian side. After all, there are documents which by their terms allot 100% of the risk to the debtor: bonds. Although they may be denominated in US dollars, although they may stipulate absolute obligations to pay, it still makes a difference whether the issuer is Switzerland or Swaziland.'

[61] See *Process and Industrial Developments Ltd v Nigeria* [2019] EWHC 2241 (Comm).

[62] *Bridas SAPIC and Others v Government of Turkmenistan and Others*, ICC Case No 9058/FMS/KGA, Final Award (26 January 2001) [7].

It is tempting to view such decisions as evidence of the economic illiteracy of some arbitrators overwhelmed by slick investor-side presentations.[63] There is probably more to it than that. It is not credible that arbitrators generally cannot appreciate the cognitive dissonance at the heart of most claimants' damages submissions. That is, arbitrators have to be able to see through the investor's quest, on the one hand, for indemnification against any number of existing and future risks of sovereign action and the investor's insistence, on the other, that project cash flows should carry low discount rates regardless of the circumstances of political risk. Even for those not at ease with economics, it should be easy to perceive that 'it's precisely because . . . [certain] host countries are riskier countries that they are attractive to investors who see the possibility of making greater returns'.[64] When such increased risks are not reflected in the discount rate in an award, the tribunal hands an undeserved windfall to the investor.

8 Getting to the Magic Figure

Imaginative claimants have ample scope to inflate claims by selective manipulation of cash-in and cash-out elements in long-term business plans, as well as by an artificially low discount rate. Yet even this may be insufficient for some ISDS claimants, who use another valuation tactic that can only be described as 'making things up'. Consider, for example, the US$30 billion claim brought by ConocoPhillips against Venezuela after the nationalization of its petroleum interests in that country in 2007.[65] From this sum, one-third (ie US$10 billion) was accounted for by income tax liabilities that ConocoPhillips would supposedly have faced in the United States had the company's claims been upheld in their entirety. These included its claims that Venezuela had taken a number of unlawful measures, therefore entitling the company to full restitution under the *Chorzów Factory* rule.[66] Shockingly, this colossal tax gross-up claim was not backed by a single document (eg one detailing ConocoPhillips' US tax position) or even a witness statement. It was as if *Chorzów* stood for the proposition that a claimant seeking restitution for an (allegedly) unlawful act need not provide evidence to support even the wildest allegations.

[63] Part of the problem with country risk discount rates is that there really is no universally accepted theory to arrive at a number. The magnitude of the 'right' number is an empirical question: ie what do real investors use. But this is a very closely held business secret.
[64] Flores and others (n 22) 80.
[65] See *ConocoPhillips* (n 50).
[66] *Case Concerning the Factory at Chorzów* (Claim for Indemnity), Permanent Court of International Justice.

Ultimately, this US$10 billion portion of the claim fell by the wayside on jurisdictional grounds.[67] This result was not, however, a vindication of the ISDS safeguards against unfounded claims or a sign of the total failure of the claim as such. Again, the yardstick of success for threadbare claims is not that they are upheld, but that they affix unreasonable figures in the mind of tribunals and the public, for anchoring purposes. Thus, they make it possible for an eventual compensation award to appear less outrageous than otherwise.[68] In domestic courts, this kind of anchoring strategy would likely founder at an early stage due to evidentiary requirements. In ISDS arbitration, many arbitrators seem indulgent about the evidentiary shortcomings, to the point that some have been willing to fill in, of their own initiative, the gaping holes at the heart of quantum claims.

This readiness by arbitrators to overlook flawed quantum submissions is most apparent for projects that never got off the ground. In such cases, as the World Bank advised,[69] the default position of tribunals should not be to use DCF in order to calculate lost profits 'for a beginning industry and unperformed work'.[70] Yet claimants constantly press tribunals to do just that. They press tribunals especially in disputes over raw materials, like copper, gold, and petroleum, that are traded in highly liquid markets. These constant efforts derive support from arguments—presented by valuation experts in articles published in scholarly journals—that there is nothing inherently speculative about relying on the DCF methodology to value *certain types* of enterprises that lack a track record of profitability.

Consider this opinion by a prominent valuation expert who is currently active in ISDS: '[i]n the oil and gas sector, neither being a startup company (as opposed to a going concern) nor lacking a historic record of profitability are serious impediments for using the DCF method in estimating damages'.[71] This view is supposedly credible on the basis that '[o]il and gas companies derive their primary value on the existence of reserves, and much less so on the ability to develop and extract such reserves and later sell them to the market'.[72] The conclusion drawn is that:

[67] The jurisdictional basis of this claim was that a Venezuelan investment law constituted a unilateral consent to ICSID jurisdiction, an interpretation rejected by the tribunal (*ConocoPhillips* (n 50), Decision on Jurisdiction and the Merits (2013) [261]–[262], [290]).

[68] The tribunal in *ConocoPhillips* (n 50) awarded claimants a record sum of US$8.7 billion plus interest.

[69] World Bank (n 3) 27.

[70] *Autopista Concesionada de Venezuela CA (Aucoven) v Venezuela*, ICSID Case No ARB/00/5 (23 September 2003) [360].

[71] Abdala (n 34) 551.

[72] ibid.

> [g]iven that the marketplace for crude oil is that of a tradable commodity, and given that oil companies derive their primary value from discovered certified reserves, the DCF cannot be ruled out simply because the company is a startup, or because the company has not yet established historic records of profitability. A case-by-case analysis is called for.[73]

It seems reasonable to assume that the article with the above passage was written for eventual use in arbitration proceedings (with its citation to be followed by a submission to the effect that 'the case at hand, members of the tribunal, happens to be one of those in which the use of DCF is warranted').[74] Its characterization of the oil and gas sector would be unrecognizable to anyone with any practical experience in that sector and its project execution risks, however. Indeed, it is hard to capture just how ludicrous, from the point of view of an oil and gas professional, is the premise that, provided a company has access to hydrocarbon reserves, it will therefore be able to create value, because the development, extraction, and marketing of those hydrocarbons are matters that will more or less take care of themselves.

In reality, making a petroleum find and establishing the existence of commercial reserves are only the beginning of a long process. In that process, vast amounts of cash can go up in smoke with no discernible reward and no value creation. Furthermore, the fact that a company may have been able to carry the process to a successful conclusion in one instance does not guarantee it will do so again with the next project. Cost overruns and delays in are so commonplace in the petroleum industry that, as was once jokingly remarked, projects often seem subject to two immutable laws: '[o]ne: regardless of how much has been invested, the amount still to be invested remains constant. Two: Regardless of how far the project has advanced, completion is still six months ahead.'[75]

The Kashagan project in Kazakhstan, undertaken by a string of major oil companies, is an excellent example of the absurdity of the proposition that 'oil

[73] ibid.

[74] And sure enough, as this chapter was being written, this exact scenario materialized in *Odyssey Marine Exploration Inc v Mexico*, ICSID Case No UNCT/20/1, Claimant's Reply (29 June 2021) [347], one of the rare ISDS cases where the pleadings are publicly available (albeit in redacted form). The quantum experts who cited the passage just happen to belong to the same consultancy firm as Mr Abdala.

[75] JJ Richardson, 'Problems of Controlling Public Sector Agencies: The Case of Norwegian Oil Policy' (1981) 29(1) Political Studies 35, 46. As Bent Flyvbjerg notes in 'What You Should Know About Megaprojects and Why: An Overview' (2014) 45(2) Project Management Journal 6, 11, if '[s]uccess in megaproject management is typically defined as projects being delivered on budget, time, and benefits', then only 'approximately one in a thousand projects is a success, defined as on target for all three ... This serves to illustrate what may be called the "iron law of megaprojects": over budget, over time, over and over again. Best practice is an outlier, average practice a disaster.'

and gas companies derive their primary value on the existence of reserves, and much less so on the ability to develop and extract such reserves'.[76] The project involved developing the largest oil find in the world over the past four decades, with recoverable reserves of around 13 billion barrels. It was originally meant to come on stream in 2005–2006 and reach peak production of 1.5 million barrels per day by 2015. The overall expenditure was supposed to have been around US$57 billion. Yet, development proved more complex than anticipated. Production only began in 2016, with costs ballooning to US$187 billion. One effect of the catastrophic delays and cost overruns has been that, even today, it is hard to tell whether any of the companies will ever see a return on their investment, despite the magnitude of the reserves.

Now consider this hypothetical. Dismayed by delays in the project, the government decided in 2006 to nationalize Kashagan in order to allow another operating consortium to take over development. There is no question that compensation would be due to the original group of companies and there is no dispute that the measure was lawful. However, the parties disagree over quantum, leading to an arbitration proceeding. Assuming the tribunal accepted the theory that the 'lack of a historic record of profitability is not a serious impediment for using the DCF method in estimating damages for an oil project', and taking the very high oil prices prevailing at the time, the outcome of a DCF calculation based on the original Kashagan development plan would likely support a damages award for scores of billions of dollars. In contrast, a DCF calculation based on a starting point in 2006 but incorporating what is now known about the date on which the project actually began producing (and the further costs that were necessary to get there) would likely lead to a negative number and no compensation. Put differently, a damages award that was based simply on the magnitude of the Kashagan reserves would be a complete travesty.

Sadly, the above scenario is far from rare in ISDS. A recent case concerned a multi-billion dollar award against Pakistan after a copper mining project failed to progress beyond the drilling for cores. The tribunal assigned a value of US$4.09 billion to the project, slightly less than half of the US$8.49 billion dollars originally claimed. The difference reflected reductions of US$1.84 billion to account for 'the impact of the risks and issues raised by Respondent regarding the feasibility of the project' and of US$2.56 billion for 'the systematic

[76] Current shareholders are as follows: ENI (18.52 per cent), Shell (18.52 per cent), ExxonMobil (18.52 per cent), Total (18.52 per cent), ConocoPhillips (9.26 per cent), and Inpex (8.33% per cent). The remaining 8.33 per cent of the shares is held by KazMunayGas, a Kazakh state company.

and asymmetric risks affecting the project'.[77] Presumably, these adjustments reassured the tribunal as to the reasonableness of its award. If so, it was a textbook example of anchoring at work. Even with the adjustments, the award of a vast sum for an unbuilt project, many years away from start-up, grievously affects a country like Pakistan (which the IMF needed to bail out, concurrently to the award being handed down, to the tune of US$6 billion).

9 It Never Is Just about Quantum

One further point deserves to be made in connection with claim inflation and anchoring. The headline claims figures—ie the anchors—are generally composites of factual matters, on the one hand, and legal matters, on the other. However, in the public arena, no distinction is ever drawn between the elements that make up a claim (partly because of the confidentiality of proceedings). Thus, in the media, disputes always appear to be exclusively about quantum. In reality, even quantum issues are not just about quantum.

Certain narrow jurisdictional and legal issues may actually be the main drivers of an ISDS claim's value. An example is the previously mentioned US tax gross-up claim by ConocoPhillips. Another is the determination of the valuation date in the case of nationalization. This determination depends partly on the lawfulness of the measure. If the nationalization was lawful, the valuation date is the day of its announcement; if it was unlawful, the date is when a judicial authority has decided to categorize it as unlawful.[78] For projects that serve volatile commodity markets, moving the valuation date may add hundreds of millions or even billions of dollars to a claim.[79] Likewise, the magnitude of claims will rise if claimants impugn the legality of tax or royalty measures, especially in industries such as oil, where government take represents the largest cash-out item for a project. This does not mean that claim inflation is the only motive impelling claimants to question the legality of fiscal measures. Even so, claim inflation is inevitable in this form of legal challenge (because damages are calculated on the basis of the fiscal regime as it existed before the impugned measures were enacted). Crucially, anchoring heuristics

[77] *Tethyan Copper Company v Pakistan*, ICSID Case No ARB/12/1 (2019) [1600].

[78] According to the rule in *Chorzów Factory* (n 66).

[79] In *ConocoPhillips* (n 50), the nationalization at issue was deemed unlawful and the shift in valuation date to a large extent explains the US$8.7 billion awarded. In the very similar case of *Venezuela Holdings* (n 52), the nationalization measure was deemed lawful, and the resulting award (subsequently annulled) came to US$1.6 billion.

will manifest themselves for whatever claim was originally asserted, regardless of whether the claimed compensation was informed by legal theories that are later found to be baseless. From time to time, however, one does come across claims in which the *sole* objective of the characterization of fiscal measures appears to be to inflate alleged damages, evidently with anchoring in mind.[80]

10 Conclusion

The notion that ISDS is not a 'fair, independent, and balanced method for the resolution of investment disputes and therefore should not be relied on'[81] has been around for a while. Misgivings about ISDS have also been rising sharpish of late, thanks to the sustained efforts of many arbitrators to provide investors with protections beyond anything envisaged by the drafters of investment treaties. These efforts have transformed standard clauses—on expropriation, full protection, and security, most favoured nation treatment, and 'umbrella' clauses—into veritable weapons of legal destruction. Perhaps none have been transformed as dangerously as FET clauses, whose morphing into provisions supposedly meant to safeguard investors' 'legitimate expectations'—a concept not recognized in customary international law[82]—has allowed tribunals to find treaty violations in facts that most drafters would view as legitimate state regulation.[83] This trend has set off alarm bells even in capital-exporting states. It has enfeebled the system overall because, as Kahale observes:

> [i]t is easy to champion ISDS when you don't face claims and can gain points at home for supporting your corporations doing business abroad; it's not so easy when you are on the receiving end of dozens of claims challenging what you consider to be the legitimate exercise of your sovereign powers and seeking enormous sums in damages.[84]

[80] In *ConocoPhillips v PDVSA and Others*, ICC Case No 20549/ASM/JPA (C-20550/ASM), Award (2018) [75], [165], the claims submitted came to a total of US$25.2 billion, and were predicated, inter alia, on an alleged entitlement to receive compensation for 'value-depressing [fiscal] measures' which claimants themselves characterized as non-discriminatory and, hence, non-compensable under the contract at issue.

[81] Gus Van Harten and others, *Public Statement on the International Investment Regime* (31 August 2010) <https://web.archive.org/web/20100905175026/http://www.osgoode.yorku.ca/public_statement/>.

[82] *Obligation to Negotiate Access to the Pacific Ocean (Bolivia v Chile)* Judgment [2018] ICJ Rep 507.

[83] Most poignantly illustrated by the claims connected with cigarette plain packaging legislation in a number of countries.

[84] George Kahale III, 'International Institute for Sustainable Development, 12th Annual Forum of Developing Country Investment Negotiators' (Lecture, Cartagena, Colombia, 28 February 2019) 12.

As a result, the continuity of ISDS in its present form can no longer be taken for granted. Were the regime to break down, blame would ultimately lie with its flawed legal conception and architecture. The efficient cause of such an outcome appears likely to be that of quantum or, more specifically, the way in which all the wrong turns in investment law have unmoored damages awards from the fundamentals of economics, and even from common sense.

According to Koller, '[t]he guiding principle of value creation ... and its corollary, the conservation of value, have stood the test of time ... When managers, boards of directors, and investors have forgotten these simple truths, the consequences have been disastrous.'[85] Many ISDS claimants have forgotten these simple truths, aided by many arbitrators. This amnesia will likely have disastrous consequences for the regime. Most evidently, it has led to colossal yet legally flimsy awards, whose combined weight may eventually be too much for a rickety structure to bear.

[85] Koller and others (n 37) 5.

11

Conclusion: Containing the Pernicious Regime of Investment Arbitration

M. Sornarajah

1 Introduction

To understand the 'dubious interpretive manoeuvres' on which the superstructure of international investment law has been built on investment treaty foundations, the essential conflicts in attitudes of the different peoples of the world must be understood. For the people of Latin America, for Asians and Africans generally and for the Australian aborigines, the Earth has divinity. To the Western capitalist world, the Earth merely provides natural resources to furnish production of goods for trade and profit. Western companies and their home states desecrated the bowels of the Earth for centuries during colonialism to finance their industrial revolutions. This was done forcibly by the conquest of lands of other peoples. As the use of force came to be prohibited, new avenues had to be found to retain control over those resources and over the economies of the erstwhile colonies that Western states had controlled.[1] International law became the instrument by which this feat was accomplished.

In the modern phase, the making of investment treaties and the use of arbitration to give them a compliance mechanism helps to secure the West's stranglehold over trade and investment.[2] Expansionary interpretation of the treaties alongside regular enforcement of awards based on these treaties has created a superstructure for the ongoing dominance that has existed since the colonial period. As various chapters in this book demonstrate, investment arbitrators have managed to beat back even the rudimentary efforts of some

[1] Jochen von Bernstorff and Philipp Dann (eds), *The Battle for International Law: North South Perspectives on the Development Era* (OUP 2019).

[2] For the view that the treaties create a regime see Jeswald Salacuse, *The Law of Investment Treaties* (OUP 2010). The use of the regime theory is interesting in that it keeps the area insulated and away from other areas of international law such as those on the environment and human rights.

M. Sornarajah, *Conclusion: Containing the Pernicious Regime of Investment Arbitration* In: *Rethinking Investment Law.* Edited by: David Schneiderman and Gus Van Harten, Oxford University Press.
DOI: 10.1093/oso/9780192871084.003.0011

states to remove this dominance over their economies. Alternative visions that resist the dominant framework have had little success.[3]

The unfortunate situation is that even those who recognize the pernicious injustices of the system are constrained not to confront it directly. The discipline of international law, within which these injustices are couched, is loaded against adverse criticism of the content of its rules. Yet the need for pompous niceties in discussion deflects from the obvious injustices and those 'highly qualified publicists' who maintain them. These publicists are given an untouchable status, even as humanity allegedly benefits from exposure to their views. The curtain of decorum hides a multitude of sins. It is best to deal with this subject, which has continued to cause misery to most of humankind, without any pretentious decorum.[4]

As the rich in the world get richer and fewer, the extent of the humanity that suffers grows. The rich control multinational corporations that scour the planet for yet more enrichment and control. The early multinational corporations, again controlled by the rich, were the harbingers of colonialism. They conquered the colonies. The modern multinational corporation lacks that capacity, not because it does not have it, but because norms of international law do not permit the use of force. Even so, they can still control the economies of other states by other means through international law. They are able to manipulate their home states to maintain international norms that favour them.[5] Their hegemonic power, wielded in association with their home states, manifests itself in investment arbitration, where the disposal of planetary resources is governed by rules devised and applied by mercenary arbitrators, clothed in a false garb of neutrality and unable to shake their natural predisposition to prioritize the material values of contract and property protection. The resistance that the people in the third world offer to this legal imperialism finds itself diverted by the making of new doctrines intent on showing that the rules benefit the development of the world's poor. There is an unwillingness among the elite of the developing world to move from this paradigm.[6] The World Bank and the International Monetary Fund actively propagate ostensibly altruistic economic

[3] On alternative visions see Lim Chin Leng (ed), *The Alternative Visions in the International Law on Foreign Investment* (CUP 2016)

[4] John Linarelli, Margot Salomon, and Muthucumaraswamy Sornarajah, *The Misery of International Law* (OUP 2019).

[5] Susan Sell has studied the manner in which multinational corporations have been able to influence intellectual property laws applicable globally. Susan Sell, *Private Power, Public Law: The Globalization of Intellectual Property* (CUP 2003); Claire Cutler, *Private Power and Global Authority* (CUP 2003); David Schneiderman, *Constitutionalizing Economic Globalization: Rule and Democracy's Promise* (CUP 2008).

[6] This may be explained by the active capture of the elite and its use by agencies of the West.

theories of development that are not founded on empirical evidence.[7] This divide is unbridgeable. It calls into question whether there should exist a system of investment arbitration that purveys a historical injustice, achieved by the agency of the law, by judicial similitudes, by false altruisms such as economic development, and by the employment of so-called third world arbitrators: quislings who glory in having joined the masters' select club.[8] It is a clash of people of different cultures, attitudes, and outlooks on life. Men and women, whose culture is based on the acquisition of material wealth, sit in judgment over people who may not be so inclined. Greed is not always good for all. This book illustrates the challenge of bridging the unbridgeable, especially in the arbitration of resource-based conflicts.

The resistance to these injustices comes from scholars of both the developing and the developed world, who can see the obvious injustices in investment arbitration. This convergence of views may have emerged because the third world, consisting of newly independent countries left impoverished by the imperialist states, are now fast developing or industrializing, if not yet progressing. Scholars in such states may be moving towards supporting the unjust norms that protect foreign investment.[9] In contrast, as the imperialist states lose power, scholars see how the growing poverty in these states makes them like the third world. A common cause emerges, for which some international lawyers are willing to fight. As the transnational capitalist class becomes smaller and richer, the commonality of the poor of humanity becomes clearer and its causes more vital.

The strategy of richer states to retain hegemony in international law has been to develop esoteric compartments of the law in isolated circles. That way, an epistemic community can protect its norms. The impact of competing areas, like environmental and human rights law, have confronted international law and generated alternative formulations that displace or reshape international investment law. These changes will gather steam over time, just as the rules of investment protection will work tenaciously to slow them.

[7] The main altruistic argument is that foreign investment promotes economic development and justifies the making of investment treaties that protect investments. There is no empirical proof for this proposition. Besides, the treaties have existed for nearly seventy years without bringing such development. Rather, as a result of huge damages having to be paid, they have heaped misery on developing countries.

[8] The author admits that he has sat on some investment arbitrations in which he was nominated as arbitrator by states. He has also appeared as an expert witness for states.

[9] Scholars in China and India show ambivalence towards investment treaties.

2 The Eco Oro Arbitration

The recent award in *Eco Oro v Colombia*[10] demonstrates the deep malaise gripping investment arbitration. The case concerned concession agreements and licences for mining given to the claimant, a Canadian company, in the region of the Santurbán *páramo*. Besides having a variety of minerals and resources, this region was an environmentally significant region to Colombia and the world. Licences were given to the claimant in the past, although their exact coverage was indeterminate. Further, it was well-known that environmental awareness and concern was increasing in Colombia as the dispute matured. The question that ran through the award was whether environmental considerations should precede concern for foreign investor rights and protection. This question was evident in judgments of the Colombian courts and decisions of other Colombian authorities, as well as the award itself.

Eco Oro's concession agreement underwent changes at various stages due to retroactive environmental laws. This retroactive change was to be expected. It emerged from increasing scientific knowledge of the impact of mining and from the ensuing environmental concerns. A reasonable investor would be conscious that the state would take such steps, as Colombia did, resulting in the arbitration. The tribunal considered issues of alleged direct or indirect expropriation, police powers, fair and equitable treatment, and potential damages. Each of these issues has been explored in the chapters of this book.[11]

The outcomes of investment arbitration are increasingly predictable. Unfortunately, they strike at the heart of the legitimacy of the system. In *Eco Oro*, the two party-appointed arbitrators acted according to their past records.[12] The tribunal divided over two main issues. On expropriation, no liability was found by a majority consisting of the tribunal president and the Colombia-appointed arbitrator, Philippe Sands. On the minimum standard of treatment (read to include the fair and equitable treatment), liability was found by a majority consisting of the president and the Eco Oro-appointed arbitrator, Horacio Grigera Naón. It was as if there were two distinct tribunals and awards in a single case. Curiously, similar rules were discussed in each, but applied

[10] *Eco Oro Minerals Corporations v Columbia*, ICSID Case No ARB/16/41 (16 September 2021).

[11] Apart from most favoured nation clauses and the umbrella clauses, the other themes in this book are captured in the *Eco Oro* award. The award is also discussed in the chapter by Sierra-Camargo and Suárez-Ricaurte in this volume.

[12] For Philippe Sands see his dissent in *Opera Fund Eco-Invest v Spain v Schwab Holding*, ICSID Case No ARB 15/36 (2021), which also involved issues of climate change and legitimate expectations. Professor Sands is a leading international lawyer with a wide practice in the area. Grigera Naón came to investment arbitration from commercial arbitration.

very differently. The eventual decision was left to the president, who was parachuted into the tribunal by ICSID, with little prior experience in investment arbitration. It is not satisfying when the outcome of an arbitration depends so heavily on the tribunal's composition. Studies establish cross-linkages between arbitrators and the predictability of their approaches that assist arbitrators to secure repeat appointments.[13]

Investment arbitration simply lacks the requisite neutrality to be a serious discipline. A serious legal discipline must have certainty, application of rules by persons credibly seen to be neutral, application within an institutional culture that is not prejudiced towards particular economic or political philosophies, and independent administration. In each respect, investment arbitration fails. Its neutrality is seriously to be doubted. Studies indicate that most arbitrators belong to networks that subscribe to definite tenets of investment protection. Institutions like ICSID operate within the World Bank, which is associated with the Washington Consensus and neoliberalism. They lack the requisite independence.

Eco Oro was notably the first case interpreting a 'balanced' treaty. Such treaties ostensibly constrain investment protection provisions with doctrines like police powers and host state defences to liability. They are said to represent a compromise between criticisms of inflexible investment protection and efforts to preserve the old order. This attempt is doomed to fail because the aims are not reconcilable. State regulation in the public interest sits too uneasily with the primacy of investment protection.

Already, investment arbitration has acquired a culture of investment protection. The 'balanced' treaties maintain this priority by emphasizing the rules in the old treaties over the defences of public interest considerations that motivate government intervention. It is a lazy way to pursue change. The old treaties are taken as a given, with new defences attached. This tinkering defies the primary task of any state to protect its public more than foreign investors. *Salus populi, suprema lex*. The knaves alter traps for the fools who make such treaties. They do so by promoting the belief that worthy changes have been made, even as regulatory considerations have been mostly related to defences. Yet the state's consideration of environmental and human rights protection, and of the welfare of society, emerge from a state right to take relevant measures, not a series of limited defences against liability.

[13] Sergio Puig, 'Social Capital in the Arbitration Market' (2014) 25 European Journal of International Law 387.

In any event, any balance in new treaties depends on interpretation by the arbitrators. They will also be inclined to prioritize investment protection. *Eco Oro* is an excellent case of failed efforts to balance investment protection with environmental considerations including climate change, access to water, and protection of an ecologically sensitive area. After some shadow boxing in the right direction, towards overwhelming Colombian and global interests, investment protection triumphed.

As mentioned, *Eco Oro* partly concerned the law on expropriation, especially its distinction between direct and indirect expropriation, its delineation of non-compensable regulatory measures, and the relevance of an investor's 'reasonable investment backed' expectations. As a precisely 'balanced' treaty, the Canada–Colombia investment treaty included a provision stating that indirect expropriation is non-compensable 'except in rare circumstances'. Yet the idea of a non-compensable regulatory measure necessarily truncates the concept of expropriation. Faced with this necessity, the arbitrators chose to confine the balancing doctrine by introducing extraneous, even if implied, factors, such as proportionality.

A majority in Eco Oro examined these balancing conditions and arbitrator requirements for regulatory defences to be pleaded. It upheld the Colombian measure as being in the public interest on the facts, incidentally privileging environmental over investment protection in the expropriation claim. Yet this finding made the tribunal's alternate majority decision, on the minimum standard of treatment, utterly unacceptable. The factors considered unfair in the latter mirror the factors considered, and dismissed, for the expropriation claim.

Thus, *Eco Oro* also concerns the modern meaning of the minimum standard of treatment, stated as including the fair and equitable treatment. In the treaty, the meaning of this clause was tied to customary international law. It remains a mystery why the clause would have been drafted this way. No evidence suggests that customary international law incorporates the fair and equitable standard. Little evidence suggests that the minimum standard of treatment is customary international law, except for its inclusion in American investment treaty practice. The fair and equitable standard could easily be left out, leaving the customary international minimum standard alone. This drafting approach is a vexing puzzle in North American investment treaties. Why do the states not simply drop the language of fair and equitable treatment where it causes so many problems?

There are interminable questions as to the contents of the phrase fair and equitable treatment. Every lawyer understands the subjectivity in such notions as fairness and equity. The provision can be manipulated. Like other investment treaty tribunals, *Eco Oro* draws on the provision to review decisions of domestic courts, acting as if it were an appellate body operating outside of its authority. By scrutinizing what will become a leading award, one can isolate the real issues raised in modern investment arbitration.

2.1 The False Altruism of Investment Law

Economic development is a false premise for investment treaties. It requires an asymmetric exchange of investment flows on the assumption that they will be beneficial if guarantees are provided and investment are assured by state. *Eco Oro* was a manifestation of the underlying policy clash. It is hard to see how an environmentally unsound investment in the *páramo* could benefit Colombia and its people. Some people were indeed employed in the mining project, and some small land holders benefited incidentally, but in contradiction an ecological catastrophe awaited the project's actual operation. As all the scientific evidence pointed towards a disaster, it would be unwarranted to scrutinize closely the state's procedures to avert it.

In *Eco Oro*, a 'balanced' treaty required the investor to prove its case and then allowed the state to defend itself from liability. Therefore, the state, with its constitutional right to act in the public interest, awaited the proof of liability and then pleaded its main case in defence. As structured, the balanced treaty relegated the state's justification to a late stage at which point the tribunal had already dealt with the policy clash. It did so, especially, by its substantive resolution of the law of expropriation and that of the minimum standard of treatment.

3 The Law on Expropriation

From early times, expropriation has been the principal feature of investment protection. The law was developed largely in the context of American investments in Latin America, outside of a formal colonial context. The US wanted external standards to govern expropriations, especially the payable amount of compensation, while Latin American states preferred domestic law for this purpose. After winning their independence, African and Asian states joined the dispute, arguing that adequate compensation was payable. This dispute is now dormant in the face of the apparent agreement, under investment treaties, that full compensation must be paid.[14]

It was always the law that some deprivations of property, such as the imposition of fines, taxation, and antitrust dissolutions of companies, were not regarded as compensable. The law's object would be defeated if the state had to pay compensation. With the welfare state, the need for the state to intervene in order to perform welfare functions required more interference with property rights. It was to be expected.

Consequently, attention shifted to the interpretation of what amounted to a taking. Arbitrators began to construe the liberal definitions in investment treaties[15] expansively to include acts that depreciated the value of the property and they awarded large sums when such deprivations took place. Developed countries themselves found it necessary to strike back against these expansive interpretations. Particularly in the NAFTA context, they were becoming respondents in investment arbitration while also the largest recipients of investment capital. *Methanex v US*[16] is a landmark decision that effected the change. Its facts track the *Ethyl* arbitration, which ended by Canada paying compensation and announcing that the company's product, which had been regulated on environmental grounds, was safe as a gasoline additive.[17] As the respondent in *Methanex*, the US revived the category of lawful public interest measures in the course of establishing that a taking, effected to secure a beneficial objective for the public, was not a compensable expropriation. In doing so, it relied on an existing rule that characterized certain measures, such as taxation and criminal fines, as not being tantamount to a taking. After *Methanex*, many investment treaties were drafted to reflect this position. This recognition of regulation as non-compensable took the wind out of the sails of expropriation law, at least momentarily.

In *Eco Oro*, a majority of the tribunal held that Colombia's measures were aimed at securing environmental protection of the ecologically sensitive areas

[14] The view that the treaties create customary law concretizing treaty principles is inexact. There are not enough treaties to bring about such a result. Not all investment treaties refer to such a uniform rule. Not all investments are protected by treaties (which specify the types of investments that are protected). An example is that treaties protect only such investments as are approved in accordance with domestic law.

[15] Apart from direct takings which were the conventional dispossession of property, the treaties referred to indirect expropriations and any measure "tantamount to" a taking. The latter phrase was capable of great expansion.

[16] *Methanex v US*, UNCITRAL (NAFTA) (3 August 2005).

[17] In *Ethyl Corporation v Canada*, UNCITRAL, a statement of the Canadian Minister for the Environment that she was contemplating the ban of a petroleum additive that may cause cancer was held to be tantamount to an expropriation.

of the paramo. In turn, the measures must be regarded as regulatory and non-compensable. The majority found:[18]

> [t]hat the measures were non-discriminatory and designed to protect a legitimate public welfare objective, namely the protection of the environment. They were adopted in good faith. The challenged measures were therefore an exercise of the police powers of Colombia.

Eco Oro adds to those few instances where the claim that a measure promoting a public welfare objective, in this case environmental protection, was accepted. Yet the tribunal majority's approach was also questionable. It sought first to find out whether there was an indirect expropriation and then it examined whether that expropriation had a regulatory purpose. This analysis inverted the process. Regulatory exceptions work on the basis that there is a state right to regulate in the public interest. If the state had such a right, it provides a justification for the state's measures. All other matters become superfluous, except for whether the right was exercised in good faith and was non-discriminatory. These limitations flow from general international law, not from any treaty prescription.

The issue of proportionality is problematic. It is not part of customary international law and its only relevance is that the absence of proportionality may show bad faith. Its importation into the law of expropriation lack authority as a substantive proposition except where it is incorporated into treaty text.[19] Those systems that recognize it, like the European Union, allow a wide margin of appreciation to the state. Once it is recognized that the state had a right to take the relevant measure, it becomes otiose to ask how that right was exercised unless there are prescribed means in the law which conferred the right. In *Eco Oro*, the arbitrators erred by considering other grounds of liability after finding the measure was a regulatory. As the dissenting arbitrator, Philippe Sands, pointed out, it was not open to the majority to proceed after a finding that the measures were in the public interest. Yet the majority, having stated that there must be 'a very significant aggravating element or factor in the conduct of the state and not mere bureaucratic muddle or state inefficiency' to displace the state's policy

[18] *Eco Oro* (n 10) [642]. This decision was made by a majority, the dissenting arbitrator, Philippe Sands joining with the President on this point. Incongruously, the finding of other violations was made after this holding with the support of the other arbitrator, Grigero Naón.

[19] The popular explanation is that it is a principle of German law adopted in European Human Rights Law by the European Court of Human Rights in cases involving the right to property. Hence, it is suggested that the rule has relevance in investment arbitration. There is no state consent for the making of this extension.

power, went on to search for bureaucratic inefficiencies and then brand them as a violation of fair and equitable treatment.

An integral part of expropriation analysis is the nature of the property that is subject to regulation. In Colombia, the constitution itself stresses the social function of property. The right to property is indefeasible in the face of overwhelming public interests. *Eco Oro* was concerned with domestic and global interests in the environment, which had to be weighed against property protection. It is the same for contract rights. Sanctity of contract must give way to competing public interests. The idea of stability for foreign investment, which the investment treaty stresses, is not viable in the face of other displacing social and other forces. The search for a balance is futile when, as in *Eco Oro*, the interests in environmental protection of the environment are clearly overwhelming. Given the hierarchy of interests in an unfragmented international law, foreign investment protection will rank lower than environmental and human rights protection, including indigenous rights and culture protection.

4 Looking for Liability after Finding No Taking

The arbitrators, seeing that expropriation law, the bastion of investment law, was being emasculated through the doctrine of non-compensable regulatory measures, sought to conserve what could be preserved by devising new strategies and finding new heads of liability. The most important way was to use the newly found basis of liability in the fair and equitable standard of treatment. Another was to strike at expropriation doctrine by introducing a proportionality rule requiring that there must be a reasonable relationship between the object of the expropriation and the taking. In the same vein, there was an effort to manipulate the doctrine of indirect expropriation so that the distinction between compensable and non-compensable expropriation became opaque. Yet another was to construe the old notion of denial of justice, seen in the more modern treaties as a panacea to limit arbitral expansionism, to include a category of judicial expropriation which is constituted by courts of the host state making improper decisions.[20] The latter category greatly expanded the scope of arbitral control over judicial pronouncements of the courts of the host state. All of these trends are in play in the *Eco Oro* award.

Once the claim of expropriation was dismissed on the ground that it was a defensible regulatory measure and, hence, carried no liability, there was an

[20] See Sattarova in this volume.

examination of the claim of the violation of the fair and equitable treatment. During the course of that examination, one finds the new majority of the tribunal letting loose all the techniques of finding liability for the violation of the rather newly resurrected fair and equitable treatment provision. Under this provision are brought a plenitude of new doctrines previously unimaginable and could possibly not have been within the contemplation of the draftsmen of the investment treaties. It is the case of interpretive exegesis gone haywire in order to serve the cause of investment protection and investment arbitration. *Eco Oro* exhibits the eagerness to keep the business of investment arbitration alive.

One aspect of the resuscitation of the police powers exception was that it paved the way towards a possible per se rule that once a regulatory purpose is shown, the expropriation should be regarded as regulatory and non-compensable. There is now an increasing body of case law and literature which identifies measures taken to protect health,[21] the environment, indigenous people, cultural property, and a residual category that is included through the use of the phrase, 'health, welfare and morals'. There was an assumption that these measures were per se regulatory. The assumption was strengthened by the fact that the state was given a wide margin of appreciation as to its view that it was taking a regulatory measure. That being so, it would have been difficult to hold that the measures taken by the Colombian government to protect the *páramo* were anything other than motivated by environmental considerations and hence, were non-compensable regulations. In the face of universal acceptance of the fact that the Columbian government was motivated by purely environmental considerations, it was inevitable that a holding that a measure was regulatory would be made. If liability was to be found, it had to be found on other grounds. This is the dilemma facing other ongoing arbitrations. It is difficult to make findings on the basis of expropriation as modern democracies would seldom act otherwise in the public interest. A law that was designed to protect against whimsical confiscations of property by dictators or capricious takings by newly established governments on ideological grounds became obsolete in the modern age. It was therefore necessary to explore other avenues to find liability.

The tussle that occurred in *Eco Oro* illustrates this ongoing clash between arbitrators inclined towards investment protection and the emergence of new factors that deter the finding of liability in the state. The tussle is between human values such as environmental protection and the material values

[21] *Methanex v US* (n 16); *Chemtura Corp v Canada*, UNCITRAL, Award (2 August 2010).

represented by inflexible investment protection. It is an ongoing struggle within international investment law.[22] Emblematic of the struggle is the effort of Colombia to advance the view that the existence of a regulatory objective should lead to an *in limine* dismissal of the claim for want of jurisdiction. This effort, summarily rejected, is discussed next before turning to tribunal's search for alternative bases of liability.

5 Environmental Measures as Ousting Jurisdiction

One interesting argument raised by Colombia must be considered from the point of view of the environmental measures as well as other measures taken in the public interest. Columbia argued that the presence of the exception in the 'balanced' treaty means that the existence of environmental reasons for the measures taken to protect the *páramo* would put these measures outside the jurisdiction of the tribunal. This innovative idea that the exceptions were really creating jurisdictional exclusions is novel. If accepted, it would have resulted in an *in limine* rejection of the arbitration as environmental measures would have been excluded. The tribunal dismissed this argument, stating that an exception had to be pleaded after liability has been established. Canada, in its amicus curiae brief, had also stated that an exception had to be pleaded only after liability is established. This was a strict interpretation of how the treaty is structured but is not theoretically sound. The fault arises from the fact that the 'balanced treaty' first contains the old investment treaty standards and then adds onto it the exceptions, thereby giving the impression that the situations indicated in the exceptions are relevant only as defences to be pleaded once liability under the first part of the treaty is established. The fault also may lie in the manner that Colombia had stated the argument.

The matter should not have been argued by reference to an exception in the treaty. Rather, the argument should have been that the state had a prior right to take measures to stem an environmental hazard. The state had a right to take measures to protect its environment both in the public interest as well as in the interest of the global public as the destruction of the ecology of the *páramo* would affect climate change. There was a duty on the part of the state to act both in terms of domestic law, which imposed on the state a constitutional

[22] Valentina Vadi spoke of the possible humanization of international investment law. It is a premature idea. Vadi herself pointed to the existence of a competing culture that emphasized materialism in Valentina Vadi, *Cultural Heritage in International Investment Law* (CUP 2012) 296.

obligation to protect the environment and, in terms of international law, which imposed obligations to prevent climate change. It was a situation of a right and a duty existing in the same entity at a given time. As such, there was a justification in the state to take measures that protected the environment. Though it is stated as an exception in the defences provided by the balanced treaty, it is already provided for in the provision on expropriation that regulatory measures taken in the public interest are non-compensable because no liability can arise from the exercise of the right of the state to act in the public (and global) interest. As in the case of necessity, it constitutes circumstances which preclude liability. Raising and establishing it must provide a situation that excludes jurisdiction of the tribunal.

Instead, the tribunal's approach that an environmental measure has to be pleaded as an exception after liability has been established would mean that the state must undergo the process of having to participate in the proceedings that establish substantive liability and then, plead the exception. This is not a necessary process, even according to the treaty text. Like in the cases of necessity and national security, the existence of situations which induce the state to take measures in the public interest, must be treated as justifications which preclude liability. Where such circumstances exist, the issue of establishing liability as a precondition for the raising of exceptions do not arise as no wrong has been committed as a result of the exercise of a right in the state.

6 Using Fair and Equitable Treatment

The recognition of legitimate public welfare measures as non-compensable emasculated expropriation as a category of liability despite incorporation of such restrictions as the proportionality rule. The building up of a law on the basis of a nebulous treatment standard, the meaning of which remains unexplored, was the way forward to keep investment arbitration alive once its most fecund basis of liability had come to be emasculated through the rediscovery of public welfare exceptions. The fair and equitable treatment standard was invested with a plethora of meanings for arbitrators to found liability on a variety of broad grounds including discrimination, non-transparency and, most vibrantly, on the ground that the state had created legitimate expectations in the foreign investor and had sundered those expectations by instituting hostile measures.[23] The idea of legitimate expectations was an import from English

[23] See Ostřanský in this volume.

administrative law where it had not been used as a substantive proposition. It gave procedural protection to situations where an administrative decision had been made without a hearing to a party in whom a prior legitimate expectation to a right or licence had been created. There was no idea that a state could not act against the expectations it had created. In investment arbitration, the rule appeared as a substantive proposition requiring the payment of compensation on the same standard as if there had been an expropriation. Consequently, an alternative strand was developed to replace expropriation.

The Argentine cases provided full rein for this view to be established and reiterated. Like-minded arbitrators had repeat appointments to ensure that the view on a substantive remedy for the violation of legitimate expectations was stabilized.[24] But, even as such expansion took place, there were efforts at restraint. No one sought to do away with the new doctrine that had been created which did not have roots in the text or in any accepted source of international law. It cannot be demonstrated to be a general principle of law. Two of the leading states that contribute to the creation of Western investment law, the United States and Canada, have routinely refused to accept the doctrine of legitimate expectations as constituting law. Yet, the doctrine sails on. The opponents have merely restrained the scope of its application without denying its existence as an applicable doctrine.

Those states showing restraint merely limit the rule by having regard to the circumstances in which the doctrine is applicable. Thus, there is examination of whether the expectation is legitimate or whether it was fanciful. Arbitrators have suggested that there should not be too high standards of governance built into the doctrine. But, direct confrontation of the doctrine or an outright refusal to apply it have not been forthcoming. The preservation of the doctrine of legitimate expectations, however lacking in foundational authority, has become the most important alternative source of liability in modern investment arbitration. *Eco Oro* is a demonstration of this trend.

In *Eco Oro*, the two arbitrators who formed the majority when considering the claim based on the fair and equitable treatment, in keeping with their pro-investment inclinations, were under pressure to find liability. The search was for a credible basis for such liability. Having found that there was no compensable expropriation, they were led to seek out external circumstances of the measures taken to pin them on to a head of liability. As the dissent pointed out,

[24] The episode illustrates the extent of law creation by arbitration in investment law. The single arbitrator, Professor Orrego-Vicuna, to whom the doctrine is traced, had repeat appointments in several Argentine and other cases; Further see Gus Van Harten, *Sovereign Choices and Sovereign Constraints: Judicial Restraint in Investment Treaty Arbitration* (OUP 2013).

it was incongruous that there should be a search for any other head of liability after a finding that the state had enacted bona fide environmental measures.

For this reason, *Eco Oro* is a strange award. As stated, it has two combinations of arbitrators. The first combination is that of the president and the nominee of Colombia, Philippe Sands. This combination rejects the claim based on expropriation. The second is that of the president and Grigero Naón, the nominee of Eco Oro. This combination accepts the claim based on the fair and equitable standard of treatment. It is bizarre that the two parts of the award simply do not sync. In the first, the arguments relating to discriminatory treatment and legitimate expectations are rejected, to a large extent on the ground that the state must be given leeway as to the making of difficult policy decisions. This is not the view taken when it comes to the fair and equitable treatment. It is difficult to see how the standards that are to be applied to similar tests can differ. The tribunal simply contradicts the views it had stated when considering expropriation. It seems to adopt new standards in the consideration of discrimination and legitimate expectations. It seems as if the president had decided to find liability and adopted a charade of dismissing one ground and accepting the other, although both grounds involve the consideration of similar principles. The outcome in *Eco Oro* indicates the truism that modern investment arbitration is tending towards the finding of liability by broadening the notion of fair and equitable treatment to the greatest extent possible.

The tribunal found that the meaning of minimum standard is not static and believed that the awards which so held had created custom. It revealed the mindset of the tribunal as arbitral awards are but a subsidiary source of international law incapable of creating custom.[25] This is either ignorance or a purposeful intent of expanding the arbitral role (it is more charitable to say that it is a result of ignorance). The tribunal then gives an expansive statement of the fair and equitable treatment by substituting words for that standard by saying that it should treat the investment in 'an even-handed and just manner'[26] as if the substitution of one amorphous phrase by another is going to enhance clarity. The tribunal engages in a discussion of police powers and, as in the case of expropriation, the tribunal holds that there is no obligation not to change existing laws. But, it finds that there would be violation of the standard if Colombia had acted in a grossly discriminatory manner. Noting that this may be difficult to prove as the state is given a high degree of deference and there must be inordinately high degree of indifference for liability to be established, the tribunal

[25] *Eco Oro* (n 10) [745].
[26] ibid [748].

is driven to return to the doctrine relating to legitimate expectations. There is considerable shadow-boxing to illustrate a degree of fairness in the thinking of the tribunal before the axe is to fall. What is difficult in the collective award is that almost all points that were considered in connection with the fair and equitable treatment had already been dealt with in case of the expropriation claim, but in a different manner.

The ground work laid for finding eventual liability for breach of the fair and equitable standard in *Eco Oro* is reminiscent of the foundation that is laid in arbitrations which adopt a similar process of reasoning. The purpose of the treaty is stated to be to bring about stability in foreign investment.[27] It is strange that the tribunal, which deemed the measures non-compensable, should in the next breath talk in terms of stability as the essence of permissible regulatory interventions in effecting change; change is the opposite of stability. It even accepted that retroactive legislation should be lawful given the need to achieve the objective of environmental protection of a sensitive region. Its later reasoning does not sit well with its earlier findings relating to regulatory expropriation. In the second part, the tribunal adopts an entirely different tack in considering the legitimate expectations doctrine. The heart of the problem is identified as the failure of the Colombian government to identify the limits of the Santurbán *páramo*.[28] If one decides on liability on the basis of an act that is 'arbitrary, grossly unfair, unjust or idiosyncratic' a surfeit of meaningless adjectives like fair and equitable, one simply finds an act and argue that it fits all those undefinable adjectives. It is not much by way of decision-making but it is what the tribunal ended up doing. It found a peg on which to hang liability because it had predetermined the issue.

7 Conclusion

The 'founding fathers' of international law were charlatans who manipulated a system that enabled elites in their states to hold power over much of humanity and pilfer their wealth. European statehood was a convenient falsehood to cloak the community interests of different elites in Europe. It created a sense of nationalism that joined sectional interests. In the post-colonial world, new methods of control over resource-rich states and the labour of poorer countries have been implemented through international law. The fraudulent altruism of

[27] ibid [770].
[28] ibid [772].

the civilizing mission has been replaced by that of economic development and prosperity for the poor. Most recently, the wedding of neoliberalism to nationalism has promoted authoritarian rule disguised as democracy.[29] Once again it enables the rich to dominate human affairs.[30] Investment treaties must be understood as part of this enterprise.

Though its modern treaty origins date to the 1950s, in the 1990s investment law took a more virulent form, enabling wide bases of jurisdiction and liability through arbitral interpretation. It soon met resistance from the very states that initially created the law. Few states have abandoned the regime, however, although it is the best solution to the system's injustices. South Africa has most clearly adopted this wise course. Other states are leaving investment arbitration as in the case of the European Union's preference for investment courts. Many states have replaced the old treaties with more 'balanced' ones. While the investment treaty establishment tinkers, substantive law reform is left to languish. Resistance to the injustice of investment treaties has been denied by accommodation, by granting fringe benefits, and by raising unimportant issues as if they were the main flaws of the system.[31]

The system is unlikely to go away. China and India are rapidly becoming large capital exporters. Both adhere to the treaties to protect their outward investments. They may well become the new oppressors. There is increasing evidence of Chinese foreign investors launching investment treaty claims. They can be expected to continue as investments are barred on grounds of national security. Thus, even as harsher aspects of investment arbitration are beaten back, for poorer countries it remains a problem. Through pressure and cajoling, they will continue to subscribe to the regime. The struggle to cope and ward off the harm continues.

[29] Nationalism can be manipulated to provide majorities that enable rule by an ethnic chauvinist to appear as democratic. Viktor Orbán in Hungary, Donald Trump in the US, and Boris Johnson in the UK are examples.

[30] Wendy Brown, *In the Ruins of Neoliberalism: The Rise of Antidemoncratic Politics in the West* (Columbia UP 2019).

[31] This is evident in the current UNCITRAL effort at changing the law. Issues like double hatting where the same lawyer performs different roles in investment arbitration divert attention from the real substantive issues that are the source of the injustices.

Index

For the benefit of digital users, indexed terms that span two pages (e.g., 52–53) may, on occasion, appear on only one of those pages.